The Risk of Economic Crisis

A National Bureau
of Economic Research
Conference Report

The Risk of
Economic Crisis

Edited and with an Introduction by

Martin Feldstein

The University of Chicago Press

Chicago and London

MARTIN FELDSTEIN is the George F. Baker Professor of Economics at Harvard University, and president and chief executive officer of the National Bureau of Economic Research.

The University of Chicago Press, Chicago 60637
The University of Chicago Press, Ltd., London
© 1991 by the National Bureau of Economic Research
All rights reserved. Published 1991
Printed in the United States of America
00 99 98 97 96 95 94 93 92 91   5 4 3 2 1

Library of Congress Cataloging-in-Publication Data

The Risk of economic crisis / edited and with an introduction by Martin Feldstein
    p. cm.   (A National Bureau of Economic Research conference report)
  Based on a special National Bureau of Economic Research conference held in Oct. 1989.
  Includes bibliographical references and indexes.
  ISBN 0-226-24090-8 (cloth).—ISBN 0-226-24091-6 (paper)
  1. Business cycles—Congresses. 2. Economic stabilization—Congresses. 3. Economic policy—Congresses. 4. Business cycles—United States—Congresses. 5. Economic stabilization—United States—Congresses. 6. United States—Economic policy—1981-   —Congresses.
I. Feldstein, Martin S. II. National Bureau of Economic Research.
III. Series: Conference report (National Bureau of Economic Research)
HB3711.R54   1991
338.5'42—dc20   91-11736
                                                                  CIP

⊗The paper used in this publication meets the minimum requirements of the American National Standard for Information Sciences—Permanence of Paper for Printed Library Materials, ANSI Z39.48–1984.

Contents

0838899   127674

Preface

As I note in the introductory chapter to this volume, the danger of a financial and economic crisis is more prominent in the thinking of policy officials and business leaders than in the research of professional economists. But although the United States has been fortunate in recent decades not to experience the kind of massive economic collapse that occurred from time to time until the worldwide depression of the 1930s, there is no doubt that the possibility of another such financial and economic crisis cannot be dismissed.

In an effort to stimulate more economic research on the causes and the possible ways of reducing the likelihood of such crises, the National Bureau of Economic Research began a series of interrelated studies. The research dealt with financial institutions, securities markets, international capital markets, and cyclical fluctuations in economic activity. Several researchers examined the antecedents of the economic decline of the 1930s. Others looked at recent problems like the less developed countries' (LDCs') debt situation and the fluctuations of exchange rates.

The findings of these studies have generally been reported in NBER working papers and subsequently published in professional journals. In addition, papers prepared as part of this project were presented at two special NBER conferences and published in separate volumes. The first group of papers on volatility in securities markets was organized by Professor Sanford Grossman and published in a special issue of *The Review of Financial Studies* (vol. 3, no. 1 [1990]). The second group of papers on financial market risks more generally was organized by Professor R. Glenn Hubbard and published in an NBER volume, *Financial Markets and Financial Crises* (University of Chicago Press, 1991).

The present volume is based on a special NBER conference that I organized in October 1989. Unlike most other NBER conferences, the participants in this meeting included not only academic researchers but also nonacademics who have played key policy roles in the past and current senior policy officials and staff. These individuals are or have been associated with the Federal Reserve System, the Federal Deposit Insurance Corporation, the International Monetary Fund, the Congressional Budget Office, the U.S. Treasury, the Council of Economic Advisers, the White House Domestic Policy Office, the Canadian Treasury Department, the Office of the British Prime Minister, and other organizations that must deal with the possibility of financial and economic crises.

The meeting was divided into three parts, the first dealing with the origin of financial crises, the second with the international aspects of financial crises, and the third with the impact of financial crises on the economy more generally. Three NBER economists prepared nontechnical papers that served as a background for the group's deliberations: Professor Benjamin Friedman on financial crises, Professor Paul Krugman on international aspects, and Professor Lawrence Summers on the economic consequences of financial crises. Each discussion session at the conference was initiated by brief personal statements from four individuals who have held key positions in the relevant area or senior academic figures who have written extensively on related issues.

This volume presents the background papers, the personal statements of the panelists, and a summary of the discussion.

I am grateful to all of the participants in this project for their contributions: the authors of the background papers for their analyses, the panelists for sharing their personal experiences and perceptions with us, the current policy officials for helping us to place the discussion in the current economic context, and Professor Douglas Elmendorf for preparing the summary of the discussions.

Financial support for the project on economic crises was provided by The Seaver Institute, The Ford Foundation, and the Lilly Endowment. Without their help, this project would not have been possible. I am grateful also to the members of the NBER staff for their assistance with all of the details involved in the planning and execution of the several meetings and conferences that were part of this project and for their work in the preparation of this volume, particularly to Kirsten Foss Davis, Ilana Hardesty, Mark Fitz-Patrick, Andrew Samwick, Kathi Smith, and Carolyn Terry.

Martin Feldstein

The Risk of Economic Crisis: Introduction

Martin Feldstein

Although cyclical fluctuations remain a problem throughout the industrial world, the depression of the 1930s was the last time that we experienced the kind of financial crisis followed by economic collapse that had been a recurrent problem in both the United States and Europe for centuries. The long period of time since the last such crisis may explain why economists have paid relatively little attention to the subject in recent decades.

Instead, economic research has focused on improving our understanding of the normal functioning of the economy and on developing policies that can make small but important improvements: bringing the inflation rate closer to zero, lowering the rate of unemployment, and reducing distortions in the use of resources. In a $5 trillion economy, even "small" improvements in overall performance can be of enormous value.

In contrast to most professional economists, policy officials and leaders of the private business sector worry a great deal about the risk of major breakdowns in the functioning of the economy. Many of the conditions and the events of the 1980s—including the failure of most of the less developed debtor countries to service their debts, the deterioration of capital among money-center banks, the large numbers of bankruptcies of the thrift institutions, the wide swings of currency exchange rates, the increase of corporate debt, and the stock market crash of 1987—have contributed to the fear of an impending major economic crisis. Rapid changes in financial markets and a dramatic increase in the complexity of financial instruments have heightened those fears.

We have graduated from the 1980s to the 1990s without any of those risks triggering a major financial crisis and economic collapse. Indeed, after an initial recession eliminated the inflationary excesses of the late 1970s, the decade of the 1980s was a time of uninterrupted growth with stable inflation.

But the risk of such an economic crisis remains. As Charles Kindleberger's distinguished and fascinating book (*Manias, Panics and Crashes: A History of Financial Crises* [Basic Books, 1978]) has ably demonstrated, economic crises have been with us as long as the market economy. At some point, greed overcomes fear and individual investors take greater risks in the pursuit of greater returns. A shock occurs and the market prices of assets begin to collapse. Bankruptcies of leveraged individuals and institutions follow. Banks and other financial institutions fail in these circumstances because they are inherently leveraged. The resulting failure of the payments mechanism and the inability to create credit bring on an economic collapse.

The potential source of financial crises is not the random excesses of investors who take on too much debt and gamble in ventures that do not succeed. Problems arise when large numbers of market participants are swept up in excessive risk taking in the same types of investments, whether it be banks lending too much to developing countries, thrifts lending too much to real estate developers in saturated markets, or individuals making leveraged investments in stocks or land at the top of a boom market.

Similarly, the reason for social concern is not that some individuals are financially hurt or even bankrupted by their bad investments. Individuals who take risks in the hopes of big returns must face the risk of commensurate losses. But a collapse of the financial institutions can hurt innocent depositors and, through the subsequent effect of financial collapse on business activity, can lead to unemployment and the loss of otherwise healthy businesses.

A pessimist might well believe that only the memory of bankruptcies deters excessive risk taking. As that collective memory fades with time, a new generation of investors takes on the excessive risks that lead to financial crisis. But an optimist would hope that improved understanding would lead to alternative institutional rules that prevent the excessive risk taking that leads to financial crises or, if such crises begin, to policies that limit the crises and prevent the evolution of economic collapse.

The public interest in avoiding the failure of banks and other financial institutions argues strongly for government regulation and supervision of these institutions. Even Adam Smith explicitly advocated the regulation of banks because he recognized that their failure would have damaging effects on the economy more generally.

The present volume is part of a broader NBER study, discussed in more detail in the preface, that aimed at increasing our understanding of the sources and propagation of economic crises and stimulating research on the general problem of reducing the risk of economic crisis. The volume divides the subject into three parts: the origins of financial crises in domestic capital markets, the international origins and transmission of financial and economic crises, and the transition from financial crises to economic collapse. For each part, an insightful background paper provides an analytic discussion of relevant issues.

Instead of summarizing either the background papers or the conference presentations, I want to look in this introduction at the four most important potential economic crises that the United States faced in the 1980s and see what lessons can be drawn, both individually and collectively, from these experiences. I will focus particular attention on the role of the government both as a source of these problems and as a force in their resolution. Although the limited space of an introduction inevitably risks oversimplification, I hope that the basic implications of our experience can emerge clearly from even this brief analysis.

The Developing Country Debt Crisis

The debt crisis for less developed countries (LDCs) began in the late summer of 1982 when the government of Mexico announced that it could no longer pay the interest and principal on its international debt and could not obtain additional funds from its creditor banks. Within months, all of the Latin American debtor nations reached a similar situation. During the decade that followed, economic growth in the debtor countries was significantly depressed. The major international banks have been forced to write off substantial amounts of the LDC debt on their books, thereby reducing the capital of the banks and weakening the financial strength of the industrial economies. The full impact of the debt crisis on the industrial nations remains to be seen.

The origins of the LDC debt problem can usefully be traced to a decade before the 1982 crisis when the OPEC countries reduced the production of oil and raised the world price of crude oil from approximately $3 a barrel to more than $12 a barrel. The rise in the price of oil created a vast pool of new savings in the hands of the governments of the oil exporting countries. Although they would eventually spend some of these funds on raising their local standard of living, most of these so-called petrodollars were invested in financial assets. The major money-center banks played a primary role in this process, borrowing funds from the OPEC governments and lending them elsewhere.

The U.S. government encouraged the American banks to recycle petrodollars to borrowers in Latin America. Government officials saw these private credits as a useful supplement to American foreign aid in stimulating economic growth in Latin America. It was not difficult to find willing borrowers throughout Latin America when an excessively easy U.S. monetary policy from the middle of the 1970s to the end of the decade raised the rate of inflation and caused short-term real interest rates to be close to or even below zero.

The major U.S. money-center banks financed the LDC loans not only with their petrodollar deposits but also by syndicating the loans to regional and local banks across the nation. Those smaller banks could add the risky LDC loans to their portfolios without increasing their cost of deposits because depositors were protected by the Federal Deposit Insurance Corporation (FDIC).

It might have been foreseen that real interest rates would eventually rise to historical levels, and that this would make it far more difficult for LDC debtors to service their dollar-denominated debts. It might also have been foreseen that the worldwide boom of the second half of the seventies would end, causing a decline in the demand for the exports of the LDCs and in the prices of their export commodities. But the financial institutions were encouraged by the institutional setting—FDIC guarantees for depositors and low capital requirements—to give inadequate attention to these risks. These same conditions encouraged excessive risk taking in other countries as well where explicit or implicit government protection of depositors substituted for the formal role of the FDIC.

When the Federal Reserve finally took strong steps in 1979 to counter the rising rate of inflation, real and nominal interest rates rose substantially and the U.S. economy experienced a pair of recessions that kept economic activity depressed from late 1979 until the end of 1982. In addition, the jump in real U.S. interest rates caused a sharp rise in the dollar, adding to the LDCs' difficulty in servicing their dollar-denominated loans. The debtor countries were able to meet the higher debt service costs only by substantial increases in their borrowing, increases that were willingly provided by the major money-center banks as late as the spring of 1982. But within a few months after that date, the nature of the debtors' problems had become sufficiently clear that they were no longer able to obtain additional credit on a voluntary basis and therefore were unable to service their debts.

Although the bank loans to these countries were not a large proportion of the banks' total lending, they were large relative to the capital of the banks. The potential losses to the banks if the debtors defaulted on their loans could significantly impair the capital of the banks. Since the deposits of the major money-center banks are primarily the large corporate deposits that are not formally insured by the FDIC, the impairment of the banks' capital entailed a serious risk that depositors would remove their funds from these banks. Such deposits could have been placed instead in foreign banks or invested directly in government securities. Major bank runs of this type could have destabilized the financial system and the economy more generally. To prevent such a collapse, the governments and money-center banks of the major industrial countries pursued the strategy of preventing default by lending some or all of the amounts needed to pay the interest on those loans. The United States and other governments were important not only in providing bridge loans until private financing could be arranged but also in pressuring the private lenders to provide new loans and to roll over old loans as they became due. Without such government pressure, the problem of "free-rider" banks that would want their old loans repaid but that refused to provide new funds would have led to a formal collapse of the repayment and lending process.

This strategy permitted the banks to claim that their LDC loans would eventually be fully repaid and to use the time to accumulate substantial reserves and additions to their capital. These developments prevented the bank runs that many feared when the LDC crisis began.

By 1989 the major money-center banks in the United States and elsewhere had accumulated large reserves and made explicit provisions for substantial losses on their LDC loans. At that point, Treasury Secretary Nicholas Brady proposed that the banks assist the debtor nations by accepting lower interest rates or substantial principal write-downs. Negotiations with Mexico, Venezuela, and the Philippines have been completed on this basis. It is generally expected that this will set the pattern for the negotiations with the other major debtor countries.

Looking back over the period of nearly a decade since the collapse of voluntary lending to the LDC debtor countries, the developments to date are certainly less cataclysmic than many initially feared. The failure of the debtors to repay their loans has not led to the collapse of U.S. money-center banks, and the runs on those banks did not occur. Nor have the debtor countries seen an economic collapse triggered by the withdrawal of international credit or by the need to make tough domestic adjustments to reduce current account deficits. Although the process of adjustment was painful for the debtor countries, the experience may have been the catalyst that caused the fundamental economic reforms in Mexico and elsewhere that now hold the promise of better economic performance in the decade ahead.

But the problems and risks created by the LDC debts are far from over. Most of the Latin America bank debt is valued on the secondary market at less than fifty cents per dollar of debt. Brazil and Argentina, the two largest debtors after Mexico, have yet to conclude satisfactory arrangements. The major money-center banks around the world remain weaker because of the write-downs that they have had to make. Their capital has been reduced by the need to record losses and to reserve for possible future losses. The equity markets' evaluation of bank stocks makes new equity capital exceedingly expensive to obtain.

Even more serious, the cost of deposits and other debt funds to the U.S. money-center banks has been increased substantially by the perception that such deposits and investments involve much greater credit risks than they did in the past. It is particularly significant that the cost of funds to money-center banks—reflecting not only the interest rates that they pay but also their mandatory capital requirements, FDIC premiums and reserve requirements—exceeds the cost of funds to major nonbank companies. These nonbank borrowers therefore bypass the banks and borrow directly from the capital markets by issuing commercial paper and corporate bonds. The banks can lend only to smaller companies and those with lower credit quality. This further increases the perceived riskiness of banks as debtors and therefore increases their cost of funds. This vicious cycle of declining portfolio quality and increasing cost of bank funds is a subject to which I shall return below.

Although it would be unwise to draw final conclusions from this experience before the existing problems are fully resolved, four general observations are possible. First, the excessive LDC debt raised fears of widespread defaults by debtor nations and massive runs by the creditors of the money-center banks. Although neither of these occurred on a scale that created a financial crisis or economic collapse, both did occur in more attenuated ways that left the banks weaker than they were when the 1980s began. Debt write-downs, debt-for-equity swaps, and interest rate reductions have reduced the capital of many U.S. and foreign banks. Creditors have not abandoned the U.S. money-center banks but now require relatively high rates of return to compensate for the increased risk. The banks have made efforts to increase capital and reserves but they continue to face new challenges. The danger remains that, in their weakened condition, their current capital and reserves may not be adequate for the challenges that lie ahead.

Second, the serious risks created by excessive LDC debt reflect the concentration of that debt in banks. If the debt had been in the form of bonds that were widely disbursed in individual and institutional portfolios, the losses associated with the failure of the debtors to pay interest and principal would not have caused the risks to the financial system that have resulted from the concentration of the loans in the banking system. That is true even though more widely distributed ownership of the debt might have precluded the provision of additional credits and thus led to greater defaults.

Third, the concentration of the debt in banks was exacerbated by government policies: the explicit encouragement to banks to recycle petrodollars to developing countries, the inadequate supervision of bank lending, and the provision of FDIC insurance that permitted small and medium-sized banks to finance LDC loans with low-cost insured deposits.

Fourth, the high and rising inflation rates of the 1970s encouraged the debtor countries to borrow excessively by temporarily depressing real interest rates. Without the rise in inflation, the accumulation of debt might have been much more modest.

The 1987 Stock Market Crash

The dramatic crash of the stock market in October 1987 was the kind of event that many in business and government had worried might start a wider financial crisis and economic collapse. In the immediate aftermath of the market's decline it was natural for the press and the public to think about the events of 1929 and the subsequent depression. Such reflection raised two questions: Would the 1987 stock market crash initiate a major economic downturn? What policies might be pursued to reduce the likelihood of such stock market collapses in the future?

The stock market crash did not precipitate a recession, let alone the kind of major downturn that many had feared. Within six months, the economy was gaining strength and real GNP rose by more than four percent in 1988. Why were we so fortunate?

It is difficult enough in economics to know why some unique event has happened. It is harder still to explain with any confidence why something has not happened. I can only speculate on the importance of two possible reasons.

First was the absence of widespread bankruptcies. Although the household sector as a whole lost more than $1 trillion of wealth, there were few personal or institutional bankruptcies. American banks, unlike those in Germany and Japan, do not have extensive equity investments. Margin requirements discourage individuals from buying stock with borrowed funds to the point where a major downturn would cause personal bankruptcy. Even the securities firms that found their liquidity impaired by the market decline were protected from bankruptcy by loans that the commercial banks were encouraged by the Federal Reserve to provide.

The absence of widespread bankruptcies was important in limiting the economic impact of the stock market decline. An individual who incurs a large capital loss but remains solvent will respond by reducing his spending over a large number of years, while a bankrupt individual will be forced to cut current spending much more sharply. Widespread bankruptcies of financial institutions could destroy the deposits of individuals who had not thought they were taking any risks and could impair the ability of the financial system to provide credit.

Second was the provision of liquidity by the Federal Reserve. Immediately after the stock market crash, Federal Reserve Chairman Alan Greenspan announced that the Federal Reserve would provide the increased liquidity demanded by the private sector. The Treasury supported this position by abandoning explicitly the goal of defending the international value of the dollar that it had pursued during the year before the stock market crash. In practice, the Federal Reserve expanded the money supply and permitted short-term interest rates to decline. The Federal Reserve had clearly learned from the studies of the 1930s, when its reduction of the money supply after the stock market crash exacerbated the economic decline.

There was much finger pointing in the search for the causes of the stock market's sharp decline and, therefore, for ways of reducing the likelihood of such declines in the future. The two principal suspects were the government and the institutional investors.

The Federal Reserve and the Treasury were blamed for pursuing an inappropriately tight monetary policy aimed at preventing a decline of the dollar. When an enlarged trade deficit was announced in early October, financial markets assumed that the Federal Reserve would again tighten monetary policy to defend the dollar. This caused interest rates to rise even before the Federal Reserve took any action. High interest rates reduced share prices directly by lowering the present value of any stream of future dividends and indirectly by increasing the risk of recession and therefore of a decline in profits.

The adverse effect of the Treasury's exchange rate policy was exacerbated by its repeated assertions about the importance of the economic policies of foreign governments for the health of the U.S. economy. When Germany and Japan indicated in October 1987 that they would not follow the policy directions that Washington wanted, financial markets interpreted that as an ominous development. The failure of the government to deal with the U.S. budget deficit as the 1988 fiscal year began also contributed to the rise of interest rates and a general unease about the economic future.

Institutional portfolio managers were blamed for program trading strategies that involved selling stock as equity prices fell. These program trading strategies probably encouraged a higher precrash level of share prices and accelerated the decline as share prices began to fall. The ability to pursue such strategies was assisted by the development of trading in index futures, which in turn was facilitated by the use of computers to manage and execute orders. These are irreversible technical developments that cannot be legislated away.

Although there have been some changes in financial regulations and in margin requirements in the wake of the stock market decline, the resiliency of the economy in 1988 and 1989 eliminated any sense of the urgency and even of the desirability of such reforms.

What lessons can be learned from this experience? First, the crash reminded us of the inherent volatility of equity markets. The stock market in every major country except Japan fell sharply in late 1987 and the Japanese market fell by nearly 50 percent in 1990. Individual investors and government policymakers must take that volatility as a starting point in all private and public decisions.

Second, structuring the ownership of equities so that even a major decline in share prices does not cause widespread bankruptcies and impair the financial system itself is important in limiting the damage of a stock market crash.

Third, a better set of macroeconomic policies—a smaller budget deficit and a monetary policy guided by domestic conditions rather than exchange rate targets—might have reduced the risk of the market decline. The Fed-Treasury decision to respond to the market crash by increasing liquidity, publicly stated in a reassuring way, probably contributed to the relatively modest economic consequences.

Fourth, although the "back door" financial help that the Federal Reserve gave to the securities firms through the commercial banks reduced the risk of an even steeper fall in share prices and of the bankruptcy of some financial institutions, the policy of pressuring commercial banks to make high risk loans weakens the ability of the Fed to hold banks' managements accountable for their lending decisions. Fortunately, this time the loans were repaid, and the banks were unscathed by these additional risks. But the precedent is a worrying one. In addition, the active role of the Federal Reserve in protecting securities firms that were on the brink of collapse may make the securities firms even less cautious in their future asset and liability decisions.

Failures of the Savings and Loan Institutions

The widespread failures of savings and loan institutions remains a subject of general public concern, not least because the taxpayers are being called upon to finance hundreds of billions of dollars of rescue costs. Although widely referred to as a "bailout" of the savings and loan institutions, it is in fact a rescue for the depositors, making good on the promise of the Federal Savings and Loan Insurance Corporation (FSLIC), which ran out of funds early in the process. The savings and loans that become insolvent are frequently closed, their senior managements lose their jobs, and their shareholders lose the entire value of their investments.

The savings and loan problem is still far from resolved. The recently created Resolution Trust Corporation (RTC) is actively acquiring insolvent thrifts and using borrowed funds, for which taxpayers will ultimately be accountable, to fill the gap between the market value of the thrifts' assets and their liabilities to depositors. Estimates of the eventual cost of this program of protecting depositors are uncertain and frequently revised upward, but an estimate of $200 billion plus the interest on the incurred debt would not be regarded as unduly pessimistic.

Why did this $200 billion problem occur? Instead of a single reason there is a series of interrelated mistakes that has led to the current situation. The root cause of the problem was the rapid inflation of the 1970s. The rising inflation rate caused a substantial rise in the interest rates paid to depositors and charged on new mortgages. Since most thrift institutions held only fixed interest rate mortgages, the market value of their mortgages fell so much that they were worth less than the value of their deposits and other obligations. To make matters worse, the interest that the thrift paid each year to depositors and other creditors exceeded the interest that it collected on its portfolio of existing mortgages. In short, these thrifts had a negative net worth and were losing more money each year.

Congress responded to these problems by enacting a series of measures designed to permit the troubled thrifts to survive in the hope that they would eventually become solvent again. This approach was based on the fact that, although old mortgages did not pay enough to cover current interest costs, new mortgages carried interest rates that exceeded the cost of funds. As old mortgages matured and were replaced by new ones, the thrifts would become profitable. This process could be helped, Congress reasoned, by faster growth of the thrifts and by investments in higher yielding assets.

To permit that rapid growth, Congress relaxed the minimum capital standards for thrifts, permitting them to increase their size without adding to their equity capital. The method of historic cost accounting permitted thrifts to keep old mortgages on their books at face value, not reflecting the decline in market value due to the rise in interest rates. As a result, the equity owners of thrifts had little or nothing invested in their institutions. They had no capital to lose if the thrift failed but much to gain if high-yield, high-risk investments were successful.

Congress permitted the thrift managements to succumb to this temptation to take substantially greater risks with their investments by relaxing the restrictions on permissible thrift assets. Instead of requiring that virtually all funds be invested in residential mortgages, thrifts were allowed to make much riskier and higher yielding investments. In a few cases, the thrift institution invested in almost nothing but high yield corporate "junk bonds." Because of the government's promise to protect the depositors through FSLIC, the thrifts' ability to attract funds was unaffected by the increased riskiness of their investments. The difference between the high interest rates paid on junk bonds and other high-risk investments and the low cost of insured deposits temporarily made this a very profitable activity.

To make it even easier for the thrifts to attract funds, Congress voted to increase the FSLIC guarantee to $100,000 per account. Thrifts eager to grow rapidly worked with securities firms to "broker" insured deposits. A securities broker would help an individual who had $1 million to invest in short-term deposits to buy ten $100,000 certificates of deposit from ten different thrifts, thus combining high yield with the complete security of government insurance. Thrifts could also use the method of brokered deposits to compete for large institutional pension accounts since the $100,000 FSLIC guarantee limit was applied to each individual participant in the pension plan.

In the end, Congress's gamble failed. Too many of the high risk loans made by the thrifts defaulted. While some of these bad investments reflected inappropriate self-dealing or even criminal activity, the failures were generally due to the excessive risks accepted in pursuit of higher yields.

The likelihood of such failures was very great in a setting where neither the depositors nor the equity owners of the thrifts had much to lose and where the equity owners and the management decision makers had the potential for substantial gains if their gambles were successful.

Moreover, since all thrifts were seeking to lend money for real estate development (including not only residential properties but also commercial real estate of all kinds), there was an inherent tendency to overbuilding. This was exacerbated by the tax rules of the early 1980s that encouraged real estate investments by generous depreciation allowances.

The process came to an end when it became clear that the mortgage borrowers for many commercial real estate investments were unable to service their debts. Faced with negative net worth, the thrifts were not able to pay off their depositors by selling their remaining mortgages in the secondary market. The FSLIC was forced to close those institutions or merge them into healthy institutions and to compensate the depositors or the acquiring thrifts. The extent of the problem was so great that the FSLIC assets were insufficient to deal with all of the insolvent thrifts. Congress voted to back the FSLIC guarantee with whatever government funds would be needed.

The Resolution Trust Corporation is now in the process of making good on that guarantee by acquiring ailing thrifts and closing them or selling them to other institutions. In many cases, the RTC is keeping the mortgages and foreclosed real estate for subsequent disposition and selling the thrift as a network of branches. The RTC then pays the purchaser the value of the deposit liabilities being assumed less a small premium for the value of the branches and the associated deposit-gathering and mortgage-lending capability.

The Office of Thrift Supervision, acting on the basis of recent legislation, is now requiring much higher capital levels of the thrift institutions and limiting the types of investments that they can make. Supervisors are also requiring that, when thrifts have assets of uncertain value, they establish reserves against the risk of future defaults, a process that reduces the thrift's capital available to meet certain of the new minimum capital requirements. The result of all of this has been to force many more thrift institutions into positions of insolvency or capital inadequacy.

Before trying to draw some general lessons from this experience, it is worth asking what would have happened if the government had taken the position that once the FSLIC had exhausted its funds no further compensation to the depositors at failed thrifts would be available.

There would of course have been the financial hardship to many of the depositors of the institutions that became insolvent. Those depositors that had spread their savings among several institutions might have suffered relatively small losses, but others could see their entire savings wiped out. A compromise solution in which the government compensated depositors only up to some lower limit once the FSLIC fund was exhausted (say $50,000 per household instead of $100,000 per account) would have prevented hardship to small savers but not to those larger investors who had used the route of brokered deposits.

But any decision not to provide the full insurance benefits that had been promised by FSLIC might have started runs on all thrift institutions, including those with adequate capital and reserves. Although the risks of the resulting disintermediation are unclear, it is certainly possible that the thrifts would have been able to retain substantial deposits by purchasing private deposit insurance (analogous to the insurance on local government bonds and on mortgages) or by paying higher interest rates in the same way that money market mutual funds do for their uninsured deposits. It is possible, however, that there would be widespread failures of thrifts and an end to thrifts as deposit-taking institutions of the type that we have today. If they could not attract depositors, their portfolios of mortgages would in the end be acquired by mutual-fund-type organizations at prices low enough to ensure that the resulting yields would be high enough to attract investors. Thrifts might continue to act as mortgage originators but would be forced to sell all of their new mortgages to mutual-fund-type organizations. The perceived risk of providing funds to finance mortgages would increase, causing the interest rates charged on mortgages to rise, perhaps substantially. This in turn could lead to a substantial decline in housing construction and a temporary economic decline.

The risks would have been even greater if the failure of the FSLIC to honor its commitments caused depositors to distrust the FDIC guarantee of bank deposits. The resulting runs on bank deposits and disintermediation of funds from the banking system would have much more severe effects on economic activity. While single-family mortgages are a relatively homogeneous product that are easily securitized, that is not true of the commercial loans that constitute the primary business of commercial banks. Eventually banks would no doubt be able to attract uninsured deposits by having much higher capital ratios and paying substantially higher real interest rates, but the period of transition could be a difficult and painful one.

Three very brief conclusions emerge from this brief summary of the thrift crisis. First, without the substantial rise in inflation from the mid-1960s to the end of the 1970s the problem would probably never have occurred. Interest rates would have remained low and the thrifts would have been able to attract funds to finance mortgages at those low interest rates.

Second, deregulation of interest ceilings, reductions in capital requirements and a broadening of permissible asset investments led to excessively risky lending and virtually unlimited leverage because capital requirements were so low and creditors were insulated from risk by the FSLIC. The problem was not deregulation as such but the combination of deregulation (of interest rates, asset composition and capital) with government guarantees to depositors.

Third, once the crisis began the government was forced to provide full insurance payments even after the insurance fund was bankrupt; this action was motivated by the fear of the systemic damage to confidence that would result from a failure to pay and of the economic consequences of the disintermediation that would result. Any transition to the narrower scope of government deposit insurance that many have urged must be done slowly if it is to avoid such risks of rapid disintermediation.

Commercial Bank Failures

Although the spotlight of public attention has focused on the thrift institutions, the risk of commercial bank failures is, if anything, an even more important problem for the economy because of the more central role that banks play.

When oil prices fell sharply in 1986, all of the major banks in Texas failed. Now declining real estate values in New England and in the mid-Atlantic states threaten bank solvency in those areas. The very low prices of bank shares relative to their reported earnings and the very high yields on the bonds of some major banks indicate financial analysts' concerns that earnings will not be maintained or that the banks will actually fail.

Why has this happened? Why are bank failures more frequent now than in past times, even when the economy is not in recession? How will government policies affect these risks in the future?

I have already noted that the LDC debt problem eroded bank capital and raised the cost of funds to banks. This reduced the ability of banks to provide loans to high-quality corporate borrowers for whom it is less expensive to raise funds directly in capital markets (through bonds and commercial paper) or from nonbank institutions like insurance companies and leasing companies. Without these high-quality corporate borrowers, banks have been driven to do more real estate lending than they did in the past.

The banks' desire to increase real estate lending came at a time when tax legislation greatly increased the attractiveness of investing in multifamily housing, in individual condominiums, and in commercial real estate of all kinds. The result has been serious overbuilding of office buildings, hotels, shopping centers, and apartment buildings. Although each prospective project seemed attractive on the basis of the existing stock of real estate and the associated level of rents, when all of the new buildings became available the rent levels were depressed.

The problem was exacerbated by the shifting regional pattern of economic weakness. The oil price declines of the mid-1980s sharply reduced the demand for all kinds of real estate in Texas and Oklahoma. More recently, the New England economy has suffered from the simultaneous decline of demand for the products of the defense, computer, and financial services industries. The result is a fall in rent levels and occupancy rates in New England.

The banks as holders of the mortgages on these properties found their earnings and balance sheets severely impaired. The high leverage ratios of banks in which equity capital is typically only about 5 percent of total assets means that unanticipated losses equal to only a few percent of total assets can leave the bank insolvent.

But the problem of the commercial banks is more fundamental than just the results of excessive lending to developing countries and real estate investors. Banks are in trouble because they have lost the low cost sources of funds in savings and checking accounts that traditionally allowed them to concentrate their lending on low-risk high-quality borrowers.

Of particular importance was the loss of the zero-interest checking account balances and low-interest savings accounts that were the basic sources of bank funds when the 1970s began. The rising rate of inflation in the 1970s and the associated increases in interest rates brought that to an end. The introduction of money market mutual funds that allowed relatively small savers to get high market interest rates forced banks to raise interest rates in order not to lose deposits. The introduction of checking facilities in money market mutual funds forced banks to pay interest on checking accounts. These changes required relaxation of regulations on bank interest rates, but these regulatory changes simply followed the market pressures. Without the regulatory changes, the banks would not have been able to hold their deposits at all.

The low-cost captive funds that had sustained banks in the past were gone. Banks had to compete directly with nonbank institutions and with the capital market for the business of the better credit risks and for pools of residential mortgages. Although the FDIC guarantees keep the cost of deposits lower than they would otherwise be, the overall cost of bank funds relative to the cost of funds provided by life insurance companies or mutual funds is increased by the premiums that the banks pay for their FDIC protection, by the need to maintain reserves with the Federal Reserve, and by the requirement to have at least a specified minimum investment of equity capital per dollar of assets.

This change in the cost of funds is changing the role of banks in our economy and, in the process, has created an excess number of banks. The large number of independent banks and of branches of individual banks keeps costs higher than they would be in a system with fewer banks and branches. The problems of the regional banks as economic downturns have shifted from one area of the country to another has highlighted the advantage that national banks would have in pooling their risks.

The process of bank consolidation that would reduce costs and risks is hampered, however, by the increased capital requirements recently agreed to at the Bank for International Settlements (BIS) meeting of the major central banks and now incorporated into U.S. banking regulations. Since few banks have extra capital, they are not able to acquire banks that have inadequate capital. The legislative rules separating banking and commerce make it impossible for nonbank corporations to acquire undercapitalized banks. As a result, a number of banks with inadequate capital are likely to fail.

The regulatory pressure on banks to increase their capital is also making banks reluctant to make new loans. This reluctance is increased by the banks' uncertainty about the amount by which the recent tightening of supervisory standards and the accompanying decline in real estate values will force them to add to their reserves against possible future loan losses. Banks are therefore reducing their lending and the amounts of their deposits in order to increase their capital-asset ratios. This process of bank-led disintermediation is making it more difficult for small and medium-size businesses to borrow and may restrict the amount of such credit when economic activity and therefore loan demand start to increase.

The combination of tougher supervisory standards and higher capital requirements may also limit the Federal Reserve's ability to expand bank credit through open market purchases of securities. Traditional expansionary open market operations lead to an increase in total bank assets and deposits equal to a substantial multiple of the funds that the Fed injects by its open market operations. But if all banks were to be at the minimum capital levels, they could not expand their total deposits and total assets. Open market operations could succeed only in substituting private loans for government securities in banks' portfolios, a much less powerful impact on the economy. Indeed, risk-based capital requirements could prevent even that small stimulative effect since banks do not need capital against government securities to satisfy risk-based capital standards but would need additional capital if those government bonds were replaced by private loans.

In short, the developments of the past decade have produced a situation in which bank failures have increased and further failures are likely among institutions that have been driven to operate with higher leverage and lower-quality assets than they did in the past. Bank lending is restrained by a lack of capital and by the need to accumulate reserves against possible future loan losses. The central role of banks in our payments system and in providing credit to those businesses that cannot have direct access to the credit markets makes such a weakening of the banking system a source of concern for the long-run health of the economy.

In addition, widespread bank failures could trigger a major economic downturn, even if the FDIC protected the value of deposits, because of the resulting cutback in business lending. As banks failed, their creditors and the FDIC would seek to collect existing loans. While some borrowers would be able to shift to other banks, the ability to borrow is often based on informal information that is difficult to transfer. This would be particularly true for smaller and middle sized borrowers. In an environment of banking failures, those banks that survive would be reluctant to take extensive risks with new customers. While everything could eventually be resolved with the same total lending and economic activity being supported by a smaller number of healthy national banks, the transition could see such a reduction of credit that economic activity would be severely curtailed.

The banking system as a whole is a "public good" that benefits the nation over and above the profits that it earns for the banks' shareholders. Systemic risks to the banking system are risks for the nation as a whole. Although the managements and shareholders of individual institutions are, of course, eager to protect the solvency of their own institutions, they do not adequately take into account the adverse effects to the nation of systemic failure. Banks left to themselves will accept more risk than is optimal from a systemic point of view. That is the basic case for government regulation of banking activity and the establishment of capital requirements.

But government rules that require more capital and less risky lending reduce the rate of return on bank capital and thus make it difficult for the banks to attract new capital. If banks cannot earn the same after-tax rate of return that investors of capital can get in other industries, it will not be possible to sustain the banking industry. Some increases in pretax returns will no doubt come about from shrinking the number of banks and thus taking advantage of the economies of scale in administration. But in the end, if the after-tax rate of return on capital in banking at the required capital ratios and risk limitations is too low, the supply of banking services in the United States will decline. Businesses with access to the capital markets will borrow directly. Smaller businesses may find that they are at such a disadvantage in raising capital that they will not survive and will be acquired by larger businesses with access to capital.

Such dire developments are not inevitable. Institutions and regulations may evolve so that banks can lend based on uninsured deposits with lower capital requirements or, like their European counterparts, with equity participation. Tax rules or the reserve requirements may change to improve the after-tax return on banking capital.

All of this is, I hope, a far too pessimistic view of what could happen. The problems of the banks have not yet reached a stage where we can predict the future or draw conclusions about the past with confidence. But, looking back, several things stand out.

First, inflation caused financial innovations that eliminated the sources of low-cost bank capital needed for banks to lend to the high-quality low-risk borrowers that have direct access to the capital market.

Second, the combination of the increased cost of funds and the additional burdens imposed by government regulations (capital requirements, Federal Reserve requirements, and FDIC charges) force many banks to compete for relatively high-risk businesses, at least as a part of their portfolio.

Third, insured depositors provide funds to the banks without worrying about the riskiness of the banks' assets because of the FDIC insurance. Major corporate depositors at the larger banks also give less attention to the riskiness of the banks' assets because of the implicit guarantee to uninsured deposits that results from the too-big-to-fail doctrine that appears to guide government policy.

Fourth, the government is seeking to limit excessive risk taking by banks through tougher supervisory standards and increased capital requirements. But this takes place in a competitive environment that forces banks to increase their risk taking because they can no longer compete for the low-risk loans that are now provided directly by the capital markets and because the high cost of funds requires correspondingly higher returns on their assets.

Fifth, the need for more bank capital per dollar of assets may continue to be frustrated by competitive market pressures that limit the ability of banks to attract capital unless they can increase the after-tax rate of return that they earn on that capital.

The result of all of this is a much higher level of risk at the center of our financial system, and, therefore, of the economy itself, than existed in the past. How well this will work in the years ahead remains to be seen.

Some Conclusions

In the decade of the 1980s the United States faced four major shocks to its financial sector and to the economy more generally. Each of these threatened to precipitate a financial crisis and a major economic downturn. Fortunately, none of these dangers materialized.

But looking back at these problems, the overall impression is that we face greater risks now than we appeared to a decade ago. My analysis of these problems also suggests that the major source of the increased risk in our economy has been a series of seemingly well-intentioned government policies.

A primary culprit identified in each of the four cases has been the rising inflation rate that resulted from the monetary and fiscal policies of the late 1960s and the second half of the 1970s. Inflation distorted real interest rates, led to excessive borrowing by LDCs, caused thrift institutions with fixed rate mortgages to become insolvent, and created fundamental changes in the commercial banking sector. All too often during the period of rising inflation economists misunderstood the serious and far-ranging adverse effects of inflation. A stable and low rate of inflation would have avoided many of the problems that have increased the risk of economic crisis.

Changes in government policies aimed at meeting new economic conditions have frequently added to the risks of economic crisis. These included the government's urging of private banks to recycle petrodollars to developing countries in the 1970s (and may include recent government pressure on banks to forgive substantial amounts of that debt), attempts at international policy coordination and exchange rate management (which not only contributed to the U.S. stock market crash of 1987 but may, by pressuring the Japanese monetary authorities into an easy monetary policy after 1987, have contributed to the collapse of Japanese share prices in 1990, which has weakened their banking system), and the relaxation of regulatory and capital standards on the thrift institutions that encouraged excessive risk taking. The consequences of institutional and regulatory arrangements are often hard to predict and create pressures that add to systemic risk.

This is certainly not to say that all government actions in the 1980s have increased the risk of economic crisis. The Federal Reserve brought down the high rate of inflation inherited from the 1970s, cajoled the commercial banks to provide enough additional lending to avoid widespread default of the LDC debts, and provided liquidity after the stock market crash. The government, through the FDIC, prevented the collapse of a major money-center bank and, through the RTC, has prevented a collapse of the thrift industry. Other examples could be added. But in virtually every case the government appears to be correcting problems of its own making and possibly sowing the seeds of future problems.

The robustness of the American financial system depends on its ability to avoid widespread personal and institutional bankruptcies; this in turn requires adequate diversification of investments relative to existing capital. Greater diversification of assets would have avoided some of the most serious risks faced in the 1980s. If LDC debts had been in the form of bonds held by individual and institutional investors instead of by the commercial banks, the losses incurred by these investors would have created no risk to the financial system as a whole. If commercial banks had geographically diversified loan portfolios, the regional problems of the American economy would not have threatened their solvency.

There are many potential sources of economic crises and much that can be done to reduce future risks. But a low rate of inflation, stable government policies, and an institutional environment that encourages sufficient diversification of risks can play a fundamental role in reducing the risk of future economic crises.

1 The Risks of Financial Crises

1. *Benjamin M. Friedman*
2. *E. Gerald Corrigan*
3. *Irvine H. Sprague*
4. *Norman Strunk*
5. *Joseph A. Grundfest*

1. *Benjamin M. Friedman*

Views on the Likelihood of Financial Crisis

Financial crises have traditionally attracted a peculiar fascination. It is difficult to specify with precision just what a financial crisis is, but most people in the business and financial world apparently sense that they would recognize one if they experienced it. More important, the fear of financial crisis is often a key motivation underlying actions in both the private and public policy spheres.

Concern about the likelihood of a financial crisis in the United States has become more widespread in recent years for several reasons. First, the wave of restructurings and reorganizations that has affected much of U.S. corporate business in the 1980s has, in one way or another, typically involved the substitution of debt for equity capitalization. As a result, the corporate sector's interest burden has risen sharply compared to its earnings, thereby prompting questions about the ability of more heavily indebted firms to meet their obligations in the event of a general slowdown in nonfinancial economic activity. This substitution of debt for equity has not merely involved a few individual transactions large enough to attract attention under any circumstances—$25 billion for RJR Nabisco, for example—but has also reached a scale that is hard to ignore at the aggregate level. During the six years between 1984 and 1989, the volume of equity that U.S. firms in nonfinancial lines of business retired, through various restructuring transactions, exceeded the gross proceeds of nonfinancial firms' new equity issues by $575 billion.

The author is grateful to Thierry Wizman for research assistance; to Charles Kindleberger for helpful comments on an earlier draft; and to the National Science Foundation, the General Electric Foundation, and the Harvard Program for Financial Research for research support.

Second, the actual record of failures of both nonfinancial firms and financial intermediaries has been extraordinary in the 1980s. The business expansion following the severe 1981–82 recession was the first on record in which
the failure rate among nonfinancial businesses continued to rise long after the
recession ended, rather than dropping back to pre-recession levels. Moreover,
on inspection it is clear that this phenomenon has not been merely the natural
counterpart of an unusually large number of new business start-ups. (Contrary
to popular impressions, the 1980s has not been an unusually fertile period for
new business formation activity in the United States.) Within the financial
intermediary system, both the actual failure experience and the perceived
threat of further failures have been unprecedented since the 1930s. More than
1,000 commercial banks failed during 1981–89—including 206 in 1989
alone—versus only 79 during the 1970s and just 91 from the end of World
War II through 1970. Hundreds of savings and loan institutions became insolvent in the 1980s, yet continued to operate anyway because the FSLIC (unlike
the FDIC) lacked the resources to close them; in 1989 Congress voted a bailout plan for the thrift industry that will cost far in excess of $100 billion.

Yet a third reason for the increased worry about a financial crisis is the
shock of the October 1987 stock market crash. Unlike many previous dramatic declines in stock prices, the drop of 23% in one day (or 33% compared
to the peak two months earlier) led to neither a financial crisis nor a business
recession. But the crash vividly demonstrated that the vulnerability of values
already experienced in recent years in the markets for more specialized assets—for example, farm land, oil reserves, and loans to developing countries—also extended to so general a class of assets as ownership claims on all
of American business. Further, the manifest failure of various "portfolio insurance" schemes to serve their intended purpose cured many institutional
investors of the illusion that even if a financial crisis did bring a broadly based
decline in asset values, their own holdings would somehow be insulated.

These developments notwithstanding, prevailing attitudes toward the possibility of financial crisis are neither unanimous nor unambiguous. The most
familiar concern is that some contractionary disturbance to business activity
could result in a cumulative inability of debtors to meet their obligations, possibly leading to some form of rupture in the financial system that in turn might
further depress the nonfinancial economy. But no one (to my knowledge) has
clearly indicated what set of circumstances would lead to such an outcome,
much less suggested how probable those circumstances now are. In addition,
there are some arguments for discounting the importance of the changes that
have taken place in this regard in the 1980s. For example, some observers
have argued that most of the substitution of debt for equity in recent years has
occurred in the context of reorganizations that are likely to promote business
efficiency and hence provide the higher earnings with which to service the
added debt; also, that these transactions are explicitly designed to minimize
conventional bankruptcy problems in the event that the anticipated higher

earnings do not materialize. Others have pointed out that even after the refinancings of the 1980s, U.S. corporations on average remain much less highly levered than their counterparts abroad.

Whether or not they are valid under today's specific circumstances, concerns about the likelihood of a financial crisis do reflect a long history of such events playing a major role in the most visible and memorable business fluctuations. The most severe business downturns that have occurred in the United States—for example, those commonly called "depressions"—have in every case been either preceded or accompanied by a recognizable financial crisis. Moreover, while each financial crisis is idiosyncratic in some respects, according to at least some lines of thinking the role of financial crises in this context is not accidental but fundamental to economic behavior in an investment-oriented private enterprise system. At the same time, there is widespread recognition that the likelihood that such a system will experience a financial crisis under any given set of circumstances also depends on institutional safeguards and other factors subject at least in part to influence by public policy.

The object of this paper is to review some of the major lines of thinking about the likelihood of a financial crisis that have emerged in response to the events of the 1980s. Section 1.1 briefly sets this review in context by referring to the long-standing tradition of emphasis on financial crises and their real economic consequences. Section 1.2 outlines the view that the large-scale substitution of debt for equity by U.S. nonfinancial corporations during the 1980s reduced the economy's ability to sustain fluctuations in business activity without borrowers' defaulting on their obligations in unusually great numbers and volume. By contrast, section 1.3 examines several different arguments for rejecting concerns about borrowers' ability to meet their obligations. Section 1.4 shifts the focus from borrowers to lenders and considers the ability of both commercial banks and thrift institutions to withstand a default experience of major proportion. Section 1.5 summarizes the paper's principal conclusions.

1.1   Financial Crises in Historical Perspective

Few students of economics or business are not familiar with some of the major episodes in the past that are easily recognizable as financial crises. The bursting of the "tulip mania" in 1636 and of the "South Sea Bubble" in 1720, the East Indian Company crisis in 1772, the collapse of the railway boom in 1846, the failure of Union Generale in 1881 and of Baring Brothers in 1890, the U.S. banking panics of 1873, 1893, and 1907, the failure of the Creditanstalt in 1931 and the worldwide bank collapse of the next two years, and, of course, Black Thursday in October 1929: all this is standard lore, typically related nowadays with substantial color and even sometimes a hint of nostalgia.[1] In fact, although financial crises as such are more difficult to recognize in more primitive institutional environments, the history of such episodes is substantially more ancient.[2]

The typical features of these events include, in Minsky's classic description, "large-scale defaults by both financial and nonfinancial units, as well as sharply falling incomes and prices" (1963, 101). Beyond that, however, it is difficult to generalize. Some financial crises have been the inevitable (at least in retrospect) end product of speculative excesses that carried asset prices to levels far beyond any plausible relationship to the corresponding fundamental values. Others—especially those that have followed the onset of war or other major political events—have themselves presumably resulted from sudden reassessments of fundamental values. Still others have resulted from foolish decisions, or bad luck, at specific financial institutions that were large enough and central enough to impair the system as a whole when they failed to honor their commitments. Yet another entire range of influences, not mutually exclusive with any of the above, has typically arisen from the nonfinancial economy. Incomes can and do decline for reasons other than financial crisis. And when they do, on a sufficient scale, the ensuing defaults have at times led to crises in the financial system.

While events in the nonfinancial economy may or may not be the proximate cause of financial crises, the main reason why financial crises are of such great interest from a public policy perspective is presumably the impact that they in turn exert on nonfinancial economic activity. The idea of influences running in this direction is also well known, even if the substantive nature of the behavioral mechanisms involved is not. Of the six U.S. economic downturns during 1867–1960 considered by Friedman and Schwartz (1963) to have been severe, banking crises either preceded or accompanied the onset of four—those beginning in 1873, 1893, 1907, and 1929.[3] The bank panic of 1837 also apparently played a major role in accounting for the severe economic downturn that began in that year (Temin 1969). Sharp declines in stock prices also occurred in each of these five years. Among U.S. economic downturns of lesser magnitude, banking panics occurred in conjunction with (although not necessarily at the inception of) those beginning in 1857, 1882, 1899 and 1902.

It is not surprising that growing awareness of the effect of financial crises on the nonfinancial economy has often prompted a policy response. The two leading examples in the United States within the twentieth century are the

1. The best general reference is Kindleberger (1978). Sprague (1910) and Friedman and Schwartz (1963) provide useful chronologies for the United States. Galbraith's (1954) account of the 1929 stock market crash and its aftermath is a jewel.

2. See, e.g., Gibbon's ([1776] 1932) discussion of financial developments in the later Roman period.

3. The two exceptions were the recessions beginning in 1920 and 1937. See the useful tables in Schwert (1989, 102, 105).

establishment of the Federal Reserve System in the aftermath of the panic of 1907 and the severe recession of 1907–8, and the separation and reform of the banking and securities industries after the 1929–33 depression. Minsky's (1963, 102) interpretation of the post-Depression banking changes is especially apt: "As the institutions were reformed at a time when the lack of effectiveness and perhaps even the perverse behavior of the Federal Reserve System during the great downswing was obvious, the changes created special institutions, such as the various deposit and mortgage insurance schemes, which both made some of the initial lender of last resort functions automatic and removed their administration from the Federal Reserve System."

Despite the general agreement on the desirability of shielding the nonfinancial economy from effects due to financial crises, the way in which these effects operate remains unclear. Friedman and Schwartz (1963) emphasized the role of financial crises in creating sudden reductions in the quantity of money held by the public, especially during episodes involving widespread bank failures or (as in the panics of both 1893 and 1907) suspensions of convertibility of deposits into currency. By contrast, Fisher's (1933) notion of "debt deflation" focused on the market for credit rather than money. More recently, Bernanke (1983) and Mankiw (1986) have further developed Fisher's idea by making explicit the role of banks as specialized institutions able to allocate credit on the basis of their superior ability to collect and process relevant information about would-be borrowers and their prospects. By compromising banks' (and perhaps other specialized lenders') ability to serve this function, a financial crisis therefore removes a necessary ingredient to many spending decisions.

Not everyone has regarded the nonfinancial consequences of occasional financial crises as wholly bad, however. Schumpeter (1934), for example, focused on the role of severe business downturns in freeing economic resources to move to more productive uses. Without a fairly severe downturn from time to time, the varied relationships and habits that make up the fabric of everyday business dealings would tend to lock both people and capital in place, even if technology and other conditions determining the best allocation of the society's resources were changing over time. According to Schumpeter the positive role of occasional financial crises, including especially the widespread abrogation of contracts, is to provide enough pressure to break through these rigidities.

Finally, under any of these notions of how financial crises affect nonfinancial economic activity—the money-destruction view of Friedman and Schwartz, or Fisher's debt-deflation alternative, or even Schumpeter's more benign perspective—there remains the question of whether financial crises themselves occur in a purely random fashion or more systematically. The most intriguing idea advanced along these lines, and the one that bears most directly on the current situation in the United States, is Minsky's "financial instability hypothesis," according to which as time passes since the last financial crisis, the relevant behavior changes in such a way as to increase the likelihood of the next crisis.[4] In particular, either borrowers take on more debt relative to their earnings, or they (and perhaps lenders too) hold relatively less liquidity, or both. But, for a shock of any given size to the typical borrower's earnings, the probability of experiencing defaults on a scale sufficient to impair the functioning of the system as a whole depends both on the volume of debt to be serviced and on the reserve of liquidity behind it. For a given distribution of shocks to which the economy is subject in the ordinary course of events, therefore, the likelihood of a financial crisis rises over time as the memory of the last such crisis fades. Whether the specific changes in the behavior of borrowers and lenders that have attracted so much attention during the 1980s correspond well or poorly to Minsky's hypothesis remains an open question.

1.2 Concerns about Corporate Indebtedness

The phenomenon of the 1980s that has accounted for the greatest part of the spreading concern about the U.S. economy's vulnerability to financial crisis is the leveraging of the nonfinancial corporate business sector. As Kaufman (1986a, 1986b) and Friedman (1986, 1988) (among others) have emphasized, corporate borrowing in the last decade has differed from prior experience both in scale and in purpose. U.S. businesses have not only borrowed in far greater volume than in the past, but have used a much greater share of the proceeds of that borrowing to pay down their own and other companies' equity rather than to put in place new earning assets. As a result, the share of earnings, or cash flow, that the typical company needs to devote to keeping current on its debt service has risen to record levels.

Figure 1.1 documents this increased interest drain at the aggregate level by showing the ratio of interest payments to available earnings before interest and taxes, since World War II, for corporate and noncorporate firms engaged in nonfinancial lines of business in the United States. For purposes of comparison, the figure also shows the ratio of personal interest payments to pretax personal income.

Especially for the corporate sector, the deterioration of interest coverage since 1980 has been dramatic. On average during the 1950s and 1960s, it took 16¢ of every dollar of pretax (and pre-interest) earnings to pay corporations' interest bills. The corresponding average for the 1970s was 33¢. Thus far in the 1980s it has been 55¢. In no year since 1981 has the interest share of earnings been below 50¢ on the dollar.

Indeed, the corporate sector's experience in this regard since 1981 vividly

---

4. See Minsky (1963, 1964, 1972, 1977). The rationale motivating the behavioral changes that drive the "financial instability hypothesis" is not fully specified in Minsky's work; see Friedman and Laibson (1989) for one possible explicit rendering.

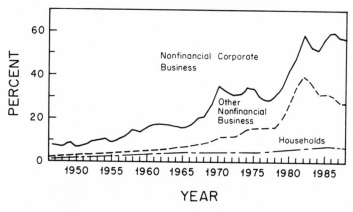

Fig. 1.1   Interest payments as a share of available earnings, 1946–88
Source: Bureau of Economic Analysis.

demonstrates the impact of continued massive borrowing for purposes of equity substitution rather than asset creation. In 1982, at the bottom of the most severe business downturn since the 1930s, aggregate pretax corporate earnings (before interest payments) were depressed by 11% from year-earlier levels, and the interest rate on short-term business borrowing reached a record 16.66% (in May). Not surprisingly, the share of corporations' earnings required to meet their interest bills also rose to a record level, 59¢ out of every dollar. By 1986 earnings had rebounded by 25%, and the average short-term borrowing rate was down to 6.39%. But by then corporations had taken on so much additional debt that, in 1986, interest payments were up to 60¢ of every dollar of earnings, yet a new record. By 1989 earnings had risen still further, to 42% above the 1986 level, and the average short-term borrowing rate was 8.80%. But with the further borrowing that had taken place, interest payments still stood at 57¢ of every dollar of earnings.

   The experience of unincorporated businesses resembled that of corporations until the 1980s, but since then it has differed sharply. Mirroring the corporate sector's interest-to-earnings ratio, the noncorporate sector's interest payments rose from only 6¢ of every dollar of pretax (and pre-interest) earnings on average in the 1950s and 1960s to 17¢ on average in the 1970s, and 33¢ in the 1980s. But after peaking at 40¢ on the dollar in 1982—to recall, the bottom of the recession—interest payments as a share of earnings dropped to only 30¢ on the dollar by 1989.

   In contrast to corporations or unincorporated businesses, the trend of household-sector interest payments in the 1980s has shown no noticeable break with prior experience. Personal interest payments averaged 4¢ of every dollar of pretax (and pre-interest) personal income in the 1950s and 1960s, and 5¢ in the 1970s. Thus far in the 1980s the average has been 8¢. As of 1989 the ratio had been essentially unchanged for half a decade, with the value for every year during 1984–89 falling within the narrow range of 7.6¢–8.0¢ on the dollar.

Finally, figure 1.2 presents an alternative perspective on business borrowers' ability to meet their current obligations by showing, separately for the corporate and noncorporate sectors, the ratio of interest payments to cash flow including earnings (as in fig. 1.1) plus depreciation. Interest payments look smaller compared to this expanded measure of ability to pay, of course, but the overall trends are roughly the same as those shown in figure 1.1. Most important, the corporate sector's ratio of interest payments to cash flow also rose dramatically during the late 1970s and the back-to-back recessions of 1980 and 1981–82, and, despite the strong recovery of cash flow and the general fall in interest rates, as of 1988 it had shown no improvement whatever from the bottom of the last recession.

The basic reasons underlying the disparate patterns of interest payments compared to earnings (or cash flow) among corporations, unincorporated businesses and households are readily apparent from table 1.1, which summarizes the changes in these three sectors' respective balance sheets between 1980 and 1989 (scaled in each case relative to gross national product). Not surprisingly, since all three sectors have borrowed in record volumes during the 1980s, the heart of the issue in the resulting comparisons is their differing use of the proceeds of borrowing.

Between 1980 and 1989 the corporate sector increased its overall debt by nearly one-fourth and its market debt by more than one-third, relative to the size of the economy. By contrast, with investment unusually weak during the 1980s (presumably as a result, at least in part, of the extraordinarily large federal budget deficit, which persisted long after the economy had recovered from the recession that began the decade), total corporate asset holdings declined by about one-tenth compared to the size of the economy, and corporate

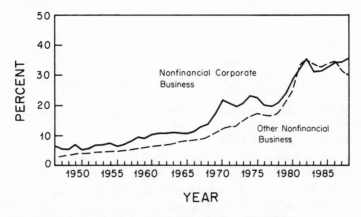

Fig. 1.2   Interest payments as a share of cash flow, 1946–88
Source: Bureau of Economic Analysis.

Table 1.1   **Balance Sheet Changes, 1980–89**

	1980	1989	Change	% Change
Corporate sector:				
Assets	140.5	126.3	−14.2	−10.1
Tangible	104.9	91.4	−13.5	−12.9
Financial	35.6	34.9	−.7	−2.0
Liabilities	45.1	56.3	11.2	24.8
Market	29.1	39.3	10.2	35.1
Other	16.0	17.0	1.0	6.2
Net worth	95.4	70.0	−25.4	−26.6
Noncorporate sector:				
Assets	60.9	63.4	2.5	4.1
Tangible	55.7	55.0	−.7	−1.3
Financial	5.2	8.5	3.3	63.5
Liabilities	18.2	27.5	9.3	51.1
Market	15.7	23.7	8.0	51.0
Other	2.5	1.3	−1.2	−48.0
Net Worth	42.7	35.9	−6.8	−15.9
Households:				
Assets	365.9	388.6	22.7	6.2
Tangible	136.0	132.1	−3.9	−2.9
Financial	229.9	256.5	26.6	11.6
Liabilities	52.3	66.5	14.2	27.2
Home mortgages	33.1	43.8	10.7	32.3
Other	19.2	22.7	3.5	18.2
Net Worth	313.6	322.1	8.5	2.7

Source: Board of Governors of the Federal Reserve System.
Note: Data (except for % changes in final column) are year-end values expressed as percentages of fourth-quarter GNP (at seasonally adjusted annual rates). Tangible assets are measured at reproduction cost for reproducible assets, and market value for land. Financial assets are measured at book value for debt and deposits, and market value for equities. Detail may not add to totals because of rounding.

holdings of tangible assets declined by somewhat more. In short, corporations were borrowing not to invest but to finance transactions—including mergers, acquisitions, stock repurchases, and leveraged buy outs (LBOs)—that merely paid down their own or other corporations' equity. As a result, the corporate sector's aggregate net worth declined by more than one-fourth compared to the size of the economy.

Both the noncorporate business sector and the household sector likewise increased their respective debt levels faster than the economy grew, but in both cases this borrowing financed at least some relative increase in asset holding. Among unincorporated businesses the increase in assets held (all of which was in financial assets) trailed well behind the increase in borrowing, so that net worth also declined substantially in relative terms—albeit not by anything like the comparable decline for corporations. Households also, at least in the aggregate, used much of their record borrowing in this decade to finance increased holdings of financial assets, so that household-sector net worth modestly increased compared to the size of the economy.[5]

It is always possible, of course, that because balance-sheet data like those summarized in table 1.1 value reproducible tangible assets at reproduction cost and exclude intangible assets ("goodwill") altogether, they understate the true earning power of assets in general and corporate assets in particular. If so, then despite the sharp rise in interest payments as a share of corporate earnings and cash flow in the recent past, earnings in the near future may increase rapidly enough to reverse the worrisome trends shown in figures 1.1 and 1.2. Investigating this possibility is far from straightforward because of the obvious difficulty of measuring assets' prospective earning power. (Standard book values are irrelevant for this purpose.) Nevertheless, the possibility of undermeasurement of assets in this way is sufficiently important to warrant making at least some attempt to grapple with the issue.

The stock market, where prices in principle reflect market participants' collective judgment about future earnings, provides one way of doing so for the corporate sector. Figure 1.3 plots the ratio of the book value of debt to the market value of equity for the aggregate of U.S. nonfarm nonfinancial business corporations, for year-end values since World War II and two other selected dates: 25 August 1987 (the stock market peak), and 19 October 1987 (the market crash).[6] The results of this calculation shed little new light on the issue at hand, however. As of year-end 1989, the corporate sector's market-value leverage remained well below the postwar record level (above 1.0) set in 1974, when firms borrowed heavily and then the stock market crashed. But it likewise remained substantially above the average level that prevailed before then. Viewed from another perspective, aggregate leverage at year-end 1989 stood about where it did at year-end 1980, or at the end of the 1981–82 recession, despite that fact that by December 1989 stock prices had fully regained the record level previously reached in August 1987.

It is also always possible that the impression given by the sector-aggregate data in figures 1.1–1.3, or in table 1.1, may not correspond to the reality of borrowing and asset accumulation by individual firms and families. The fact that the household sector as a whole has accumulated substantial assets to match its record issuance of debt in the 1980s would be of limited help in the event of an economic downturn if the families who had bought the assets had little or no overlap with the families that had issued the debt. For analogous

5. Moreover, the additional financial assets taken on by households included not only equities but large amounts of deposits, government securities, and other credit market debt instruments.

6. Year-end values are taken directly from the Federal Reserve System's Flow of Funds Accounts. Values for other dates are based on interpolation or extrapolation of the corporate borrowing data in the Flow of Funds Accounts, in conjunction with a simple equation that relates the Standard & Poor's stock price index to the Flow of Funds estimate of the market value of equity for the entire nonfarm nonfinancial corporate business sector.

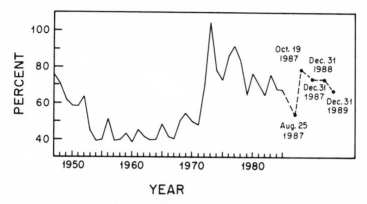

Fig. 1.3   Debt-equity ratio, U.S. nonfarm nonfinancial corporate business sector, 1948–86, and selected dates, 1987–89
Sources: Board of Governors of the Federal Reserve System, Flow of Funds Accounts, and author's calculations.

reasons, the fact that the corporate sector as a whole has borrowed far in excess of its creation of new assets in the 1980s would not increase the economy's financial fragility if the firms that had done the borrowing were mostly ones that had had only little debt, or excess liquidity, to begin with. Investigating the possibility of such a divergence between the aggregate data and the disaggregated reality is difficult for the household sector because of the paucity of available information on individual families' holdings.[7] By contrast, disaggregated data on the corporate sector are readily available, at least for the larger firms.

Bernanke and Campbell (1988) and Bernanke et al. (1990) used data from the Compustat files to study the detailed balance sheet and earnings record of some 1,400 U.S. corporations for years beginning in 1969. On the whole, their findings from these disaggregated data reinforce rather than contradict the impressions drawn above on the basis of aggregate data. For the median firm in their sample, interest expense rose from 13¢ of every dollar of cash flow in 1969 to 22¢ in 1988. For firms in the 90th percentile for this ratio, however, interest expense rose from 34¢ of every dollar of earnings in 1969 to $1.86 in 1988. (In other words, by 1988 more than one firm in 10 was not earning its interest due.) Nor did this sharp deterioration reflect merely the vagaries of one year's earnings. Compared to a trailing three-year average of earnings, interest expense for firms in the 90th percentile rose from 44¢ on the dollar of earnings in 1971 to $1.48 in 1988.

An especially interesting exercise carried out by Bernanke et al. was to "replay" the 1981–82 recession in the sense of considering the implications of

7. See Friedman (1986) for a brief examination of the Federal Reserve's 1983 Survey of Consumer Finances from this perspective.

the actual 1981–82 percentage decline in firms' earnings in the context of the typically higher debt levels taken on by 1988. The results indicated that, in the absence of some offsetting factor, default levels in such an event would have substantially exceeded those experienced during the 1981–82 recession itself. By the second year of the recession, for example, firms in the 90th percentile of indebtedness would have had negative cash flow, and firms in the 75th percentile would have had interest due equal to 72¢ of every dollar of cash flow.

These results are all the more striking in that firms in the Compustat sample apparently did much less borrowing than the average U.S. corporation and likewise accounted for a disproportionately small share of equity repurchases. In 1988, for example, firms in Bernanke et al.'s sample raised just $41 billion from debt issues (net of repayments) versus $198 billion for the nonfarm non-financial corporate business sector as a whole (as measured by the Flow of Funds accounts). Similarly, firms in their sample repurchased only $26 billion of equity in 1988 versus $131 billion for the nonfinancial corporate sector overall.

In sum, the concerns raised by Kaufman and Friedman on the basis of sector-aggregate data for balance sheets as well as interest expense compared to earnings (or cash flow) appear to stand up not only against correction for market value of firms' equity but also against the use of individual firm data.

1.3   Contrasting Viewpoints

Public discussion of the developments summarized in section 1.2 has not reflected a one-sided conclusion that these trends represent any threat to the U.S. economy, however. Both academic researchers and financial practitioners have advanced a series of arguments to the effect that the increasing reliance on debt by U.S. business corporations in the 1980s has not yet exposed the economy to any significant risk of financial fragility and is not likely to do so in the foreseeable future.

1.3.1   Perspectives on Debt Aggregates

To begin, Summers (1986, 1989) has emphasized the fact that the increasing aggregate indebtedness of both business and household borrowers in the 1980s has represented no more than a continuation of trends that had already prevailed over most of the post–World War II period. Figure 1.4 shows the total outstanding indebtedness of all U.S. borrowers other than financial intermediaries, scaled in relation to gross national product, for year-end values since the end of the Korean War. The behavior of the economy's *total* debt ratio was certainly extraordinary in the 1980s. Until the last decade, one of the most striking features of U.S. postwar financial behavior had been the stable relationship between debt and economic activity. The debt ratio measured in this way fluctuated within a very narrow range, with no evident trend

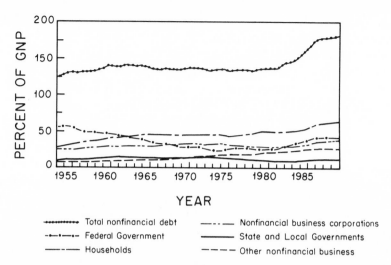

Fig. 1.4   **Outstanding debt of U.S. nonfinancial borrowers, 1953–89**
Source: Board of Governors of the Federal Reserve System.

either up or down. By contrast, since 1980 outstanding debt has risen by one-third compared to the size of the economy.[8] But as table 1.2 shows, a rising ratio of debt to income is not new for private borrowers. The outstanding debt of unincorporated businesses has risen, relative to the size of the economy, in every decade since World War II. So has that of households. Corporate debt has risen relative to gross national product in each postwar decade except the 1970s. For each of these three borrowing sectors, therefore, it is difficult to look at figure 1.4 and identify the 1980s as a clear departure from prior postwar experience.

Instead, what stands out in this regard is primarily the extraordinary behavior of the federal government's debt ratio. Not only in the postwar period but in the entire history of the United States, back to 1789, the only sustained increases in the outstanding federal debt compared to the size of the economy took place during major wars and during the depression of the 1930s (when the economy itself was shrinking). With the huge budget deficit that the government ran throughout the 1980s, however—notwithstanding the absence of either war or depression—the federal debt ratio increased sharply in every year from 1981 through 1986, and then held roughly steady through 1989. This extraordinary fiscal imbalance has probably affected the U.S. economy in a variety of ways, but increasing the likelihood of financial crisis is presumably not one of them. Even after the increase of the 1980s, the federal debt ratio is still just back to where it was (on the way down, after World War II) in

8. The mean debt ratio during 1953–80 was $135.70 of debt for every dollar of income, with standard deviation (based on annual data) of only $2.90. At year-end 1980 the ratio was $137.10. At year-end 1989 it was $183.60.

Table 1.2   Debt Ratios for Private-Sector Borrowers, 1928–89

	Nonfarm Nonfinancial Business Corporations	Other Nonfarm Nonfinancial Businesses	Households
1928	.45	.34	.24
1945	.20	.06	.13
1950	.23	.07	.24
1960	.30	.09	.43
1970	.34	.14	.47
1980	.29	.16	.50
1989	.39	.24	.64

Sources: U.S. Department of Commerce and Board of Governors of the Federal Reserve System.
Note: Values shown are ratios of year-end debt outstanding to fourth-quarter GNP (at seasonally adjusted annual rates).

1962, and to date no one has voiced serious concern over the government's ability to meet its obligations.

Taggart (1985) has pointed out that, among private borrowers, sector-aggregate debt ratios in the 1980s have reached record levels for households but not for businesses. Precise comparisons to the prewar (and pre-Depression) experience are difficult to draw for several reasons, of which the most immediate in this context is that a greater fraction of the nation's business activity is now conducted via corporations than was the case 60 years ago. As table 1.2 shows, however, the combined debt of corporations and unincorporated businesses is still well below the relative level that prevailed during the 1920s.

Just what to make of these comparisons is unclear. Summers's interpretation of the 1980s as mostly a continuation of prior postwar trends is, in the end, unreassuring because of the lack of any benchmark for judging how high is up. Carried to its logical conclusion, this argument implies that no level of debt compared to income would be worrisome as long as borrowers got there by increasing their indebtedness along a continuation of their respective postwar trend lines. Nor is Taggart's comparison to the 1920s ultimately persuasive in light of the debt default experience of the 1930s.

1.3.2 Perspectives on Firm Behavior

In contrast to these arguments on the basis of aggregate data, Jensen (1984, 1986, 1988, 1989a, 1989b) has developed a series of arguments about the behavior of individual firms, all to the effect that the nature of the transactions by which U.S. corporations have substituted debt for equity in the 1980s is such as to minimize, or even alleviate altogether, the risks that have normally been attendant on high indebtedness in the past.

First, Jensen has argued that the "value" created for investors in leveraged buy outs and other forms of corporate acquisitions—value that is apparent in the typically large premium paid over the previously prevailing market price of the acquired firm's stock—is a reflection of prospective gains in operating efficiency. In the case of leveraged buy outs in particular, Jensen has argued that these gains in efficiency are due to the replacement of an inferior organizational form of management, the conventional large (and often diversified) corporate structure, with the superior organizational form represented by the "LBO association." Further, even apart from changes in organizational form, Jensen's "free cash flow" theory of corporate behavior holds that a higher debt level increases managers' incentive to achieve operating efficiencies: "Debt creation, *without retention of proceeds of the issue,* enables managers to bond their promise to pay out future cash flows. . . . The exchange of debt for stock helps managers overcome the normal organizational resistance to retrenchment that the payout of free cash flow often requires. The threat of failure to make debt-service payments serves as a strong motivating force to make such organizations more efficient" (Jensen 1988, 29–30; emphasis in original.)

While this first argument implies that increased earnings are likely to be forthcoming to support firms' newly increased leverage, Jensen has also presented a second argument to the effect that the highly levered capital structure itself reduces creditors' incentive to force liquidation of the firm in the event that the anticipated efficiency gains and consequent higher earnings do not materialize. The heart of this claim is that higher leverage also increases the value at risk in any bankruptcy proceeding, which in turn "provides larger incentives to bring about private reorganization outside of the courts" (Jensen 1989a, 413). Hence even if the firm fails to achieve greater efficiency and faster earnings growth, and therefore cannot meet the increased debt-service payments promised, the outcome is unlikely to be a traditional default and bankruptcy of the kind that in the past has resulted in workers laid off, orders to suppliers canceled, and losses recorded on creditors' balance sheets.

Third, Jensen has also argued that several recent advances in financing technology have further reduced the likelihood of a bankruptcy that would result in any of these undesired outcomes. One example is the use of "strip financing," in which each participant in a reorganization purchases an identical set of (inseparable) claims against the firm, ranging from secured debt to senior unsecured debt to junior unsecured debt to equity. The object of strip financing, from this perspective, is to make the creditors senior to any possible dividing line identical to those junior to it and thereby to preclude the emergence of an adversarial situation that could lead to one party's putting the firm into bankruptcy. Examples of other financial innovations that reduce the ordinary risks attendant on high debt-service ratios are the purchase of interest rate "caps," which limit the potential increase in payments that a firm is obligated to make, and "swaps," which in effect convert nominally floating rate debt into fixed-rate debt.

Roach (1989) has advanced an additional argument that further buttresses Jensen's confidence that the corporations that have greatly increased their leverage in the 1980s have, for the most part, done so under specific circumstances that do not represent greater financial fragility. According to Roach's data, firms involved in leveraged buy outs have been disproportionately engaged in lines of business typically subject to smaller than average fluctuation of earnings over the course of ordinary business cycles. Food and tobacco companies, for example, accounted for more than 20% of all LBO transactions effected during 1978–88 (measured by dollar size), and companies in retail trade accounted for nearly another 19%. By contrast, such cyclically sensitive industries as mining, construction, and manufacturing of most durable goods have experienced relatively less LBO activity. As a result, the exposure of the newly leveraged firms to potential inability to meet their debt-service payments in the event of recession should be smaller than if these firms had been uniformly distributed throughout the U.S. corporate business sector.

Once again, it is difficult to know what confidence to place in these arguments. As of the time of writing, it appears as if new patterns of LBO activity are beginning to deviate from the concentration on noncyclical industries emphasized by Roach.[9] (The two most recent large transactions both involve airlines.) Because Jensen's arguments are strictly forward-looking, however, they are much more difficult to evaluate.

1.3.3   International Comparisons

Finally, yet another line of argument downplaying the significance of the great increase in business indebtedness in the 1980s has emphasized the fact that, even today, most U.S. corporations remain less highly leveraged than their European or Japanese counterparts.[10] If businesses elsewhere can sustain much greater debt burdens, the reasoning goes, why cannot ours?

Simple comparisons between corporate capital structures here and abroad fail to take into account differences in the institutional, legal, and philosophical environment that are potentially of great significance in this context. Foreign financial markets and financial institutions are typically structured very differently than those in the United States. Ownership of corporate debt and equity securities is typically more highly concentrated than it is here, and—unlike the case in the United States—major lenders are also often major equity holders in the businesses to which they lend. As a result, the entire relationship between the financial sector and nonfinancial industry has a sharply different character.

9. Fox (1990) has shown that firms undergoing leveraged buy outs before around 1986 differed in this and other respects from those that have done so since then.

10. As French and Poterba (1989) have shown, however, because of the great increase in Japanese equity prices in the 1980s, since 1986 the market-value debt-equity ratio of the average corporation has been *lower* in Japan than in the United States.

At the same time, foreign attitudes toward competition versus cooperation (or even cartelization) within industry have traditionally differed from attitudes in the United States. So have attitudes toward the relationship between the private sector as a whole and the government, including, in particular, the willingness of both financial institutions and nonfinancial firms to accede to various forms of governmental guidance. In some cases, a close corollary of this willingness has been a different set of presumptions about the government's readiness to intervene, if necessary, to rescue distressed private firms.

No one knows just how important any or all of these differences have been in accounting for the historically higher leverage of European and Japanese firms. Much systematic research needs to be done on such questions. The findings of that research may indicate, for example, that specific changes in U.S. legal and institutional structures would be useful, in that they would then permit corporations to adopt, with safety, debt burdens more nearly comparable to those abroad. In the absence of such changes, however—indeed, in the absence even of knowledge about just which differences between institutions here and abroad are most important in this regard—the simple fact that U.S. corporations' debt burdens have not yet risen as high as those of foreign firms is also not reassuring.

1.3.4   Bankruptcies and Defaults in the 1980s

Given the uncertainty surrounding each of these disparate sets of arguments, the actual record of bankruptcy and default by U.S. businesses in the 1980s may be instructive. As figure 1.5 shows, this experience has already been beyond all prior comparable experience since World War II, despite the sustained economic expansion that began in 1983. Bankruptcies and defaults have usually increased during and immediately after business recessions, but in prior postwar experience both had then fallen back to pre-recession levels not long after the recession ended. After the 1981–82 recession, however, both bankruptcies and defaults continued to rise for four years during the ensuing expansion, and even by 1988 the bankruptcy and default rates remained far above any previous postwar level.[11] (By contrast, neither the level nor the persistence of delinquencies on consumer loans was at all out of the ordinary during or following the 1981–82 recession.)

The fact that not only the business failure rate but the default rate too have been extraordinary in the 1980s is of particular significance. Popular discussion of the increase in business bankruptcies has sometimes suggested—erroneously—that this phenomenon is merely the reflection of an especially fertile climate for new business start-ups created by tax reduction and deregulation since 1980. Since new start-ups are much more likely to fail than

11. The data shown are the number of bankruptcies per 10,000 concerns, and the dollar volume of liabilities in business failures expressed as a percentage of gross national product. Data are from Dun and Bradstreet. I have adjusted values plotted for 1984–88 for a series break after 1983.

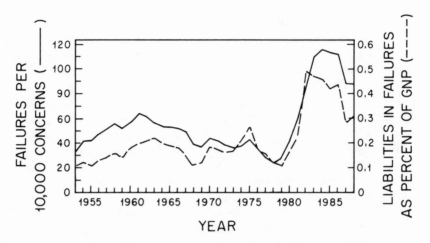

Fig. 1.5   Bankruptcy rates and default rates, 1953–88
Source: Dun and Bradstreet; coverage does not include all industry sectors.

going concerns, any period in which start-ups increase rapidly will also be a period in which failures increase rapidly, and hence the higher failure rate in the 1980s is supposedly a healthy sign rather than a danger signal. If all that were true, however, the failure rate would be high but not the default rate. New start-ups typically do not have large amounts of liabilities. (Moreover, popular impressions notwithstanding, it is also not true that the pace of business start-ups was unusually rapid in the 1980s. The number of new businesses incorporated each year rose at just 2.7% per annum on average during 1980–89, vs. 6.0% per annum during 1950–80.)[12]

The specific default experience of the high-yield unsecured debt ("junk bonds") typically issued in the course of leveraged buy outs and other corporate acquisitions has in particular been subject to substantial debate. Most researchers have agreed that the overall default rate on such securities has been modest.[13] By contrast, Asquith et al. (1989) have shown that this finding hinges on the great increase in the volume of such securities issued in recent years, together with the tendency for most defaults to occur only several years after the time of issue. Although the default rate for high-yield bonds that have been outstanding for several years or more is high, the "universe" of bonds outstanding at any point in time consists disproportionately of bonds issued only recently, and therefore exhibits only the familiar modest default rate *overall*.

Table 1.3, reproduced from Asquith et al. (1989, table 2), shows that the cumulative default rate, measured for bonds issued *in each year* rises from

12. The data are from Dun and Bradstreet.
13. See, e.g., Altman and Nammacher (1985) and subsequent annual issues.

Table 1.3   Aged Defaults for High-Yield Bonds Grouped by Year of Issue

Panel A: % of Par Amount Defaulted in nth Year After Issue:

Issue Year	1st	2d	3d	4th	5th	6th	7th	8th	9th	10th	11th	12th	Total
1977	.00	.00	.00	.00	.00	.00	.00	7.71	3.63	19.27	3.30	.00[a]	33.92
1978	.00	8.32	.00	1.39	.00	7.91	4.85	3.12	5.55	1.39	1.73[a]		34.26
1979	.00	.00	5.54	1.11	2.38	6.73	1.98	.00	5.78	1.19[a]			24.70
1980	.00	.57	2.45	.00	.00	13.90	6.30	1.88	2.45[a]				27.56
1981	.00	6.05	.00	8.06	6.85	.00	.00	.00[a]					20.97
1982	1.00	2.41	1.61	11.49	.00	9.44	.00[a]						25.94
1983	.00	.00	6.08	7.83	4.80	.50[a]							19.21
1984	2.29	1.99	2.03	3.06	.00[a]								9.38
1985	.00	.80	2.28	.45[a]									3.53
1986	2.73	3.84	1.57[a]										8.14

Panel B: Cumulated % of Par Amount Defaulted for x Years After Issue:

Issue Year	1st	2d	3d	4th	5th	6th	7th	8th	9th	10th	11th	12th	Total
1977	.00	.00	.00	.00	.00	.00	.00	7.71	11.34	30.62	33.92	33.92[a]	33.92
1978	.00	8.32	8.32	9.71	9.71	17.61	22.47	25.59	31.14	32.52	34.26[a]		34.26
1979	.00	.00	5.54	6.65	9.03	15.76	17.74	17.74	23.52	24.70[a]			24.70
1980	.00	.57	3.03	3.03	3.03	16.93	23.22	25.10	27.56[a]				27.56
1981	.00	6.05	6.05	14.11	20.97	20.97	20.97	20.97[a]					20.97
1982	1.00	3.41	5.02	16.51	16.51	25.95	25.94[a]						25.94
1983	.00	.00	6.08	13.91	18.71	19.21[a]							19.21
1984	2.29	4.28	6.32	9.38	9.38[a]								9.38
1985	.00	.80	3.08	3.53[a]									3.53
1986	2.73	6.57	8.14[a]										8.14

Source: Asquith et al. (1989).

Note: In this table an *n*th year default is defined as a default within *n* × 365 days of the issue date. High-yield bonds are all bonds rated below investment grade at issue date by Moody's and Standard & Poor (S&P). Defaults are defined as a declaration of default by the bond's trustee, filing of bankruptcy by the firm, or assignment of a D rating by S&P for a missed coupon payment.

[a]May be incomplete, i.e., entire sample may not have been outstanding for *x* years.

only 3%–8% after three years to 25%–33% after 10 years. Nevertheless, with $31 billion of junk bonds issued in 1986 and $13 billion per annum on average in 1984–85 versus only $1 billion per annum on average during 1977–82, the overall default rate for all bonds issued during 1977–86 remains just 8%. No doubt the patterns shown in table 1.3 reflect not just the passage of time per se but also the fact that firms issuing bonds since 1983 have not had to face the burden of meeting debt-service payments during a recession. At least until the next recession occurs, however, separating out these two factors will remain difficult if not impossible.

1.4 Focus on the Banks

The evidence and arguments presented in sections 1.2 and 1.3 bear entirely on the question of whether, and under what circumstances, the borrowers that have taken on greatly enlarged debt-service burdens in the 1980s may be unable to meet their commitments. In some contexts—for example, setting the right price on junk bond portfolios or evaluating the prospects for specific borrowers or even specific industries—this is all that matters. From the broader perspective of assessing the likelihood of financial crisis, however, the ability of *lenders* to absorb portfolio losses is also crucial. Given the history of financial crises, the strength of those lenders that also function as financial intermediaries is of particular importance in this regard.

Financial crises in the past have invariably involved not just debt defaults by nonfinancial borrowers but either the threat or the actuality of a rupture of the financial system. Indeed, as long as financial intermediaries continue both to create deposits and to extend credit, the economy as a whole is likely to remain insulated from a cumulative default experience capable of sharply curtailing nonfinancial economic activity. After all, that is why the "lender of last resort" policies of central banks (and, occasionally, other governmental agencies) usually focus on avoiding the failure of financial institutions, even though their underlying public policy objective is far broader. Although the solvency of the U.S. financial intermediary system has already received enormous attention elsewhere—banks, primarily, in the context of loans to developing countries, thrift institutions in the context of the recent plague of insolvencies and the subsequent multihundred billion dollar bailout—the issue is important enough to warrant at least some attention here as well.

Table 1.4, adapted from Brumbaugh et al. (1989), shows how the $2.9 trillion of assets—and hence deposits—held as of September 1988 at all U.S. commercial banks of size greater than $50 million was distributed among banks according to each bank's ratio of risk-adjusted capital to total assets.[14]

---

14. See Brumbaugh et al. (1989), table 5. "Risk-adjusted capital" is defined as equity plus perpetual preferred stock plus subordinated debt and limited preferred stock, minus investments in unconsolidated subsidiaries.

Table 1.4   **Distribution of Bank Assets by Capital-Asset Ratio**

Ratio of Risk-adjusted Capital to Total Assets	Number of Banks	Assets ($)
Negative	28	22.5
0%–3%	48	43.4
3%–6%	150	926.0
6% +	5,094	1,894.5
Total	5,320	2,886.4

Source: Brumbaugh et al. (1989).
Note: Asset figures are in billions of dollars. Data are for September 1988.

Almost $1 trillion of this total was held at banks with capital-asset ratios below 6%, and, in some cases, far below that percentage even with all bank assets counted at full book value.

What makes this situation either more or less likely to lead to a potential problem, depending on one's perspective, is the extreme concentration of this $1 trillion of assets among the nation's largest banks. Individual banks' year-end data for fiscal years ending in 1988 showed a total of $833 billion of assets—well over a quarter of the $2.9 trillion shown in table 1.4—held by the largest 15 banks. Again with all bank assets counted at full book value, these banks had capital-asset ratios ranging from 1.49% (NCNB of Texas) to 6.89% (Morgan Guaranty Trust Co.). The average capital-asset ratio for all 15 banks, weighted by assets, was 4.34%. But merely assuming a reserve for LDC loan losses equal to 50% of each bank's exposure reduced the average capital-asset ratio for the group to 3.17%, and for the more exposed banks the erosion consequent on allowing a 50% reserve against LDC loans was even greater. For Manufacturers Hanover, for example, allowing this reserve reduced the capital-asset ratio from 5.31% to 1.44%. Doing so for Bank of America reduced its ratio from 3.71% to 1.48%.[15]

Further, these same banks are also among the most heavily committed to financing leveraged buy outs. As of the most recent available data, 12 of the nation's 15 largest banks each had more than $1 billion in LBO exposure, including loans already outstanding plus unfunded commitments. Total exposure among these 12 amounted to $37 billion—more than their combined total capital, even including all LDC loans at full book value. Manufacturers Hanover, for example, which had $3.3 billion of capital as reported, or only $900 million after allowing a 50% reserve against LDC loans, had $5.1 billion in LBO exposure including $3.5 billion of loans already outstanding. Bankers Trust, which had $2.6 billion of reported capital, or $1.5 billion after a 50% reserve against LDC loans, had $5.0 billion of total LBO exposure including $3.6 billion in loans already outstanding.[16]

15. Data described here are from Brumbaugh et al. (1989), table 6.
16. Data described here are from Quint (1989).

In sum, the largest U.S. banks' holdings of debt issued in the course of leveraged buy outs alone—not to mention other corporate reorganizations also involving the substitution of debt for equity capitalization—already bulks large compared to these banks' thin margins of capital. Because other lenders (e.g., life insurance companies) have also participated heavily in financing corporate reorganizations, while most developing countries have been able to borrow only from banks, banks' total LBO exposure remains well below their total LDC exposure (see Krugman in this volume). Nevertheless, exposure to risk via LBO debt and other high-leverage corporate situations has grown to a magnitude that also represents a potential problem in the event of any systemic default experience. Moreover, the circumstances under which large numbers of highly levered U.S. corporations would be unable to meet their obligations—a severe business recession, for example—overlap considerably with circumstances under which many developing countries would find servicing their debts even more problematic than is already the case.

By contrast, debt securities issued in corporate reorganizations are apparently less of a factor in the current troubled situation of U.S. thrift institutions. The Garn–St. Germain Depository Institutions Act of 1982 authorized federally chartered thrift institutions to hold up to 11% of their assets in junk bonds, and state-chartered institutions have faced more generous limitations in some cases. California, for example, in principle imposes a 15% limit (although one large California institution had 29% of its consolidated assets in junk bonds as of March 1988). Nevertheless, as of September 1988 only 161 of the more than 3,000 FSLIC-insured thrift institutions owned any junk bonds at all, and among those that did, in most cases their holdings were well within these limits.

Thrifts that became insolvent in 1987, for example, held only 0.2% of their combined total assets in junk bonds, and only 1.9% in commercial loans of all kinds (see Brumbaugh et al. 1989, table 13). As of September 1988, all thrift institutions combined held only $13 billion of junk bonds, or about 5% of the universe of junk bonds outstanding. These holdings were highly concentrated, with 76% of the thrift industry total held at just 10 institutions and 91% at 25 institutions. Although this concentration pattern raises questions about the few institutions that do have junk bond holdings, a recent GAO inspection found no apparently greater risk of insolvency at these institutions on that account (see General Accounting Office 1989). Indeed, some of the 10 thrift institutions with the largest junk bond holdings have been unusually profitable.

1.5   Summary of Conclusions

The evidence and arguments reviewed in this paper support several specific conclusions. First, financial crises have historically had a major role in large fluctuations in business activity. A financial crisis has occurred either just prior to, or at the inception of, each of the half dozen or so most severe recorded declines in U.S. economic activity. Before World War II financial crises occurred in conjunction with most other business downturns as well.

Second, the proclivity of private borrowers to take on debt in the 1980s has been extraordinary by postwar standards. Among business borrowers, including especially corporations, much of the proceeds of this surge in debt issuance has gone to pay down equity (either the borrower's or another company's) rather than to put in place new earning assets. As a result, interest payments have risen dramatically compared to either earnings or cash flow. The corporate business sector's debt-service burden, relative to either earnings or cash flow, rose to record highs in the early 1980s and has remained at record levels despite sharp declines in nominal interest rates and a sustained expansion of business profits.

Although there are arguments both for and against the view that this increase in business leverage raises the prospective threat of widespread default in the event of a generalized decline in earnings, as would presumably occur during a major recession, a third conclusion that is clear from the record to date is that the rate at which U.S. businesses have gone bankrupt and defaulted on their liabilities in the 1980s is already far out of line with any experience since the 1930s. The business failure rate not only rose to a postwar record level during the 1981–82 recession but—in contradiction to prior cyclical patterns—continued to rise through the first four years of the ensuing recovery. The volume of defaulted liabilities, measured relative to the size of the economy, behaved in a parallel way (thereby contradicting the notion that the businesses that failed were primarily new start-ups, of a small enough size not to matter much from the perspective of systemic risk).

Fourth, the largest U.S. banks' exposure to debt issued in the course of leveraged buy outs or other transactions substituting debt for equity capitalization now exceeds their risk-adjusted capital, even with all bank assets (including loans to developing countries) counted at book value. Although this exposure is not (yet) as large as that due to banks' LDC loans, the two sets of risks are not independent.

The implications of these developments for public policy in the United States are, at least potentially, profound. If these trends of the 1980s together constitute an increase in the economy's financial fragility, they increase not only the likelihood that the government will have to act in its capacity as lender of last resort but also the likely magnitude of lender-of-last-resort action should such be necessary. The responsibility for such actions has been decentralized since the 1930s, however, and some of the responsible governmental agencies are themselves less secure than used to be the case. For example, the gross insufficiency of the FSLIC's resources has already necessitated a multihundred billion dollar bailout of insolvent and potentially insolvent thrift institutions, a bailout which is to be financed in large part by new federal government borrowing. And in both 1988 and 1989, the FDIC experienced losses—in other words, had to draw down its capital—for the first time since its inception in 1934. Responding to a renewed insolvency problem in the thrift industry, or, even more so, to a proportionately equivalent problem in the commercial banking system, would therefore be extremely challenging.

At the same time, the Federal Reserve System also retains some responsibility to act in a lender-of-last-resort capacity. Indeed, the basic rationale for the system's creation, stated clearly in the 1913 Federal Reserve Act, was "to provide an elastic currency"—precisely so as to avoid financial crises. Should the exercise of this responsibility become necessary, doing so in a fashion consistent with other Federal Reserve objectives, like maintaining price stability, will also be challenging to say the least.

References

Altman, Edward I., and Scott A. Nammacher. 1985. *The Anatomy of the High Yield Debt Market*. New York: Morgan Stanley.

Asquith, Paul, David W. Mullins, Jr., and Eric D. Wolff. 1989. Original Issue High Yield Bonds: Aging Analyses of Defaults, Exchanges, and Calls. *Journal of Finance* 43 (September): 923–52.

Bernanke, Ben S. 1983. Nonmonetary Effects of the Financial Crisis in the Propagation of the Great Depression. *American Economic Review* 73 (June): 257–76.

Bernanke, Ben S., and John Y. Campbell. 1988. Is There a Corporate Debt Crisis? *Brookings Papers on Economic Activity*, no. 1, 83–125.

Bernanke, Ben S., John Y. Campbell, and Toni M. Whited. 1990. U.S. Corporate Leverage: Developments in 1987 and 1988. *Brookings Papers on Economic Activity*, no. 1, 255–86.

Brumbaugh, R. Dan, Jr., Andrew S. Carron, and Robert E. Litan. 1989. Cleaning Up the Depository Institutions Mess. *Brookings Papers on Economic Activity*, no. 1, 243–84.

Fisher, Irving. 1933. The Debt-Deflation Theory of Great Depressions. *Econometrica* 1 (October): 337–57.

Fox, Christopher J. 1990. *Changes in the Insolvency Risk of LBO Transactions: Evidence from the 1980's*. A.B. thesis, Harvard University.

French, Kenneth, and James Poterba. 1989. Are Japanese Stock Prices too High? National Bureau of Economic Research, Mimeo.

Friedman, Benjamin M. 1986. Increasing Indebtedness and Financial Instability in the United States. In *Debt, Financial Stability, and Public Policy*. Kansas City: Federal Reserve Bank of Kansas City.

———. 1988. The Corporate Debt Problem. In *Economic Vulnerabilities: Challenges for Policymakers*. Washington, D.C.: Curry Foundation.

Friedman, Benjamin M., and David I. Laibson. 1989. Economic Implications of Extraordinary Movements in Stock Prices. *Brookings Papers on Economic Activity*, no. 2, 137–89.

Friedman, Milton, and Anna J. Schwartz. 1963. *A Monetary History of the United States, 1867–1960*. Princeton, N.J.: Princeton University Press.

Galbraith, John Kenneth. 1954. *The Great Crash, 1929*. Boston: Houghton Mifflin.

General Accounting Office. 1989. *High Yield Bonds: Issues Concerning Thrift Investments in High Yield Bonds*. Washington, D.C.: Government Printing Office.

Gibbon, Edward. (1776) 1932. *The Decline and Fall of the Roman Empire*, 6 vols. New York: Modern Library.

Jensen, Michael C. 1984. Takeovers: Folklore and Science. *Harvard Business Review* 62 (November–December): 109–21.

———. 1986. Agency Costs of Free Cash Flow, Corporate Finance and Takeovers. *American Economic Review* 76 (May): 323–29.

———. 1988. Takeovers: Their Causes and Consequences. *Journal of Economic Perspectives* 2 (Winter): 21–48.

———. 1989a. The Effects of LBOs and Corporate Debt on the Economy. In *Tax Policy Aspects of Mergers and Acquisitions*, pt. 1. Hearings held by U.S. Congress, House of Representatives, Committee on Ways and Means (101st Congress, 1st Sess.). Washington, D.C.: Government Printing Office.

———. 1989b. Eclipse of the Public Corporation. *Harvard Business Review* 67 (September–October): 61–74.

Kaufman, Henry. 1986a. *Interest Rates, the Markets, and the New Financial World.* New York: Times Books.

———. 1986b. Debt: The Threat to Financial Stability. In *Debt, Financial Stability, and Public Policy.* Kansas City: Federal Reserve Bank of Kansas City.

Kindleberger, Charles P. 1978. *Manias, Panics and Crashes: A History of Financial Crises.* New York: Basic Books.

Mankiw, N. Gregory, 1986. The Allocation of Credit and Financial Collapse. *Quarterly Journal of Economics* 101 (August): 455–70.

Minsky, Hyman P. 1963. Can "It" Happen Again? In *Banking and Monetary Studies,* ed. Deane Carson. Homewood, Ill.: Irwin.

———. 1964. Longer Waves in Financial Relations: Financial Factors in the More Severe Depressions. *American Economic Review* 54 (May): 324–32.

———. 1972. Financial Stability Revisited: The Economics of Disaster. In *Reappraisal of the Discount Mechanism*, vol. 3. Washington, D.C.: Board of Governors of the Federal Reserve System.

———. 1977. The Financial Instability Hypothesis: An Interpretation of Keynes and an Alternative to "Standard" Theory. *Nebraska Journal of Economics and Business* 16 (Winter): 5–16.

Quint, Michael. 1989. Banks Cast a Hard Eye on Buyouts. *New York Times* (September 10), sec. 3, pp. 1–14.

Roach, Stephen S. 1989. Living with Corporate Debt. *Journal of Applied Corporate Finance* 2 (Spring): 19–30.

Schumpeter, Joseph A. 1934. *The Theory of Economic Development.* Cambridge, Mass.: Harvard University Press.

Schwert, G. William. 1989. Business Cycles, Financial Crises and Stock Volatility. *Carnegie-Rochester Conference Series on Public Policy* 31 (Autumn): 83–125.

Sprague, O. M. W. 1910. *History of Crises under the National Banking System.* Washington, D.C.: Government Printing Office.

Summers, Lawrence H. 1986. Debt Problems and Macroeconomic Policies. In *Debt, Financial Stability, and Public Policy.* Kansas City: Federal Reserve Bank of Kansas City.

———. 1989. Taxation and Corporate Debt. *Journal of Applied Corporate Finance* 2 (Spring): 45–51.

Taggart, Robert A., Jr. 1985. Secular Patterns in the Financing of U.S. Corporations. In *Corporate Capital Structures in the United States*, ed. Benjamin Friedman. Chicago: University of Chicago Press.

Temin, Peter. 1969. *The Jacksonian Economy.* New York: Norton.

2. *E. Gerald Corrigan*

The Risk of a Financial Crisis

I am delighted to contribute to this important volume if for no other reason than to find that I am not alone in my worries about the vulnerabilities of the economic and financial system. I should also say at the outset that the three background papers prepared by Ben Friedman, Paul Krugman, and Larry Summers have bolstered my confidence in the work being done by academic economists. All three papers are first rate; they are readable, coherent, institutionally sensitive but, most of all, they offer pragmatic guidance to someone like me who must bridge the gap between theory and practice. What is also striking about these three papers is that none dismisses the possibility that a serious financial disruption could occur, although each comes to that view from a somewhat different vantage point.

Overview

My task, as I understand it, is to add something of my own personal perspective to the discussion as a whole. With that in mind, let me start with several general comments.

First, all three of the background papers grapple with the definition of "crisis," and to varying degrees they attempt to distinguish between types of crises. While I have great difficulty coming up with neat definitions in this area, some useful distinctions can be made. For example, "financial disruptions" can be distinguished from "financial crises" by means of the extent of the damage they inflict on the real economy. That is, the term "crises" should be reserved for those episodes that cause clear and significant damage to the real economy. However, even that distinction may be misleading in that it may ignore or unduly play down the extent to which a financial disruption has the potential to inflict serious damage on the real economy if left unattended or if handled irresponsibly.

Second, with the above distinction in mind, my personal perspective is one that is tempered by direct experience in dealing with quite a few financial disruptions but no financial crises since even the 1987 stock market disruption seems to have had little or no effect on the real economy. However, as suggested above, the line between "disruption" and "crisis" can be fine indeed since it is not at all difficult to imagine circumstances in which specific "disruptions" of the past 10 or 15 years could have tripped into the category of "crises." Indeed, I can readily think of a number of examples of "financial

Due to the press of events, E. Gerald Corrigan was not able to attend the October 1989 conference. This paper was submitted subsequently for inclusion in the published record of the conference.

disruptions" that clearly had at least the potential for causing serious if not systemic damage.

Some might feel that this is an exaggeration. Perhaps so, but the hard fact is that when the phone rings, informed judgments have to be made and often they have to be made very quickly in the face of limited and conflicting information. Those initial judgments almost always center on an assessment of whether a given situation has systemic implications and, if so, the nature and extent of such implications. Those initial assessments are also always made in a context in which you know that losses and even failures provide a necessary element of discipline to the system. Thus, efforts to protect the system should not protect those whose miscalculations or misdeeds caused the problem in the first instance.

Third, as I see it, the past 15 years have witnessed a greater number of financial disruptions with potential systemic implications than was the case over the postwar period before 1974. And, if we divide the 1974–89 period roughly in half, the latter half of that interval has seen more disruptions than the former, especially in a context in which the last seven years have been characterized by uninterrupted economic expansion—a point Ben Friedman stresses above. At the risk of oversimplification I believe there are three reasons why the past 15 years have seen such a high incidence of financial disruptions: first, macroeconomic policies and performance—perhaps especially the tacit acceptance of deficits, debt, and inflation—have contributed both directly and indirectly to elements of volatility and risk taking in financial markets and in other elements of economic activity; second, financial innovation and technological advances in financial markets are two-edged swords. These developments clearly provide important new choices and benefits to savers and investors alike, but they are also the source of new elements of risk and volatility; finally, there is far, far too much emphasis on short-term returns and rewards, surely here in the United States, but elsewhere as well.

The *last* general point I would make is that I believe that, looking forward, the risks of financial crises—as distinct from financial disruptions, which are sure to occur—are something more than zero. Since that may be interpreted as a provocative statement, I will elaborate. It is probably fair to say that automatic stabilizers and other institutional changes have—as suggested in all three background papers—reduced the statistical probabilities of a financial disruption turning into a crisis. But, and this is a very big but, if a crisis were to develop, I believe its capacity to generate major damage to the real economy may be greater today than it was in the past. The fundamental reason for this is the nature, speed, and complexity of the operational, liquidity, and credit interdependencies that bind together all major financial institutions and markets in the world. In Bagehot's day, and long before, the first precept in banking and finance was, "Know your counterparty." Today, that is not nearly good enough. Indeed, in Bagehot's day, the managers of financial institutions understood very well the nature of the transactions that were generating income and profits; today that is often not the case. That, of course, raises the question of whether financial management has fully caught up with today's incredibly complex financial marketplace.

Some Diagnostics of Recent Financial Disruptions

Against that general background let me now turn to some diagnostics of the financial disruptions to which I have had some direct exposure over the past 15 years to see what common denominators—if any—may be present. Such an exercise may be helpful in identifying approaches and policies that, at the very least, can help check problems when they arise but maybe—just maybe—also help in the formulation of approaches that can reduce the incidence of such disruptions.

I have already touched on the first factor I want to cite in this regard; that, of course, is macroeconomic policy and performance. There is no question in my mind that the seeds of many of the financial disruptions we have seen in recent years were sown in the decade between 1969 and 1979, when attitudes about inflation were all too sanguine. More recently we have made the implicit decision that we can live with huge internal and external deficits and corresponding high levels of public and private debt. Directly and indirectly, the resulting economic and financial environment produces patterns of behavior and expectations that surely work to increase risk and fragility in the financial system.

The second factor I would note is concentrations of activities or exposures by financial institutions. Concentrations take many forms: exposures to a single borrower, exposures to a single industry, exposures to a single instrument, exposures to a single class of borrower, or exposures to a single commodity. However defined, I am hard-pressed to think of a single episode of financial disruption in recent years that did not entail some element of concentration on the part of the institution or institutions that got into trouble.

A third factor is what Paul Krugman calls the "bandwagon" effect. Beyond its obvious forms, there is a curious twist on this phenomenon. Namely, financial innovations (new instruments, trading strategies, etc.) that initially produce high rates of return for the innovator tend to be very short-lived in the financial sector because they are so easy to duplicate. However, the bandwagon effect, reinforced by the illusion of permanent high rates of returns, tends to draw relatively unsophisticated players into such activities at just the wrong time. As a further extension of the bandwagon effect, there is another phenomenon which I call the "illusion of liquidity." That is, the belief—obviously unfounded—held by many market participants that they are that much smarter, that much quicker, or that their stop-loss strategy is that much better, that they will be able to take profits and get out when markets turn while others take the losses.

A fourth factor that has been present in most financial disruptions of the past 15 years is the threat of dislocation in payment, settlement, or clearing systems. This has been reasonably well documented in the case of the stock market crash, but very difficult and potentially very serious problems with payment and settlement systems have also been encountered in other episodes over the past 15 years. For example, both the Herstatt situation in 1974 and the silver market disruption in 1980 presented major problems of this nature. Needless to say, payment and settlement systems are of special importance because such systems can be the vehicle through which a localized problem can very quickly be transmitted to others, thereby taking on systemic implications.

A fifth factor I would cite, but with some trepidation, is the possibility that financial markets—or at least some segments of financial markets—may be characterized by a condition of overcrowding such that spreads and returns do not fully compensate for risks. In saying this, I know full well that the textbooks would say this condition cannot exist for long. The textbooks would also say that the solution to overcrowding is exit—graceful or otherwise. That is of course, one of the things I worry about. Namely, if the overcrowding hypothesis is correct, can the implied shrinkage and consolidation occur in an orderly way, when we recognize the fact that financial institutions are not gas stations?

A sixth factor that must be mentioned is plain old-fashioned greed, which in all too many cases has given rise to fraud and other elements of criminal activity. Indeed, we have seen cases in which widespread violations of criminal statutes have occurred; there are numerous other examples of reckless and irresponsible behavior that I find utterly shocking. Needless to say, the problem of blatantly excessive risk taking is more likely to be a problem in the case of thinly capitalized institutions since the owners have so little to lose if things go sour.

A seventh and final factor that must be cited relates to supervisory gaps or, even worse, breakdowns in the supervisory process. The worst example of this, by far, is to be found in the thrift industry situation, which saw not only a breakdown in the supervisory process but a public sector "bailout" of incredible proportions. However, the silver market disruption, the Ohio thrift problem, and the stock market crash all revealed at least some troubling elements of supervisory gaps or shortcomings in the supervisory process itself. Even today, I regard the absence of any form of consolidated oversight of major securities companies as a defect in the supervisory framework in the United States.

In this context, I am mindful that questions have also been raised about the effectiveness of the bank supervisory process in cases such as that of Continental Illinois and the major Texas bank failures. More specifically, the question is often asked as to why the bank supervisors were not able to identify and stop the patterns of behavior that gave rise to these problems before they reached the proportions that ultimately caused failures and large costs to the deposit insurance fund.

While each of the financial disruptions of the past 15 years is very distinct, every episode I can think of had elements of most of the seven factors listed above associated with it. Having said that, I wish to stress that the diagnostics of financial disruption are useful only up to a point. What may be even more important are the traits of firms or markets that have generally avoided problems or the patterns of behavior that have permitted firms to overcome problems without reliance on public funds or other forms of public support. Here it is clear that comfortable margins of capital and liquidity, combined with diversification of activities and exposures and strong management and control systems, are the keys to success in avoiding problems and overcoming them when they arise.

Some Myths about Financial Disruptions

Having shed some light on common denominators that have been present in most if not all of the financial disruptions of the past 15 years, I would now like to turn my attention to several of what I regard as popular myths that tend to be associated with the folklore of financial disruptions. I will cite seven such myths.

First, there is the view that systemic concerns are uniquely associated with large financial institutions or, more particularly, large banks. That is simply not true on two counts: first, large securities houses present many of the same systemic issues that arise with large banks; and second, troubled institutions need not be large *or* be banks to raise systemic concerns. The best illustration of this is to be found in the chain of events triggered in 1985 by the failure of E.S.M., a small government securities firm in Florida. That seemingly inconsequential failure triggered the Ohio and Maryland thrift problems and the failure of B.B.S. (a small government securities dealer in New Jersey), placed in jeopardy several insurance companies, and came very close to producing full-scale gridlock in the entire mortgage-backed securities market. This sequence of events produced headlines in newspapers throughout the world, uncovered hundreds of millions of dollars in losses for the affected institutions, and resulted in a number of individuals being convicted of criminal violations. However, none of the institutions involved was "large," none was a bank, and none had federal deposit insurance. Yet by any definition, the sequence of events had the clear potential to produce systemic damage.

The second myth I want to touch on is the bank "bailout" myth in general and more specifically the "too-big-to-fail" myth. For these purposes I want to draw a sharp distinction between banks and thrifts because I believe it important that the banking sector not be penalized unjustly by virtue of the problems in the thrift industry and the extraordinary blend of circumstances that gave rise to those problems.

In banking, as historically defined, the term "bailout" is a misnomer, and I believe there is more to the distinction than semantics. In point of fact, banks—including large banks—have failed, and, in the process, the shareholders and management have not been bailed out. To be sure, the process of closing, merging, and/or recapitalizing problem or failed banks has cost money, but the funds used for these purposes have, virtually without exception, been provided out of the deposit insurance fund, which is funded by the banking industry itself.

Having said that, there is no question that large, financially troubled institutions present special difficulties simply because they, by definition, carry with them greater systemic risks and greater threats to public confidence. For these reasons, governments at all times and in all places have been reluctant to run the risks of the sudden and uncontrolled failure of large depository institutions—a pattern we see even in countries that have no formal deposit insurance system. The problem, however, is not so much that large institutions are too large to fail, for large institutions have failed. Rather, the problem is that authorities are reluctant to tolerate the sudden and uncontrolled failure of large institutions and therefore generally opt for managed shrinkage, merger, or recapitalization in a context in which shareholders and management are generally wiped out.

Viewed in that light, neither equity holders nor senior managers of failed institutions—including large institutions—have any reason to believe they will be "bailed out." Yet, we are all acutely sensitive to the so-called moral hazard problem which, in effect, postulates that banking and financial market participants take on undue elements of risk in the belief that public authorities will somehow protect them from the risks of loss and/or failure.

There can be no doubt that the moral hazard problem is quite real, just as there can be no doubt that the failure of large institutions presents special problems for the authorities. However, neither of these considerations need imply that any institution is too large to fail or that owners and managers—at the least—of such institutions will not be severely penalized by virtue of such failures. Perhaps the balance of risks and rewards is somewhat out of kilter—at least at the margin—but even if this is true, it does not justify the all too widely held view that the authorities in this country—to say nothing about other countries—systematically and irresponsibly bailout financial institutions, small or large. That is not to say, however, that there is not greater room in the process for market discipline, for surely there is.

The third myth I want to comment on is the one that says disclosure—or more disclosure—is something of a panacea that can solve the market discipline problem. While I am obviously all in favor of disclosure, I think it is sheer fantasy to assume that individual investors and depositors—and perhaps even large and relatively sophisticated investors and depositors—can make truly informed credit judgments about highly complex financial instruments and institutions. Even now, we may have a condition of information overload in a setting in which even the professional rating agencies have their problems. Continental Illinois and the major Texas banks were investment-grade rated during the time interval in which they were acquiring the assets and the concentrations that led to their demise. Once again, this is not to say that disclosure or better forms of disclosure cannot play a useful and constructive role in helping the market discipline process along, but only to suggest that the benefits of even the most optimal forms of disclosure are not as great as is assumed by many commentators.

Fourth, there is the view that fire walls are fail-safe and can fully insulate the insured depository or the registered broker-dealer from the misfortunes of its parent or affiliated companies. Not only is that view highly questionable in practice but, in the extreme, fire walls can increase risk rather than contain it. That is if we depend excessively on legislative or regulatory fire walls we may encourage riskier types of behavior or we may construct barriers that stand in the way of prudent intracompany flows of liquidity or capital that can, in particular circumstances, help to minimize problems. Because of this, I believe strongly in the principle of consolidated supervision, and I resist the combinations of banking and commercial firms. Finally, while fire walls may work the wrong way on safety and soundness grounds, I do believe they play a very necessary and useful role in limiting conflicts of interest and unfair competition.

While on the subject of fire walls, I should also acknowledge that in the eyes of many practitioners the presence of complex regulatory fire walls in the context of the bank holding-company structure places U.S. firms at a significant competitive disadvantage in relation to their international competitors. While there is something to this view, it is very difficult to judge how important this factor may be in competitive terms. What is clear, however, is that the differences in structure do introduce political tensions in the application of national treatment principles to banking and securities firms operating in foreign markets.

Fifth, there is a myth that market participants, or even the central bank, can readily distinguish liquidity problems from terminal financial problems in the very short run. This is simply not always the case. This reality has enormous implications for the way market participants will behave in the face of uncertainty. For example, had it been clear from the outset that the stock market crash of 1987 would not result in any solvency problems of consequence, the near-gridlock conditions that prevailed in financial markets at times in the days after October 19 would not have occurred. However, in the face of uncertainty, market participants may tend to hold back on credit extensions, delay payments, or hold back on the delivery of securities or collateral, such as suggested in Larry Summers' October 1991 scenario. Unfortunately, in these circumstances what may start out as a liquidity problem can all too easily become a far more serious problem, ultimately giving rise to the risk of failures or insolvencies.

The inability to distinguish liquidity from solvency problems in the very short run can also have implications for the supervisors and the lender of last resort. For the supervisor, the problem can be the legal and policy ramifications of closing or taking over a troubled institution in a context in which it may be clearly capital deficient but not so clearly insolvent. For the lender of last resort, there is the danger of violating Bagehot's first principle of "never lending to unsound people." I might add in this context that the problem of distinguishing between liquidity and solvency becomes all the more difficult in a globally integrated financial system in which large institutions may have dozens, if not hundreds, of branches, subsidiaries, and affiliates scattered throughout the world.

The sixth myth I want to discuss is the view that there is something fatally and irreversibly flawed with the U.S. system of deposit insurance that, in turn, seriously complicates the moral hazard problem. Here again, I want to focus particularly on commercial bank deposit insurance. The argument is rather straightforward: namely, the mere presence of a system of officially supported deposit insurance—but especially one that has gravitated toward full insurance of all deposits—largely eliminates market discipline and promotes excessive risk taking.

It seems to me that, at least in its extreme form, this argument can be challenged on several grounds: first, in a number of other countries even where there is no system of deposit insurance, the authorities are generally no more willing to allow depositors to incur losses than they are in this country, and, if anything, in many cases they may tend to be more cautious insofar as their willingness to permit banks or other financial firms to fail in a disorderly manner; second, in every case of a severely troubled bank—including those that have overcome problems—we have seen significant deposit outflows. This, of course, suggests that at least some depositors—typically large and/or overseas depositors—do not fully accept the notion of full insurance; finally, as noted earlier, shareholders and managers of failed banks have, in fact, been systematically and seriously penalized for their mistakes.

These remarks should not be construed to imply that I believe that there are no constructive opportunities to strengthen the workings of the deposit insurance system. Rather, the point is that we should be careful in approaching the task of reform. For example, the suggestion of subjecting offshore deposits in branches of U.S. banks to insurance premiums—whatever its merits on other grounds—runs the clear risk of further broadening the appearance of de facto full insurance, thereby changing the behavior of the one class of depositor that clearly exerts a powerful element of market discipline on major banks. I have similar reservations about risk-based deposit insurance premiums on the grounds that they may simply be viewed by some as a license to be even more prone to take risks in their activities.

On the other hand, proposals to deal with the obvious abuses of the brokered deposit market, to find faster and surer ways to merge, close or take over seriously troubled institutions, and to strengthen both the amount and structure of capital, all warrant careful study in a context in which the 1989 Financial Institutions Reform, Recovery, and Enforcement Act (FIRREA) has already put in place a number of constructive reforms. At the end of the day, however, the keys are the factors I cited earlier: abundant amounts of capital—especially equity-like and unencumbered debt capital—and a strong yet flexible supervisory apparatus.

The seventh and final myth I want to mention is the idea that central banks can "solve" financial disruptions simply by providing individual institutions or the market at large with ample liquidity. Before going into this subject further, it is important to recognize that the contemporary central bank can provide liquidity in *at least* two ways; one is the traditional lender-of-last-resort function via the discount window and a second is through open market operations. Depending on the nature and source of the disruption either or both may be appropriate and either or both can provide important elements of flexibility. However, in the face of major uncertainties—especially relating to the credit worthiness of major institutions—there is no guarantee that even the provision of generous amounts of central bank liquidity can necessarily prevent a "disruption" from becoming a "crisis." Larry Summers's paper makes it plain that others recognize this possibility when he raises questions about the extent of moral suasion (arm twisting) on major banks in the wake of the October 1987 market break. You will understand why I object to phrases like "arm twisting" but I hope that you will also understand my conviction that in times of stress the central bank must be prepared to provide not just liquidity but also leadership—consistent, of course, with the exercise of individual credit and business judgments by particular institutions in the marketplace. But, for observers and practitioners to assume that central banks have a magic wand of liquidity and moral suasion that can overcome each and every problem is simply wrong and, even worse, dangerous.

Having said all of that, there is another side to the lender of last resort issue which is raised by both Friedman and Krugman. Specifically, Friedman raises the specter that the central bank will have to "cave" on inflation in order to avoid financial disorder, while Krugman suggests the possibility that the process of providing liquidity to contain a financial disruption could trigger an international run on the dollar. These dangers are very real, but I believe it is possible to provide needed amounts of liquidity in the short run without necessarily having to compromise the basic thrust of monetary policy, and I believe that the events of October 1987 can be looked at in precisely that light. Needless to say, however, if a "disruption" tilts into a crisis, the balancing act becomes all the more difficult, although in those circumstances, immediate concerns about current and prospective inflation would be significantly dampened, if not eliminated.

Conclusion

The focus of this paper is diagnostic rather than remedial. Therefore, I will not, at this time, attempt to outline a long or short list of public or private initiatives that could reduce elements of fragility and volatility in financial markets. Nevertheless, throughout the text there are numerous comments that point in the directions in which I believe public policy should be moving. The first would be the importance of sound overall macroeconomic and structural policies, keeping in mind that the roots of many of the financial problems we have seen can be traced to the policy fundamentals—fundamentals that include the need to reform and modernize the structure of the financial system. The second would be that we not lose sight of the fact that the primary burden of securing the safety and integrity of financial institutions and markets lies not with the authorities but with financial market practitioners and, most especially, the directors and senior management of individual firms.

---

3. Irvine H. Sprague

Financial Risks and Crises

First, I would like to congratulate Benjamin Friedman for his concise, lucid, very readable exposition of where we have been, where we are now, and how we got here.

I am particularly pleased to see Hyman Minsky on the program. He and I spoke two weeks ago at a somewhat similar conference of economists at Terni, Italy. To me it was most revealing. After those of us on the panel presented our papers, the moderator would ask for questions from the audience. Someone would come up to the microphone and give a short speech and sit down. Then the moderator asked for another "question," and so on. Sometimes the speeches related to what we were talking about. I am more used to speaking in the United States where audiences are not reluctant to challenge the speaker or at least to ask a question. I see no shrinking violets in this gathering.

When Martin Feldstein invited me to this conference he said to leave the scholarly research papers to the economists—"just talk about your judgments based on your personal experience," he said. That I will do.

We all have thought a great deal about where we should go with regulation, supervision, and insurance for the financial industry. I perceive that opinions as they have jelled so far range from reregulation to complete deregulation and from removing all insurance protection to allow "market discipline" to police the system to those who would extend the insurance to 100 percent coverage for all. I take the middle ground. Leave things as they are for the time being.

There are two hazards in seeking any change, and they are formidable.

My proposal certainly is not what I expected to come up with when I began to think seriously about the process after Congress enacted the thrift bailout legislation this summer. It is a particularly unusual theory coming from one who proudly worked in the White House and who spent more than a quarter century in various positions serving Congress.

My thesis is that the two principal hazards are the president and Congress, and we should avoid any situation that would give them an invitation to meddle. I can illustrate my meaning with two examples.

In 1970, during the days of Regulation Q, we regulators removed all interest rate ceilings on deposits of $100,000 and up. This was in response to the Penn Central collapse.[1]

No problem. This deregulation stayed on the books for a decade with no noticeable adverse impact. Then, in 1980, Congress got involved—disastrously.

Deposit insurance had increased in increments from $2,500 to $5,000 to $10,000 to $20,000 to $40,000 over the years. This time, Congress jumped it all the way to $100,000 in a precipitous and irresponsible move. At the time I proposed an increase to $70,000 to keep abreast of inflation. The House supported this position, but the Senate was taken in by the savings and loan lobbyists who wanted a vehicle to draw in funds by the billions to their institutions.

We all know what happened. The juxtaposition of $100,000 insurance coverage and no interest rate restrictions at $100,000 created an irresistible invitation to speculators and outright crooks. As we know, all interest rate restrictions were lifted during the 1980s, but the damage was done. Sharpies and get-rich-quick operators, as well as serious investors, were already drawn into the savings and loan web, where they would remain until the final disintegration.

After the 1980 legislation, money brokers could put together $100,000 deposit packages and in all honesty say: "Not to worry—if anything goes wrong the government will be the patsy." How right they were.

The money brokers did not limit their sales efforts to savings at home. Many banks were closed after money brokers swelled their deposit base. Penn Square, a good example, grew from a $30 million shopping center bank to a $500 million disaster.

Greed, of course, was the driving force, but raising the insurance coverage was only step one by Congress. The thrifts now had a vehicle for drawing in

---

1. To my knowledge this was the only time ever that all 13 regulators have gathered in one room. Federal Reserve Chairman Arthur Burns called us together—seven Fed members, the Comptroller, two others from the FDIC, and three from the Bank Board. We acted unanimously.

deposits; they did not have complete freedom to spend the money they were accumulating.

No problem. Congress obliged in the 1980 law—the one that gave us $100,000 insurance—with a slight crack in the door for thrifts to expand their horizons, and they opened the door wide and threw away the key two years later in the Garn–St. Germain Act. Now the thrifts could embark on a frenzy of speculation and fraud, gambling with and stealing from depositors' money. Many did.

One line I particularly enjoyed in the Senate committee report on the 1982 bill was a statement that the experience of the deregulated thrifts in Texas was so rewarding that "these benefits" should be extended to all thrifts, state and national chartered alike. Texas as a role model—unbelievable. So much for Congress; now the president.

Drawing up a rescue plan for the thrifts was difficult enough, but it was just about impossible to do it legitimately because of the president's obsession with his ill-conceived campaign pledge of "no new taxes."

Prior to the 1988 election you economists knew the thrifts were in trouble, but the public could not tell this fact from the administration's silence. The White House managers were terrified at the thought that the true situation would be revealed before the election. Then—surprise—just a week after the election the White House discovered there indeed was a problem and it would cost the taxpayers billions of dollars. How many billions became a moving target as the administration gingerly started with a lowball figure and then scaled the numbers in increments. Today I believe their fantasy is that it can be handled with $167 billion. Don't you believe it.

When the Financial Institutions Reform, Recovery and Enforcement Act of 1989 was drafted, the president insisted that none of the rescue funds come from taxes that could be *immediately identified* and that none of the cost be counted against the Gramm-Rudman budget ceilings. We were going to spend a great deal of money and pretend it did not happen.

The president's insistence that all the costs be hidden off-budget is already causing problems and will continue to do so. One telling effect is that the taxpayers will be stuck with an unnecessarily large bill, payable, of course, in later administrations. It is too early to know with precision how much the no-new-tax pledge is going to cost the taxpayers. Certainly plenty.

Knowledgeable people like Dan Rostenkowski and Leon Panetta tried to derail this maneuver, but the bill was being considered on the last day before the August recess and nothing will deter a congressman from catching his plane home for a recess. While running the White House office, I coined the phrase "District work period" for these recesses, so I guess we all resort to deception from time to time.

A "compromise" was adopted. Twenty billion dollars would be on-budget and raised by Treasury. The catch was that all of the money would have to be spent prior to October 1 so it would not count in the Gramm-Rudman computations. The other $30 billion would be off-budget and here again it would not count against Gramm-Rudman. How is that for open and honest accounting?

Another provision to dupe the public is allowing the Resolution Trust Corporation (RTC) to borrow on up to 85 percent of the market value of the assets it holds. This allows administration witnesses to testify as they already have, with tongue in cheek, that they have no idea of the true cost of the bail out and will not know until the assets are finally disposed of. Translation: we will not have to confirm the true cost until the next election.

Even more damaging is the provision that chips away at the traditional independence of the FDIC. Treasury now controls two of the five seats on the expanded board, and with the president signaling who will be chairman, the administration gains a heavy hand.

Worse yet, the Office of Management and the Budget (OMB) finally gets some kind of a handle on the Federal Deposit Insurance Corporation (FDIC). For as long as I can remember OMB has tried to squeeze the FDIC, demanding to pre-clear testimony, asking that the number of field examiners be cut back just at the time the banking crisis of the 1980s was unfolding, and generally pecking away at the corporation's independence. We always stopped their efforts, but the financial structuring of the RTC may give them the opening they so long have yearned for.

The FDIC is used to acting quickly, handling as many as six bank failures over a weekend. The RTC already is delaying the process, probably to establish the fact that it is the boss.

An independent FDIC is crucial. The principal reason for the shocking difference between the FDIC and the Home Loan Bank Board was that the FDIC, operating with nonappropriated funds and acting at arm's length from the banking industry, has been able to withstand pressures from Congress, the White House, and the industry they regulated.[2]

Already the fancy White House maneuvering is coming unraveled. Seeking to meet the October 1 spending deadline for the first $20 billion, Bill Seidman of the FDIC loaned the $8 billion he had not yet committed to five thrifts on September 30, just beating the deadline.

The thrifts, selected because they were next in line to be unloaded by the RTC, were to get rid of high cost CDs and buy government securities, which the RTC was to hold as collateral. The deal held for about 24 hours when Treasury Secretary Nicholas Brady ruled that Federal law makes it illegal to invest appropriated funds in interest bearing instruments. This created an acute embarrassment.

Another problem occurs because, in their efforts to hold down the admitted cost of the rescue, Congress and the president did not make any provision for

---

2. Efforts to crack the FDIC independence recur like clockwork. Don Regan was particularly aggressive in the Interest Rate Deregulation Committee and during the Continental Illinois travails. It was not a party matter. I withstood extraordinary Democratic White House pressure when they wanted to name my general counsel—the person who selects law firms throughout the nation for the very, very lucrative business of representing the FDIC.

working capital. The RTC projections might possibly be accurate, but they do not take into account the fact that the RTC must pay for illiquid assets up front. The asset disposition takes time. Under the FDIC guidelines, now being used by the RTC, an asset is not considered "dumped" if it is marketed for up to six months. Already pressures are building to force the FDIC to hang on to distressed properties for a much longer period.

Seidman told Congress last week that he will need at least $25 billion in working capital above the amounts provided for in the legislation.

A further problem is created by the fact that Danny Wall's pumpkin deals in the final hours of the year are coming unraveled and many will probably have to be rerescued at a cost nobody knows. As we all know, a pumpkin deal must be done before midnight or you will turn into a pumpkin.

We always had a rule of thumb when I was with the FDIC—the situation at a failed institution would turn out to be worse than anticipated when you got inside the door for a good look at the books. With nearly 300 thrifts already turned over the RTC and another 300 likely to appear in the near future, there will be a bountiful harvest of surprises.

So we have the threats from two sides—Congress and the president. If any legislation begins to move there is no telling how it would be embellished by these two.

The only sensible solution is to sit back and not support any legislation now. Let the dust settle and see how the situation unwinds. Perhaps we need a radical restructuring of the system, perhaps not. I know the urge to "do something" is in all of us. The hardest task of all is to sit tight.

A final note. Keep criticizing the regulators. It is good for their soul.

In that context I give you a story to think about. After the events surrounding the Continental failure, I was talking with someone who is here today and was told that we should have let Continental close its doors, an opinion shared by many economists. He said: "It would be a great intellectual exercise. We could finally know whether or not the domino theory is true and whether the collapse of a money-center bank really would destroy the economy of the nation."

4. *Norman Strunk*

The Savings and Loan Story

Even casual readers of the daily newspapers know a lot about the savings and loan problems of the past five years. Much has been written and said with respect to the origins of the problems and the resulting costs both to the thrift system and to the American taxpayer.

Some years ago, I coauthored a book with Fred Case, professor emeritus of

real estate at the University of California in Los Angeles, titled *Where Deregulation Went Wrong—a Look at the Causes behind the Savings and Loan
Failures in the 1980s* (Chicago: U.S. League of Savings Institutions, 1988).
In this book we listed 15 different reasons for these failures. Today I will
certainly not review this written record, but for what lessons it might have for
us within the theme of this conference I will offer a five-minute summary of
what, in my view, were the major reasons for this cataclysmic decade in the
history of our specialized institutions.

I begin by pointing out that the savings and loan business was structured
for a different period in our economic history—one not characterized by high
and volatile interest rates and downward sloping yield curves. It was created
for the special purpose of providing an assured source of reasonably priced
housing credit for American families when upgrading our nation's housing
standard of living was considered an appropriate public policy objective.

It did well in a simpler economy without today's technology with respect to
systems of communication and the use of computers in the conduct of the
banking business, a fact that has, for example, permitted the securitization of
the mortgage market.

Unfortunately, the savings and loan business did not change with the times.
For this there were many reasons. The Hunt Commission, which functioned
during the first term of the Nixon administration, advocated major changes,
including a phase-out of Regulation Q. This general prescription for change
was rejected by the business, which felt very comfortable with the status quo.
It was rejected by the Realtors of America and the home builders, groups that
wished to preserve our institutions as a captive source of credit. It was rejected
by the Congress, which also was concerned with preserving a certain source
of credit for housing. It is quite clear that the business relied for too many
years on Regulation Q and the one-quarter of 1% price advantage that this
program gave to our institutions.

As a bit of history, you may be surprised to know that the U.S. League did
not ask for or lobby for the imposition of Regulation Q when it was extended
from the banking business to the thrift institutions in 1966. In fact, we re-
quested the two-year sunset provision in the original law. Once our business
had Regulation Q, of course, it did not want to give it up.

In the free-wheeling, deregulated environment of the 1980s, the business
clearly had inadequate supervision, both in terms of the authority provided in
the basic law and from a woefully inadequate supervisory and examination
staff. The basic supervisory law was written by Congress in the Johnson administration. The law was not looked at as to its adequacy in the Reagan era
of deregulation: the new permissive law of Garn–St. Germain and the very
liberal lending and investment authority for state-chartered associations
granted by many state legislatures, primarily California, Florida, Texas, and
Arizona. Requests for a larger and better-paid examination and supervisory
staff and revised supervisory law to give the supervisors what I have referred

to as a "fast whistle" did not come until 1984, during the chairmanship of Ed Gray. Chairman Gray's requests for additional supervisory capability, both in terms of personnel and supervisory authority, did not receive support from the administration or the banking agencies, and Congress did not act on it. For the record, it should be noted that the savings and loan business, through the U.S. League, strongly supported Chairman Gray's successful program to upgrade the examination and supervisory staff and endorsed a limited revision of the supervisory law to improve the ability of the board to use its cease-and-desist authority.

It is obvious that deregulation came first on the wrong side of the balance sheet. There has been much finger pointing as to whose fault this was, but the fact is that deposit rates were freed while the business was sitting with some 80% of its assets in fixed rate, long-term mortgage loans—all made when interest rates were much lower. This led to a decline in the *tangible* net worth of the business from $32.2 billion at the end of 1980 to $3.8 billion two years later. The business never really recovered from this destruction of its net worth. Many of the failures we have seen the last two years have come as a result of this earnings tragedy of the early 1980s and the inability of many institutions to take advantage of the breathing space provided by what I have called the creative accounting arrangements allowed by the Federal Home Loan Bank Board in the 1982–84 period. These were intended to avoid the type of financial crisis that we are discussing at this conference—a crisis as to the deposit insurance provided by the FSLIC, which could well have spread to the Federal Deposit Insurance Corporation (FDIC). This type of "forbearance" was similar in its intent to that provided by the State of New York in the early 1930s with respect to the book valuation of the assets of the state's life insurance companies and savings banks.

There were many regulations issued by the Federal Home Loan Bank Board under Chairman Pratt in the early 1980s, most of them of a liberalizing nature, with two of them being particularly unwise. One permitted an unlimited amount of money solicited by the security brokers to be received under the cover of FSLIC insurance.

The other damaging regulation, less obvious to students of our history, reduced the minimum number of stockholders from 400 to one and canceled the rule that no one individual could own more than 25% of the stock. The board also eliminated the requirement that the boards of directors of these institutions be composed of a variety of individuals from the community or communities served by the institution.

To this very brief summary of the causes of savings and loan failures of the 1980s must added, of course, the precipitous decline in the price of oil and the collapse of the real estate economy in Texas, Louisiana, Arkansas, Colorado, and Arizona—which caused many bank failures—as well as the collapse of the savings and loan system in those states.

In the context of this discussion today and the background paper by Benjamin Friedman, it is perhaps useful to note that the savings and loan crises of the 1980s did not stem from any one or a few unavoidable causes but, rather from many—most of which, with hindsight, were avoidable. It should also be noted that (as costly as it may eventually prove to be) the savings and loan failures did not spread to our financial system at large or, in fact, even cause a significant downturn in the real estate and home-building sector of our economy.

I ask the question whether this "non-event" as to our nation's economy as a whole came from the fact that our financial institutions up to this point essentially have been compartmentalized into several different systems and from the public's confidence in the integrity of the system of federal insurance of deposits. In both instances I think the answer is yes, which may have some lessons in our efforts to reduce the risk of financial crises.

I have been asked to express some views as to the effectiveness of the reforms of the thrift system enacted this past year by Congress. I would say that the reforms will certainly reduce the risk of any new wave of expensive failures in the savings and loan system. This is true in part because the reforms were significant; additionally, I am not sure how much of a savings and loan business will be in existence five years from now to pose a risk to our broader financial system.

Let me list quickly the reforms enacted by Congress this past year. First, there is now a separation of the function of insurance from the function of chartering and supervision. I really do not see how this reduces the risk of institution failure, but many think it does. The insurance function, as you know, is now provided by the FDIC. We hope it proves as good as its reputation. Supervision has been put into the Treasury under the Office of Thrift Supervision, which functions in a manner compatible to the Comptroller of the Currency.

The record of the Comptroller's office over the years suggests this will be a risk-reducing agency rearrangement. The personnel of the Federal Home Loan Banks will no longer be involved in supervision, and the bank presidents will no longer be the chief supervisory officers in the field. There will, I believe, be more Treasury Department involvement in the Federal Home Loan Bank System, although the new law does not provide so specifically.

The supervisory law has been revised to provide at least a "faster whistle" in the use of cease-and-desist orders and orders to remove officers and directors. This has been provided to the bank supervisory establishment as well as to the Office of Thrift Supervision. Much of this new supervisory authority follows the changes asked for by Bank Board Chairman Gray for five years and unfortunately not given to him. There are, as you know, higher net worth standards, which, in effect, limit the authority of supervisory people to grant forbearance to those institutions that fall below reasonable minimums. The practical effect of this is yet to be seen. I think it will be very helpful. Few may remember that the savings and loan business for years had a 5% minimum tangible net worth requirement, except for new institutions. In the late 1970s, and again in the Reagan era, this minimum was reduced as a pragmatic way to keep mortgage money flowing into the Sunbelt and to reduce the regulatory case load.

The laws have been tightened, wisely, with respect to the ability of institutions to make loans or investments for land development, to engage in home building, and to invest in junk bonds. Intelligent limits have been placed on loans to one borrower. The FDIC has been given authority, in effect, to override state laws with respect to the lending and investment activities of state-chartered savings and loans. One more reform is needed, and it can be accomplished by regulation. The use of money from brokers should be limited to, say, 5% of total deposits, the rule from 1963 to 1982.

In my view, the legislation enacted by Congress this year should substantially reduce the risk of savings and loan failures and any possible threat to our financial system. There is rightful concern, however, that we may have a case of "overkill." Reducing the investment flexibility may be harmful rather than helpful to the financial health of the remaining institutions. I am concerned about the effect of the higher limits on the percent of assets that must be invested in residential related assets, the so-called qualified thrift lender test.

The savings and loan problem may well be back before Congress, but not because of failures of institutions that today are alive and solvent. It will be back before Congress because of the inadequacy of the funding and the operations of the Resolution Trust Corporation.

I suggested earlier that this new law together with the events of the past few years in our financial system generally may well mean the disappearance of the savings institutions as a certain and specialized source of home mortgage credit for middle-class America. Opinions will differ whether this might, or might not, be a desirable result from the standpoint of the functioning of the free market in this country, but it will not be a good result from the standpoint of our nation's standard of living in housing.

From the broader standpoint of our financial system and the risks of financial crises, there will be increasing talk about deposit insurance reform. I personally do not think it is politically realistic to expect much of a change. I do not think Congress will lower the $100,000 insurance limit. I do not think that a coinsurance system is politically feasible. I do not think it is practical to expect any administration to fail to provide de facto 100% deposit insurance for the large banks. When crunch time comes, I believe the government officials involved will conclude that some banks are, in fact, too large to fail.

I am concerned with the increasingly broad scope of commercial bank operations and the virtual collapse of Glass-Steagall. Things move too fast in banking these days for examiners and supervisors to detect and stop bad practices in time to prevent major losses. I have seen in the savings and loan system the effect of examiners and supervisors not understanding what is going on and not dealing with problems in a timely manner. I fear the same thing can happen in our commercial banking system.

Further, let me say that the major banks in Texas did not survive the economy in that state of the 1980s. I am concerned as to what would happen if conditions, such as we have seen in Texas, became common in several parts of our economy at the same time or if we have that long-overdue major economic downturn.

As pointed out in the last chapter of the Strunk-Case book, major problems arose with respect to the system of deposit insurance operating in a deregulated environment. As I have said, I do not think that substantive changes in deposit insurance are politically possible. I hope that the alternative of effective supervision and qualified people in supervision will be able to avoid the problems that deregulation with deposit insurance created for the savings and loan system.

A "tough cop" mentality is needed in supervision. I personally think that there is still too much "due process" protection to owners and management built into the supervisory law. The call of the supervisory officials in the field should not be subject to an "instant replay" review by a panel of judges in the press box.

I also feel that much more use should be made of the powers granted the supervisory agencies by the Change in Control Law, and maybe that law needs to be strengthened, although it was revised just three years ago. Banking-type institutions should not be the plaything of takeover artists or speculators, nor should they be subject to leveraged buy outs. I have seen too many bad results from the wrong kind of owners of our savings and loan associations. The same thing must not be allowed to happen in commercial banking.

---

5. *Joseph A. Grundfest*

When Markets Crash: The Consequences of Information Failure in the Market for Liquidity

Few topics capture the public eye as effectively as a stock market "crash." Whenever stock prices drop sharply—even if only for a very short period of time—Congress, regulators, and the press quickly demand an explanation and begin a hunt for culprits who can be blamed for the market's woes. These

---

The views expressed in this paper are those of Commissioner Grundfest and do not necessarily reflect the views of the Securities and Exchange Commission, other commissioners, or the commission's staff. Commissioner Grundfest resigned from the commission on 18 January 1990.

efforts are invariably accompanied by calls for new regulatory safeguards to prevent crashes from ever happening again.

By now, the political minuet danced in the wake of a crash is well understood. The Securities and Exchange Commission (SEC) and the Commodity Futures Trading Commission (CFTC) are charged to provide studies of the crash. Self-regulatory organizations, such as the New York Stock Exchange (NYSE) and Chicago Mercantile Exchange, empanel commissions to analyze the crash and to propose remedies. Meanwhile, many traders busy themselves blaming other traders for the market's woes: traditional "fundamentalists" blame indexers, indexers blame specialists, specialists blame the futures markets, and everyone finds reason to blame Congress and the regulators.

Though this sequence of events is quite predictable, the political demand for an explanation of market volatility nonetheless repeatedly manages to create an intellectual vacuum in Washington, D.C. Inasmuch as nature abhors a vacuum, the demand for explanation is quickly filled by legions of Wall Streeters, academics, and journalists who supply a groaning smorgasbord of diagnoses. These diagnoses typically range from the hilariously implausible to the rigorously indecipherable. Indeed, with so many explanations to choose from, many policymakers have little trouble finding rationalizations that mesh with politically convenient predispositions.

Many of the explanations proferred in the wake of a crash are perfectly credible attempts to make sense of an infrequent, complex, short-lived, and turbulent phenomenon. Other explanations are, however, tinged with self-interest. In particular, it is clear that if the federal government can be persuaded that a particular group is responsible for market volatility, or that a specific form of intervention might cure the market's ills, then some traders' positions can be strengthened at the expense of others'. Rent-seeking behavior of this sort is hardly unusual, and the market volatility debate would surely set a record if all its participants were interested solely in the public good.

Reasons for Caution When Attempting to Explain Recent Market Volatility

The specter of self-interest is not, however, the only reason to approach the volatility debate with care. It is important to recognize that the very nature of the volatility that is the subject of the debate limits the degree of confidence that we can have in any explanation of the market's behavior. These limits on our ability to explain market behavior also limit the degree of confidence we can have in recommendations for market reform. By my count, there are at least five factors beyond the customary political machinations that counsel intellectual caution in the volatility debate.

First, despite the great attention devoted to recent market volatility, instances of sharp market declines remain few and far between. Since 1987, stock market declines have drawn widespread public attention on fewer than 1 percent of all trading days. When these declines occur, they also tend to last for relatively short periods of time. Efforts to explain market crashes are thus constrained by a small-numbers problem caused by the infrequency of market crashes and by the brevity of the events sought to be explained.

Second, not all crashes are alike. Crashes happen for several different reasons and express themselves through several different mechanisms of action. Efforts to generalize about market behavior during periods of sharp, transitory decline can therefore overemphasize apparent similarities while brushing aside subtle but critical distinctions. More fundamentally, however, we must remember that markets learn as a result of crash experiences. For example, the market's behavior during the crash of 13 October 1989, was influenced by its experience of 19 October 1987. In this sense, crashes are fundamentally nonreplicable events. The market's inherent inability ever to suffer the same crash twice thus makes the task of explaining market volatility more difficult than it might otherwise be.

Third, recent history teaches that, even if the markets could experience the same crash twice, the government and self-regulatory organizations stand ready to prevent any repetition. In particular, following the October 1987 crash, the markets adopted a new set of trading-halt rules popularly known as "circuit breakers." The presence of these circuit breakers changed market behavior in October 1989 and introduced a level of noncomparability with the earlier 1987 experience. Following the October 1989 crash, circuit breakers were again modified to address perceived weaknesses in the level of intermarket coordination. Accordingly, it is already a sure bet that the regulatory environment accompanying the next crash will be different from the environment that existed during the October 1987 and October 1989 crashes.

It is also a safe bet that, if and when the next crash occurs, the rules of the game will once again be changed as a result of that crash experience. Efforts to explain market crashes will therefore inevitably become embroiled in debates over the extent to which changes in the regulatory process either exacerbated or ameliorated the market's woes.

This process of perpetual regulatory adjustment happens for perfectly understandable political reasons and is easily explained: to many policymakers, the unspoken objective of the regulatory process is to eliminate the possibility of a crash and not simply to assure that crashes are, in some sense, equitable, rational, efficient, or justifiable. Crashes are politically unacceptable. The fact that a crash has recurred is interpreted as evidence that the preexisting regulatory environment was somehow deficient. Accordingly, further regulatory tinkering is necessary to prevent a repetition of extreme market volatility. Thus, just as the market's internal learning process causes sequential crashes to be noncomparable (at least to some degree), the process of regulatory tinkering compounds the challenge of explaining market behavior.

Fourth, the variables most central to any explanation of market behavior during a crash are extraordinarily difficult to quantify. Financial market behavior is fueled by expectations. Expectations, however, are not directly observable during the market's gyrations and are only imperfectly measured after the fact. Economic analyses of market crashes, therefore, generally rely on observable measures of price and volume that reflect the consequence of the interaction of underlying market expectations, and not the underlying expectations themselves.[1] Like physicists inferring the existence of subatomic particles from droplets in cloud chambers, economists are often forced to infer expectations structures from observable stock market price and volume data.

Physicists have, however, done quite credible work by tracking droplets in cloud chambers. Similarly, economists have made substantial contributions to the understanding of crashes by analyzing the path of prices and volumes during market declines. Although these analyses are quite useful in debunking many theories about market behavior, and although they can support powerful inferences about the forces that give rise to market crashes, there is a level of explanatory power that studies based on price and volume data are unlikely ever to achieve.

In particular, given the rapid pace at which expectations can change during market crashes and the extent to which individual expectations can be influenced by perceptions of the expectations held by others, there is a level of cause and effect that will be difficult if not impossible to divine from observable price and volume data. This inability to measure underlying expectations, combined with the difficulties encountered in conclusively demonstrating the mechanisms of action that define the observed path of market prices, leaves the door open for policymakers to rely extensively on anecdotal evidence. It also provides a basis for some policymakers to dismiss economic studies as not having come to grips with the forces of fear and greed that politicians often perceive as dominating market behavior during crashes. Put another way, it is easy for politicians to believe that "animal spirits" dominate the market during periods of sharp decline, and it can be difficult for economists to dissuade policymakers from these animist beliefs.

Finally, and perhaps most significantly, economists have reason to be cautious in their explanations of crash behavior because of the current state of the art in economics. Economics is simply not as advanced in explaining the adjustment process whereby markets move from one equilibrium to another as it is in many other areas. As Franklin Fisher observed, "Economic theory is preeminently a matter of equilibrium analysis. . . . We have no similarly elegant theory of what happens *out* of equilibrium, of how agents behave when their plans are frustrated. . . . Unless one robs words of their meaning and defines

---

1. It should be noted that not all economists limit their analyses to studies of price and volume data. For example, in the wake of the 13 October 1989 crash, Robert Shiller and William Feltus surveyed market participants to find out about the expectation structures that gave rise to their behavior. See R. J. Shiller and W. J. Feltus, "Fear of the Crash Caused the Crash," *New York Times* (29 October 1989, sec. 3, p. 3, col. 1).

every state of the world an 'equilibrium' in the sense that agents do what they do instead of doing something else, there is no disguising the fact that this is a major lacuna in economic analysis."[2]

The fact that economics is not as advanced in explaining adjustment processes as it is in describing equilibria does not, however, justify intellectual nihilism. In particular, it does not mean that "anything goes" in the effort to explain market crashes, or that any explanation is as credible as any other explanation. It suggests, instead, that a certain degree of humility may well be appropriate for anyone who ventures into the difficult and highly contentious political arena in which the volatility debate is likely to be fought.

Why Crashes Happen: A Tentative and Partial Explanation

Having described five reasons for caution in any effort to explain market behavior during a crash, I will now ignore my own advice and attempt to offer an explanation for certain aspects of recent market volatility. In defense of this obviously impetuous decision, I can only point out that my call for caution is certain to be ignored widely in Washington and elsewhere. Thus, rather than be left totally out of the race to explain recent market volatility, I will suggest a tentative and partial explanation and then take comfort in the distinguished company I am sure to share when it comes time to name those who have been so bold as to attempt to explain the behavior of the stock market.

More seriously, however, the explanation I am about to offer differs from many others in at least three respects. First, the explanation is consciously tentative—unlike some other explanations, which are presented as powerful solutions to a great mystery, what I present is more in the nature of a hypothesis to be mulled than of a truth revealed. Indeed, I will not feel overly embarrassed if further analysis proves my explanation wide of the mark.

Second, the explanation is consciously partial—even if the explanation is eventually accepted as accurate, there is much still left unexplained and much work remains to be done in order to understand market behavior during crashes. Because the explanation is partial it is also not necessarily inconsistent with several other explanations that have already been offered for the market's behavior. Nor is it necessarily inconsistent with explanations yet to be offered.

Third, the explanation is politically neutral in the sense that it points a finger neither at New York nor at Chicago as the source of the market's problems. Instead, the explanation suggests that the conditions leading to recent market volatility could well be the result of more fundamental problems shared by the

2. F. M. Fisher, "Adjustment Processes and Stability," in John Eatwell, Murray Milgate, and Peter Newman, eds., *The New Palgrave: General Equilibrium* (New York: Norton, 1989), 36; emphasis in original. Recently, some economists have explored the application of the chaos theory to instances of market volatility. It is, I believe, too soon to judge whether these efforts will bear meaningful fruit.

equities and futures markets alike. Effective remedies for the market's woes might therefore lie in measures that address broader questions of market structure and performance—particularly matters related to the availability of information regarding order flows during times of high volume and volatility. Measures of this sort do not, however, currently appear to be high on the list of remedies being considered in the policymaking process.

A Thumbnail Sketch of the Model

Simply put, I suggest that a large component of recent market volatility is the rational result of an "information failure" in the market for liquidity rather than the consequence of rapid and irrational changes in the market's assessment of the value of securities traded on America's stock exchanges. Information is the lifeblood of the market.[3] In order to set stable prices, markets need information both about the business prospects of the companies whose shares are traded *and* about the demand for short-term trading services in the markets where those instruments are traded. The lack of information about *either* fundamental business prospects *or* about the magnitude and composition of an atypically large demand for immediate trading can be sufficient to induce substantial market volatility. Indeed, as I later demonstrate, even informationless trading can cause substantial price volatility, if the trading is sufficiently large and is of sufficiently uncertain magnitude and composition.[4]

During recent crashes, the markets have suffered from a serious lack of information about an anticipated spike in the demand for short-term trading activity.[5] The markets have been uncertain about the magnitude of the expected demand, about the reasons why certain traders are selling, and about the price levels at which substantial buying interest might appear. This lack of information makes trading quite risky. In response to this quantitative and qualitative uncertainty over the anticipated demand for short-term liquidity, which is in the nature of a highly uncertain peak-load demand on traditional liquidity providers, the price of liquidity rises sharply—that is, it becomes quite expensive to purchase the immediate right to sell shares or futures. This sharp increase in the price of liquidity is reflected in a simultaneous widening of spreads and in a general price decline in the equities and futures market alike.[6] Indeed, in an environment in which the cost of trading rises sharply, as does the perceived probability of having to trade more frequently, liquidity-

---

3. See, generally, R. Gilson and R. Kraakman, "The Mechanisms of Market Efficiency," *Virginia Law Review* 70 (1984): 549–644.

4. See discussion of the "S&P 500 effect" and of volatility during "triple witching hours" in this text around nn. 12–13 and n. 17, respectively.

5. This spike in demand for trading can, of course, occur simultaneously with uncertainty over fundamental valuations, as discussed below.

6. In this regard, it may also be useful to observe that some economic models suggest that "traders' impatience" can affect the terms of trade, particularly in dynamic markets. See, e.g., R. B. Wilson, "Exchange," in J. Eatwell, M. Milgate, and P. Newman, eds., *The New Palgrave: Allocation, Information, and Markets* (New York: Norton, 1989), 87.

related transactions costs can have significant effects on stock prices.[7] Once sufficient information comes to the market describing expected short-term trading flows, and once the returns to providing liquidity become high enough, the peak-load nature of the demand subsides, the risk involved in trading is reduced, the price of liquidity declines, spreads narrow, and equity prices recover a large portion of their losses.

This explanation of market volatility, which relies on information failure in the market for short-term liquidity, is not inconsistent with the efficient market hypothesis (EMH). Among other assumptions, the EMH is based on the specific understanding that "(1) information be available to a 'sufficient' number of investors; [and] (2) that transactions costs be 'low.'"[8] The uncertainty surrounding peak-load trading demands suggests that information relevant to setting the price of liquidity may not be available to a sufficient number of traders. It also suggests that transactions costs are not low because of the uncertainty generated by the information failure. Thus, if the information failure argument presented herein is correct, certain conditions necessary for the application of the EMH may not be satisfied during some sharp market declines. The information failure argument can thus be viewed as complementary to the traditional EMH, not as a challenge to or rejection of the EMH.

The need to analyze separately the structure of information flows about "fundamental" valuations and about liquidity demands is, I think, the critical link missing in many currently popular explanations of market behavior. Related observations have appeared in academic analyses of market volatility.[9] Unfortunately, these analyses appear not to have made a substantial change in policymakers' approaches to the volatility debate beyond the somewhat simplistic and perhaps overly hopeful view that circuit breakers can slow trading sufficiently so as to allow more deliberate decision making to restore a semblance of equilibrium at prices reasonably close to those that prevailed prior to the market's dislocation.

The analysis presented herein suggests, however, that circuit breakers, in and of themselves, are not as important as the quality of information brought to the markets either while trading is halted or ongoing. Remember that the markets had a two-day trading halt between October 16 and October 19, 1987. That two-day halt, popularly known as a weekend, did little if anything to prevent the market's precipitous decline because, it is suggested, nothing was

7. See, e.g., Y. Amihud and H. Mendelson, "Liquidity and Cost of Capital: Implications for Corporate Management," *Journal of Applied Corporate Finance* 2 (Fall 1989): 65 (estimating that, at a turnover rate of once every two years, a 4 percent transaction cost reduces an asset's net present value by 28 percent).

8. James Lorie and Mary Hamilton, *The Stock Market: Theories and Evidence* (Homewood, Ill.: Irwin, 1973), 80.

9. See, e.g., Grossman, "Insurance Seen and Unseen: The Impact on Markets," *Journal of Portfolio Management* 14 (Summer 1988): 5–8; Gennotte and Leland, *Market Liquidity, Hedging, and Crashes* (School of Business Administration, University of California at Berkeley, May 1989).

done to address the huge uncertainties about the demand for short-term trading that had accumulated over the weekend. Indeed, from a broader perspective, the analysis presented herein suggests that many other frequently proposed solutions to the volatility problem are also likely to be ineffective unless they too address the information failure problems that can arise in the market for liquidity.

Crashes and Crashettes

This thumbnail sketch of market behavior suggests a distinction that I have found useful in certain policy-related conversations: it is the difference between "crashes" and "crashettes." A "crash," under my proposed nomenclature, reflects a sharp, fundamental downward reassessment of the intrinsic value of a financial instrument. Crashes can happen suddenly, but they are not transitory phenomena because asset prices are likely to remain depressed for substantial periods of time following the initial sharp decline. In contrast, "crashettes" reflect transitory uncertainties and peak-load demands that result from failures in the trading systems in which financial assets are exchanged. A crashette can come and go with prices returning to pre-crashette levels in relatively short order.

Rapid changes in stock prices need not, however, be purely the result of a crash or crashette. Changes in fundamental information are also often correlated with sudden liquidity spikes. Any given instance of market volatility can thus be viewed as a combination of crash and crashette behavior, with the crashette component having varying degrees of significance.

Theory aside, there is reason to believe that a significant portion of the market's recent volatility is much better described as the result of a series of crashettes rather than as the consequence of several market crashes. Obviously, the problems presented by crashes are quite different from those presented by crashettes, and the policy process would be making a serious error if it sought to treat crashettes with remedies that might be appropriate for crashes, and vice versa.

A Closer Look at Liquidity

In order for this information and liquidity-related explanation of recent market behavior to be credible, there must be some friction in the process by which liquidity is drawn into equity-related markets. If liquidity were freely and instantaneously available to respond to any level of short-term trading demand, then the notion of a sharp price decline due to uncertainty in the market for liquidity would lose much of its persuasive force.

This is neither an obvious nor noncontroversial proposition. To the average small investor, the whole notion of a market for liquidity is something of a cipher. The average investor who picks up the morning paper and reads the stock quotes sees lengthy tables depicting the prices at which individual stocks are traded. There are no tables describing the price of liquidity. Indeed, the vast majority of small investors are largely unaware that whenever they buy or sell stock, futures, or options they are paying a price for liquidity.

Similarly, the traditional approach to market analysis incorporated in the capital asset pricing model, and other valuation models, does not address the possibility that sudden, large, and uncertain demands for trading, even when those demands are "informationless," can so deeply influence the market's infrastructure that prices are rapidly thrown out of equilibrium. The notion that uncertainty in the market for liquidity can cause rapid, transitory price disturbances is not inconsistent with accepted pricing models; rather it is a consideration complementary to and distinct from those models.

To explain the importance of liquidity in the equities and index-futures markets, it helps to revisit some basic principles and to consider a hypothetical situation in which the only factor influencing market pricing is a massive short-term change in the demand for liquidity. When attempting to explain the notion of liquidity to small investors, I often draw an analogy to the used car market. If I want to sell my car quickly, it is highly unlikely that I will know someone immediately interested in buying my car at a price anything close to the price I could get if I advertised for a couple of weeks. Under these circumstances, if I want to sell my car quickly, or if it simply is not worth my time to try to sell it on my own, I am likely to sell the car to a used car dealer who will hold it in inventory until he finds a suitable buyer. The used car dealer is providing a liquidity service by paying me immediately for the car that he holds in inventory until a buyer comes along to take it off his hands.

Used car dealerships are not, however, charitable institutions. They provide liquidity only for a fee. That fee is measured by the difference between the price at which they buy and sell the same car. This spread between buying and selling prices is never posted on a big sign at used car lots and is never advertised in the paper. However, the fact that the spread is not obvious does not mean that liquidity is free or that the size of the spread is immune to the forces of supply and demand. In particular, if used car dealers expect a sudden rush of immediate selling interest by owners of used cars they will likely respond by lowering the price they offer to sellers even though the quality of the used cars they acquire remains unchanged and even though they expect to remarket those cars within a relatively short period at preexisting prices.

Just as there are firms that specialize in providing liquidity to the used car market, there are firms that specialize in providing liquidity to the equity and futures markets. Thus, even if there is no "long-term" investor who immediately wants to buy the 500 shares of General Mills that I want to sell, there is a "used stock dealer" who, for a fee, will buy those shares and hold them in inventory until an interested buyer comes along.[10]

10. Accordingly, there is a sense in which the equities and futures markets cease to behave as "spot" markets during periods of extreme volatility because the size and risk of inventory rises quite sharply.

The amount of capital ready to provide liquidity in the equity and futures markets at any one point in time is, however, finite and is determined by the risk-adjusted rate of return provided to that activity. In addition, there is reason to believe that the total pool of liquidity capital, while large in absolute dollar terms, is actually quite small when measured as a percentage of the value of the assets traded in the equities and futures markets.

For example, the Brady Commission found that the total capitalization of specialists on the floor of the NYSE is approximately $3 billion.[11] While $3 billion is a lot of money by some measures, it is less than one-tenth of 1 percent of the outstanding value of equity investments.[12] No doubt, the liquidity provided by specialists is supplemented by locals in Chicago's pits, over-the-counter market makers, and upstairs block positioners. However, I strongly suspect that even if accurate data about the quantity of liquidity capital available from these sources were available, we would find that immediately available liquidity capital is only a small percentage of the total value of equity instruments, open futures interest, and open options interest that could be traded on the market.

In the vast majority of situations, the amount of capital available for liquidity purposes is adequate and the typical trader barely notices the price that is charged for the temporary use of the market's liquidity capital. However, when suppliers of liquidity capital have reason to believe that there will be a sudden and sharp increase in demand for transaction services, and when there is substantial uncertainty over the magnitude and qualitative contour of that demand, a totally different scenario emerges.

The Origins of Crashettes

There is, by now, widespread agreement that instances of market volatility typically begin with one or more pieces of news that disturb preexisting price levels and suggest that some equity prices should be lower. Debate continues to rage, however, about whether these pieces of news are really powerful enough to cause multibillion dollar changes in valuation across the entire spectrum of equity investments traded in U.S. markets. This debate can, I think, be cut short if, instead of examining the effect of certain news items on the fundamental valuation of equity, futures, and options markets, we focus on the effect that news has on the demand for liquidity services.

Given current market structures, it is not difficult to conceive of situations in which news items suggest that relatively moderate changes in fundamental valuations might be accompanied by substantial short-term demands for liquidity. This may be particularly true under circumstances in which liquidity

---

11. Presidential Task Force, *Report of the Presidential Task Force on Market Mechanisms* (Washington, D.C.: Government Printing Office, 1988), VI–40.

12. The Wilshire Associates Equity Index, which measures the market value of NYSE, AMEX, and OTC issues, stood at $3,419.879 billion as of 29 December 1989. See Market Indicators, *New York Times* (30 December 1989, p. 21, col. 3).

suppliers believe that (*a*) a significant percentage of asset holders intend to follow mechanistic trading rules that cause investors to sell as prices decline (stop-loss rules or portfolio insurance strategies would fit into this category) or (*b*) the need to meet margin requirements is so substantial that a meaningful amount of selling will ensue as a result of wealth constraints and leverage effects. Whether these beliefs are accurate is, in a sense, beside the point so long as the beliefs are widely held and acted upon.

The belief that risk arbitrageurs will quickly have to sell billions of dollars of stock to cover losses resulting from one "busted" deal is an example of a scenario that describes the latter situation. This scenario also fits many popular descriptions of market behavior at about the time of the October 13, 1989 market crash. The belief that portfolio insurance would swamp the market in October 1987 fits the former scenario and is also consistent with widespread press reports prevalent at that time.

It is interesting that the key variable in each of these scenarios is the *expected demand for short-term trading services*. It is not the actual demand for trading services as later observed in the market, or the aggregate anticipated price change based on "fundamentals" that is expected to result from the new information coming to market. This is a critical distinction that is supported by several collateral observations.

Studies have, for example, demonstrated that statistically significant price changes accompany the announcement that a particular issuer's shares are to be added to the Standard and Poor (S&P) 500 Index. Typically, the price of these shares increases for a relatively short period of time and then gradually declines. These price changes occur even though there is absolutely no change in the fundamental information describing the issuer's business. Instead, the short-lived price increase is generally ascribed to a transitory liquidity effect that results from a large demand by index funds for immediate possession of the issuer's shares so as to minimize the tracking error between their fund's behavior and the behavior of the S&P 500 Index.[13]

These studies have important implications for the analysis of market volatility because they demonstrate that "informationless" trading can induce stock price volatility provided that the trading creates a sufficiently unanticipated demand for liquidity. Indeed, this effect, which has been clearly demonstrated for a single issuer's shares, may well be generalizable to the entire market, as I now explain.

The Purest Crashette

The existence of a measurable stock price effect attributable solely to an informationless demand for liquidity suggests an interesting *Gedankenexperiment*. Suppose that, instead of changing one stock in the composition of the

---

13. See, e.g., Harris and Gurel, "Price and Volume Effects Associated with Changes in the S&P List," *Journal of Finance* 41 (1986): 815–29; C. Lamoureux and J. Wansley, *Market Effects of Changes in the S&P 500 Index* (Department of Finance, Louisiana State University, February 1986); Standard & Poor's Corporation, *S&P 500:1989 Directory* (New York, 1989), 91–102.

S&P 500, Standard and Poor's announced an immediate reconstitution of the entire S&P 500 Index with significant changes in the weighting and composition of that benchmark portfolio. The result would likely be great uncertainty in the short-term trading market as participants scrambled to guess how index funds would attempt to rebalance their portfolios. This uncertainty would be compounded by a lack of information about the likely trading strategies of "closet indexers" and of other investors whose portfolio compositions are, one way or another, keyed to the composition of the S&P 500 Index.

In all probability, the price of short-term liquidity would rise in response both to the expected marketwide demand for immediate portfolio rebalancing and to the great uncertainty associated with the pace and potential magnitude of the rebalancing activity. The prices of some shares would increase as a result of an increased weighting in the index while the price of shares whose weighting was reduced would likely suffer a transitory decline. On balance, however, the increase in the price of liquidity caused by massive rebalancing would be reflected in a decline in average stock prices which would likely be reversed once all the rebalancing had been accomplished. In other words, after all is said and done, the prices of IBM and GM shares should not change much, if at all,[14] as a result of the reconstitution of the S&P 500 Index, but there may well be an interim period during which prices could be higher or lower depending on whether the issue's weighting has increased or decreased. The result would be the purest of all crashettes: a transitory price decline wholly unrelated to any change in the fundamental valuation of any asset.

The critical point to note, however, is that a crashette need not occur even under these extreme circumstances if Standard and Poor's provides the market with sufficient advance warning of the changes that it intends to make in the composition of its benchmark portfolio. Such advance warning would provide market participants an opportunity to eliminate much of the uncertainty associated with anticipated liquidity demands and thereby reduce the risk premium demanded by liquidity providers. It would also allow portfolio managers to moderate the pace at which they rebalance their portfolios and thereby avoid generating peak load demands on the supply of immediately available liquidity.

Attracting More Liquidity: Why Doesn't It Happen Faster?

No doubt, when crashettes visit the market the rate of return to liquidity providers increases substantially. Why then does more money not quickly rush into the market and thereby rapidly restore a semblance of order? There appear to be at least two answers to this question.[15]

---

14. Whether prices change at all depends on whether there is a longer-term S&P effect. See, e.g., P. C. Jain, "The Effect on Stock Price of Inclusion in or Exclusion from the S&P 500," *Financial Analysis Journal* 43 (January–February 1987): 58–65.

15. A parallel question can, of course, be asked about the opposite side of the market: if the price of liquidity rises so substantially and quickly, why do sellers keep demanding liquidity? Information failure among sellers provides at least a partial answer to this question. Sellers who

First, although the absolute return to liquidity providers trading during crashettes might seem substantial when measured in hindsight, the risk-adjusted rate of return, given the uncertainty that exists at the time of the crashette, is not necessarily out of line with other prevailing risk-adjusted rates of return. Indeed, there is reason to believe that the uncertainty during a crashette can become so great that the price of short-term Treasury instruments experiences a transitory run-up as a consequence of a "flight to quality." This observable price change in what is probably the most liquid financial market in the world, combined with anecdotal indications that some large traders pull back from the market at least during the initial phases of volatility, suggests that the uncertainty causing a crashette can be of a sufficient calibre to force liquidity out of the market precisely at the time the market needs it the most.

Second, it is important to recognize that the process of providing liquidity to the market can involve a relatively high degree of specialization that is not quickly acquired. Experience in judging the information content associated with certain patterns of order flows, as well as the ability quickly to gather reliable information from the cash and derivative products markets, can be extraordinarily valuable in managing funds during periods of market volatility. Simply put, many investment managers who pride themselves on their ability to pick "winners" and avoid "losers" (though in reality they may do neither) do not believe they have a comparative advantage in trading during periods of volatility. Moreover, these investment managers are either unwilling to provide capital to traders with that specialized expertise or are unaware of traders who have the necessary skills.

The observation that there are gains from specialization that result from experience in judging the informational content of order flow is hardly unique. The observation appears in analyses of specialist and market-maker behavior. It also appears in studies that hypothesize the existence of "informed" and "noise" traders.[16] For present purposes, however, the essential

---

are concerned that there is a tremendous overhang of selling yet to come may be willing to pay a high current price for liquidity in order to avoid an anticipated price that is even higher. Sellers who have decided not to sell because of the high price of liquidity do not, however, have a practical means of signaling that they have no interest in adding to the demand for liquidity. In particular, the prospect of massive legal liability could well deter major traders from announcing a policy of abstinence during periods of volatility because, if market conditions changed and the grader decided that he wanted to sell, he would open himself to allegations of market manipulation and fraud. Thus, it is possible for sellers to be demanding liquidity in order to avoid a selling wave that will not come.

There is reason to believe that such behavior may have been at work during October 1987's market volatility. The volume of selling by portfolio insurers was substantially less than some traders had feared, but there were no practical means for insurers to signal that they would not be selling the anticipated volumes at prevailing market prices. Accordingly, many traders may have generated a demand for liquidity based on expectations that were incorrect but that could not be promptly adjusted.

16. For example, Gennotte and Leland (see n. 9 above), hypothesize the existence of three classes of investors: uninformed investors who observe only the prevailing equilibrium price; price-informed investors who also have access to unbiased predictors of future price; and supply-

observation is that not all investors are equally well-situated to trade during a crashette. Models that assume rapid and continuous entry by "fundamental" or "value-oriented" investors may therefore oversimplify some of the informational difficulties that arise during periods of unusual volatility.

Strategic Behavior and the Possibility of "Crazy Eddie" Pricing

There is also reason to believe that, during market crashettes, at least some traders engage in a form of strategic behavior that links stock prices much more closely to liquidity considerations than to any assessment of the market's underlying value. These strategic considerations are perhaps best described by way of an example.

Suppose the Dow Jones average stands at 2600 immediately before the arrival of information that triggers a crashette. A trader estimates that, after the market absorbs the news, prices will reequilibrate at a Dow of 2500. To compensate for the risk that this estimate is incorrect, the trader decides not to buy until prices drop as low as 2550.

However, suppose the trader also perceives that the price of short-term liquidity is about to skyrocket as a result of both the peak-load nature of the demand for trading services and the uncertainty associated with the magnitude and composition of that demand. Under those circumstances, liquidity-related considerations could well cause prices to fall below the 2550 level at which the trader would be induced to buy on the basis of fundamentals alone. From the trader's perspective, if he is happy buying at a price of 2550, he's even happier buying at a price of 2450, or 2300, or 2200. As long as the trader believes that liquidity considerations are likely to force prices even lower, the trader has little incentive to buy even though he believes the market is oversold on the basis of "fundamentals." (This example assumes, of course, that the trader does not change his estimate of post-shock pricing as a consequence of the information he subsequently observes in the market—surely an unrealistic assumption, but one that simplifies the example.)

When will such a trader enter the market and start buying? When he believes that, given the immediate supply and demand for liquidity, prices are so low that unless he starts buying now he may not find prices as good after the market recovers. Equivalent prices will be unavailable because the market is so thin that his orders are unlikely to be filled at better prices during the recovery. Put another way, the trader may estimate that the peak price of liquidity is about to be reached and that the discounts associated with the demand for

---

informed investors who observe order flow information. They find that the presence of an adequate number of supply-informed investors is critical to avoiding crashette-type behavior. The point I am suggesting is that, given usual trading patterns, there is an optimal amount of capital that is allocated to supply-informed traders. This amount of capital is not, however, so large that it is able to absorb the peak-load demand for trading that accompanies a crashette. Moreover, there are perfectly understandable institutional reasons why more capital does not quickly flow to these investors during times of market stress.

liquidity are about to decline. Under either circumstance, the trader's decision to buy stock or futures is determined by conditions in the market for immediate liquidity rather than assessments of postequilibrium stock market values.

This explanation of trading behavior may provide a rational basis for the observation that prices during crashettes no longer reflect assessments solely of the "fundamental" value of shares traded on an exchange. That does not, however, mean that the prices observed during crashettes are irrational because crashette prices may be sending more information about liquidity conditions than about fundamental values. Given the level of uncertainty and the peak-load nature of demand for liquidity that accompanies a crashette, short-term price declines may be perfectly understandable, if uncomfortable, consequences of rational market forces.

This behavior pattern can be described in a somewhat more colorful fashion that will be particularly familiar to New Yorkers. For many years, New York's airwaves were filled with advertisements starring a pitchman for "Crazy Eddie," an electronics and appliance retailer who claimed to have prices so low that they were "insane." The message was that Crazy Eddie's prices were so good that you could not afford not to shop at his store. That, in a sense, may describe the price signal sent during a crashette that triggers some traders' decision to reenter the market—prices are so low (because the price of liquidity is so high) that it makes sense to buy even if there is a chance that prices might drop lower still.

Information Problems and Information Solutions

If this analysis is generally correct, it suggests that recent incidents of short-term volatility have been caused, at least in part, by information problems in the market for immediate liquidity. Thus, it seems reasonable to suggest that we might want to look for information solutions to these information problems.

Interestingly, this is an area where regulators have actually experienced a modicum of success. During 1985 and 1986 the most significant complaints about market volatility were caused by "triple witching hours." These quarterly events were the result of the simultaneous expiration of futures and options contracts that created informationless peak-load demands for liquidity at precisely the market's closing price. Market participants knew beforehand exactly when there would be large liquidity demands but did not know the magnitude of those demands or the specific stocks in which the demands would be greatest.

To reduce the volatility associated with triple witching hours, regulators and self-regulatory organizations modified trading procedures in the futures, options, and equities markets. Contract expirations were moved from the close to the open, new requirements were introduced calling for earlier submission of trading orders, and new opening procedures were adopted that gave the market a better view of the volumes likely to be bought or sold at the open. As a result of these measures, traders had better estimates prior to the open of just how much demand for trading was likely to arise and of just where that demand would likely be centered. In other words, the regulatory environment was changed so as to generate more information about the demand for a very particular and immediate form of liquidity.

These relatively simple measures appear to have eliminated most of the volatility associated with triple witching hours. Moreover, triple-witch volatility appears to have been eliminated at very low cost and with no perceptible market inefficiency or dislocation.

There is a lesson to be learned here. Regulators have already successfully eliminated a particular form of liquidity-induced volatility by increasing the amount of information available to the market. Granted, this task is particularly easy when the peak-load demand on liquidity happens like clockwork because of the structure of contracts traded on futures and options markets. Reducing volatility through information solutions at other times will be more difficult, but it might not be impossible.

What is needed is more information about the magnitude and composition of the demand for liquidity, particularly when the market experiences substantial volatility. This information can be provided through a variety of channels. In no special order, and recognizing that other approaches may be preferable, I will describe two possible means of increasing liquidity-related information in the event of extreme volatility. Moreover, I should emphasize that I am not endorsing either of these proposals as measures that should be adopted. Instead, the primary purpose of articulating these information-related remedies is to stimulate consideration of approaches that have not been broadly explored or debated.

The first and perhaps simplest approach would be to require that, in the event of unusual volatility, traders announce their orders ahead of trading and perhaps also identify themselves if their orders are sufficiently large. Such a requirement would provide the market with information about the forthcoming demand for liquidity and not just about present and past demand. It would also provide the market with information about sellers' identities, from which the market could infer both the extent to which selling is informationless and the extent to which more selling might be forthcoming.[17]

This proposal could, of course, be modified in a variety of ways. The preannouncement period could either be quite short (e.g., requiring announcement immediately before the actual entry of an order) or it could be relatively long

17. A similar proposal is discussed by Gary Becker; see "Lassoing Herd Instinct for the Good of the Market," *Business Week* (20 November 1989), 20. ("If booms and busts in stock prices are caused by limited information, stock performance could be improved by more of it. For example, advance announcement of large institutional orders coming to market—sunshine trading—might give investors better information about the sources of price changes.")

(e.g., requiring announcement 15 minutes or more prior to execution of an order). Longer announcement periods would have to address the possibility that traders can legitimately decide to cancel preannounced orders, as well as the possibility that some traders might behave strategically and enter orders that they never intend to execute. The proposal would also be relatively cheap to implement and would not require that regulators have any ex ante view as to whether volatility is the result of a crash or of a crashette: in either event the proposal would call forth additional information.

No doubt, a major drawback of this approach to some traders will be the loss of anonymity currently available in the market. The basic policy issue, however, is whether the benefits resulting from increased information outweigh the costs associated with the loss of anonymity in situations of extraordinary volatility.[18]

The second approach would be to halt continuous trading once a specific volatility level is reached and require that trading then be conducted through a single-price auction. In a single-price auction buyers and sellers indicate the volumes of business they would be willing to do at various prices. This information is then conveyed to all market participants in a form analogous to supply and demand curves that illustrate the prices at which markets would clear. By requiring that all trading occur through the single-price auction mechanism, the market would be guaranteed that it knows the total demand for liquidity, at least until the next single-price auction is held or until continuous trading resumes.

The single-price auction has been actively promoted by Steve Wunsch of Kidder Peabody. Although it has several appealing information characteristics, a complete single-price auction for hundreds or thousands of financial instruments might be difficult to implement, particularly during periods of great volatility when a substantial amount of price-search activity is ongoing. Moreover, single-price auction systems would also have to address the possibility of strategic behavior by buyers and sellers who might enter indications of interest that they pull before trading commences. This approach could also expect to draw opposition from locals, specialists, market makers, and other intermediaries whose services would not be needed because the auction mechanism effectively allows buyers to do business directly with sellers. In addition, this approach would require the introduction of several new electronic systems. Accordingly, a single-price auction approach might be easier to justify on a cost basis if single-price auctions were used regularly, regardless of the degree of price volatility—a possibility that may deserve consideration for reasons wholly independent of volatility concerns.

18. Certain traders who want to preserve anonymity might seek to transact offshore in markets that are not subject to equivalent disclosure requirements. Liquidity for U.S. shares in foreign markets is, however, likely to be even worse than it is in the United States, and these traders will therefore be forced to pay a substantial price to retain their anonymity.

Conclusion

There is substantial reason for caution in any attempt to explain recent market volatility. Nonetheless, there is cause to believe that a material part of the volatility recently experienced in the equity market is attributable to information failure in the market for liquidity. In particular, instances of volatility appear to be correlated with peak-load demands for immediate trading and with great uncertainty about the magnitude and composition of these demands.

This observation is supported by evidence that large volumes of informationless trading can move the price of individual equities, as well as the price of the entire equity market. This observation also supports the policy recommendation that information failures should be addressed by information solutions. Measures designed to increase the flow of information about the size and composition of the market's demand for liquidity may be particularly worthy of further debate and consideration.

Summary of Discussion

Friedman began by pointing out that the discussants' remarks were focused on financial institutions and financial markets. He emphasized that the behavior of nonfinancial entities matters too, because their behavior affects the quality of the credits held by financial institutions. He posed the question whether regulation and supervision can control the quality of those credits. Friedman added that, despite the high visibility of the breakdown of the savings and loan system, that breakdown did not result in a financial crisis, although a banking system failure might produce such a crisis.

William S. Haraf felt that the problems of savings and loans were greatly understated by the discussants' comments. The true culprit in the S&L failure is deposit insurance, which long predates the 1980–82 deregulation. He then outlined two key problems for the future of the banking system. The first is determining the extent of coverage provided by deposit insurance. He noted that since the failure of Continental Illinois, when, on grounds of fairness, contingent creditors were protected as well as depositors, regulators have adopted "too small to fail" as well as "too big to fail." Consequently, there is little market discipline left in the current system. The second problem is understanding whether regulation can prevent institutional failure, and at what efficiency cost. Haraf pointed out that various changes in the deposit insurance system have been proposed that would restore some market discipline to the banking industry.

Lawrence B. Lindsey went on to say that the beginning of the unraveling of the savings and loan industry was disintermediation and the government's re-action to the problem. Under Regulation Q, disintermediation created serious problems for the construction industry, but preserved the integrity of the savings and loan industry. Further, the process was self-correcting as the resulting recession in the construction industry cooled off loan demand, thus bringing interest rates back down to levels consistent with Regulation Q. The gradual deregulation of interest rates and the banking industry generally was an effort to limit the impact of monetary policy on construction and spread it more generally across the economy. The result was a shift in riskiness from the construction industry to savings and loans and the elimination of the self-correcting link between disintermediation and a recession in construction.

Sprague responded to Haraf that after the Penn Square failure, he had favored a "modified payoff" policy, in which insolvent banks were closed and depositors immediately received 100% of all deposits below $100,000. Depositors also receive a percentage payment on the uninsured deposits based on the expected future sale value of their share of the bank's assets. This policy was employed eight times but was ignored in May 1984 when the consensus of regulators was that Continental Illinois had to be saved.

Paul A. Volcker also answered Haraf, saying that whether banks could be "too big to fail" depended on the meaning of the word "fail"; although Continental Illinois creditors were paid, the stockholders lost. He argued that financial regulators must act differently with the current "tenuous institutional background" than with a "robust institutional background." Alternative strategies were tried with Continental Illinois but failed. It is a misinterpretation of this episode to say that no bank would ever fail. Volcker noted that small banks are essentially protected by deposit insurance alone, since they have few deposits over $100,000. He wondered how, in general, we can ensure protection from crisis without protecting inefficiencies in the banking system.

Feldstein asked Volcker whether we wanted to rely on supervision or to build in risk-sharing arrangements. *Volcker* responded that we need both and felt that lowering the $100,000 insurance limit and introducing copayments for deposit insurance made economic sense but seemed politically impossible.

Michael Mussa explained that if the increase in corporate leverage was a response to greater macroeconomic stability and thus less economic risk, it should be viewed as a good thing. So the important question is whether we have encouraged too much leverage in some way. At the end of the Civil War, equity was 40% of banks' total assets but is only about 3%–4% today. One reason for the change is risk sharing by the federal insurance agencies. If only equity and not subordinated credit is at risk in a failing bank, then only equity should count toward the capital requirements. Further, capital requirements should be large enough that the average failing bank draws no public funds.

Robert J. Shiller addressed Grundfest's remarks by agreeing that psychology was important but disagreeing with Grundfest's specific theory. Financial panics are marked not by public insanity but by rapid shifts in public opinion.

The opinions held at any one time are not unreasonable; there are usually "experts" expositing them. The problem is that people change too sharply from one expert to another. People pay closer attention to the markets when they are unstable, so they are more likely to change their minds. Closing markets is unlikely to help this problem.

Edward J. Kane returned to the issue of regulation and supervision of the banking system. The recent reform of the regulating agencies gave the agencies new powers but also established grace periods before capital requirements can be enforced, left loopholes in the capital requirements, and resulted in a diversion of personnel to handle the failing institutions. The key error at the regulatory agencies has been measuring their success in the short run by failure rates rather than by the net capital reserves of the insurance funds. Savings and loans' losses developed in the mid-1960s and throughout the 1970s and early 1980s, but, until the mid-1980s, the FSLIC covered up the problems. Kane emphasized the importance of insurers' reporting *net,* not gross, capital reserves for themselves and regulated institutions based on mark-to-market asset values, with tough fraud laws to prevent deception. He proposed "escalating and predictable" penalties for a declining capital base, focusing on forcing shareholders to "buy back" the institution by investing more money or watch the institution close.

William Poole reminded the group that any proposal to make depositors bear some of the losses of a failing institution must take account of the fact that short-term assets are always subject to a run. This fundamental problem of instability cannot be overcome by programs aimed at depositors but must instead be addressed by increasing the amount of equity or long-term debt.

Sidney Jones asked the panelists to consider the sources of the regulatory failure of the savings and loans. He raised three possibilities. First, was the financial system inherently too complex to regulate? If regulators are working eight hours per day to enforce obsolete regulations and institutions are working 24 hours per day to beat the system, risk sharing arrangements will be necessary. Second, does the ability of financial institutions to move between different regulatory environments pressure regulators to soften their rules? Third, has the quality of the regulatory personnel been a problem? Jones said that, as a political appointee for 20 years, he can attest that they vary in quality. In particular, he was concerned about the turnover among appointees and their lack of previous experience. He summarized his views as a support for more supervision of institutions and less protection if they fail anyway.

Feldstein asked whether less protection for creditors is politically feasible and whether it would encourage more careful institutional behavior anyway. Individuals with less than $100,000 in bank accounts are probably not sophisticated financial analysts. Would credit rating agencies develop to help such depositors assess the risks of different institutions? *Jones* repeated his belief in limitations on deposit insurance.

Sprague responded to Jones by stating that the main difference in operation between the Federal Home Loan Bank Board (FHLBB) and the FDIC was the ability of the FDIC to ignore the special pleading of Congress and the president, an ability the FHLBB did not have.

Strunk agreed with Jones's suspicion that the FHLBB had a very inadequate examination staff in terms of size, ability, and experience. This was due to direct congressional control of the agency and low salaries. The FHLBB was also cautious in dealing with failing institutions due to a likely federal court review of their actions.

Paul A. Samuelson discussed the origin of the saving and loan problems in Congress's desire to help the real estate industry. By legislating a system with short-term deposits and long-term loans, they created the potential for honest institutions to go under water if interest rates were highly variable. This danger preceded the moral-hazard and agency problems stressed by Kane.

Richard F. Syron agreed with Jones and Samuelson that the Home Loan Bank Act of 1932 was inherently flawed, as the intent of Congress to promote home ownership became interpreted as an intent to promote the savings and loan industry. A system where the goal of the regulator was to promote the regulated industry (a majority of directors of the Home Loan Banks were from the institutions being regulated) could only work in a stressless world.

Samuelson discussed another approach to the insurance issue based on his personal money management, namely individual choice of mutual funds holding assets of varying risk.

Feldstein added that James Tobin had recently supported the so-called narrow bank concept in which individuals could have many types of mutual fund accounts but government insurance would apply only to deposits corresponding to government or AAA short-term bonds.

Grundfest went on to say that the Securities and Exchange Commission has given serious thought to popularizing the simple observation that limitless insurance is available at zero premium *if* one puts one's money into a money market mutual fund that invests in U.S. Treasury instruments. If one wants a return greater than the riskless rate, one needs to take some risk, but all of the legitimate reasons for deposit insurance can be fulfilled by money market funds that hold Treasury securities.

Richard D. Erb described other structural rigidities in the banking system that increase risks to individual institutions. The most important are limitations on asset choice, limitations based on geography because of restrictions on inter- and intrastate branch banking, limitations on the size of institutions, and the historical link between the mortgage market and the savings and loan industry. He proposed moving toward requiring a broadly defined portfolio distribution for all institutions covered by deposit insurance. Opening up the diversification possibilities for savings and loans was a good step but was too limited, as remaining geographic limitations led to concentrated high-risk investments, as in the Southwest.

Robert E. Hall raised the broader question of why default on debt is dangerous for the economy. Although the public associates default with shutdown and layoffs, in fact the company usually continues in business with a new set of shareholders, as the old shareholders are wiped out and the debt holders become shareholders. Why is this conceptually distinct from a business that operated with zero leverage and faced hard times? Hall noted that there is an alternative view that default is more costly, as David Cutler and Lawrence Summers showed that the stock market capitalized the cost of Texaco and Pennzoil's reorganization in the billions of dollars. This loss greatly exceeds the direct costs, and the source of the extra loss is unknown, but there is no evidence that combined employment fell. Further, as defaults become more common, both their perceived and actual costs will fall.

Hall continued that the crucial question for banks is whether lending continues unabated after defaults. The answer appears to be yes for real estate loans, but is less clear for business loans, for which there is no secondary market; this means that funding and loan origination are done by the same institution. The idea that a financial crisis reduces business investment because it precludes business borrowing is much less true than it used to be.

Feldstein emphasized that the conference's concern is not with individual institutional failure but with the possibility of a systemic breakdown. Has the deposit insurance system acted as a brake on that breakdown process?

Friedman concluded by asking whether systemic failures differ from individual failures in a fundamental way. If they do, then Hall's approach of thinking about one institution in a world where other institutions are operating normally will not be a sufficient analysis.

2 International Aspects of Financial Crises

1. *Paul Krugman*
2. *C. Fred Bergsten*
3. *Rudiger Dornbusch*
4. *Jacob A. Frenkel*
5. *Charles P. Kindleberger*

1. *Paul Krugman*

Financial Crises in the International Economy

The international economy since 1982 has presented a somewhat paradoxical picture. From the point of view of financial analysts, these have been the most turbulent times since the 1930s. Financial market prices have experienced both large day-to-day volatility and very large swings. To take just three examples: the price of the dollar in Japanese yen went from 250 in early 1985 to half that two years later, then rebounded to 150 in April of 1989; the Standard and Poor's index lost 22 percent of its value within a week in 1987, then regained all of that ground over the following 20 months; the average secondary market price of Third World debt dropped from about 70 percent of par in late 1985 to 30 percent in late 1987. To someone who looked only at financial data, it would seem obvious that we are living in very unstable times.

Yet away from the financial markets the economic picture has remained remarkably placid, at least in the advanced countries. The economic recovery that began in late 1982 has continued for nearly seven years without either turning into a runaway boom or stalling into a recession; at the time of this writing, widespread predictions of an imminent U.S. recession had faded away in the face of some favorable economic news. Inflation came down in all of the advanced nations in the early 1980s, and since about 1986 it has been generally stable at moderate rates (with a few exceptions, such as in Britain). In many ways economic performance remains unsatisfactory—productivity growth in the United Stated remains sluggish, unemployment in Europe remains stubbornly high—but instability has not been a major problem.

The seeming inconsistency between wildly volatile financial markets and a calm real economy admits of two interpretations. One is that it is the stability that is the essential feature of our times and that the hyperactive financial markets are of little real importance. Indeed, it can be argued that financial prices can fluctuate as much as they do precisely because they have so little real effect, an argument to which I will return late in this paper. The alternative hypothesis is, of course, more disturbing: it is that the apparent stability of the real economy is unreliable, and that there is a lurking risk of crisis arising from the financial side.

Even 60 years later, the specter of the Great Crash still looms over us. Like the 1980s, the 1920s were a time of impressive economic performance in many ways, marred by unstable financial markets. And in spite of the many unresolved debates over what really caused the Great Depression, it still seems clear that in the end financial instability undermined the real economy. Certainly anyone today who dismisses financial events with the assertion that the economy is "fundamentally sound" is aware of the slightly hollow echo of that remark, no matter how reasonable it may be.

Of particular concern in the present environment is the possibility that the destabilizing effects of financial crisis may catch us by surprise because they take place through international channels. It is often asserted that today's international markets are integrated to an unprecedented degree, thanks to modern communications and information processing. There is room for doubt on this score: both international goods and international financial markets were already highly integrated by the late nineteenth century, and it is not clear how much *economic* difference being able to carry out a transaction in a second via computer, as opposed to an hour via the telegraph, really makes. What is clear, however, is that thanks to the effects of trade liberalization, elimination of capital controls, and financial deregulation, international markets are more integrated now than at any time since the early 1930s—an observation that can be seen as ominous.

Influential commentators on the Great Depression, Charles Kindleberger most prominent among them, have long argued that the roots of the Depression lay largely in a collapse of the international financial system. They also argue that this collapse was due in large part to the absence of leadership, in particular to the failure of any one player to act as lender of last resort. In turn, the absence of leadership may be attributed to the transitional state of the international system: Britain, in relative decline, was no longer prepared to act as guarantor of the system, while the United States was still too immature to take on its appropriate role. The parallels with our own time are there if one wants to see them, in the relative decline of the United States and the problematic role of Japan.

But economic analysis cannot be made solely by loose historical analogy. The purpose of this paper is to offer a framework for thinking about the possibility that the highly integrated world markets that have emerged over the past decade present a risk of financial crisis.

The paper begins by laying out a simple typology of internationally generated crises, illustrating this typology with some "classical" historical examples. It turns next to the analysis of the major types, briefly reviewing the (generally skimpy) theoretical literature and illustrating the points with historical case. The paper then turns to present concerns: why didn't the huge swings in equity and foreign exchange markets since 1985 destabilize the real economy? Are the risks of instability still there? What can policy do to prevent crisis?

2.1 Types of International Crisis

The study of economic crises in general is relatively undeveloped, mostly because crises are difficult to model formally. There are a few scattered models, largely in the analysis of balance of payments and banking problems; I will describe these models briefly below. Most writing on crises, however, is informal and literary, drawing more on historical example than on rigorous reasoning.

In spite of this informality, the most influential writers on crisis, notably Minsky and Kindleberger, are insistent that there is a general model of crisis—that it is a mistake to try to subdivide the crisis problem into particular subcases. Kindleberger in particular is sharply critical of the idea that "the genus 'crises' should be divided into species labeled commercial, industrial, monetary, banking, fiscal, financial . . . and so on" (Kindleberger 1978, 22). They argue that there is a standard crisis story in which naive investors get pulled into an asset market by the belief that they can benefit from rising prices, thereby reinforcing that very rise; then they stampede together for the door when the price finally stabilizes or begins to decline, precipitating a price crash. This price crash then, through a variety of channels, destabilizes the macroeconomy.

I am strongly sympathetic to the desire to have a single crisis story, and I find the particular story offered by Kindleberger a very appealing one: it makes psychological sense even if it is hard to fit into standard economic models, and it fits enough historical episodes to be a useful organizing device for our thinking. Nonetheless, for the current paper it seems necessary to have at least a rudimentary typology that distinguishes one kind of crisis from another. This typology is necessary for at least two reasons. First, the way a crisis plays out depends on the actors in the market; and these actors are very different when the focus is on foreign exchange markets and the balance of payments than when the focus is on stock markets. Second, the real effects of a financial crisis depend on its type: to take the two most discussed possibilities, a crisis that begins with a run on the U.S. dollar will not look the same as one that begins with a run on the Japanese stock market.

At the risk of complicating up the subject, then, I offer here a minimalist typology of international financial crises.

2.1.1 Types of Crisis

At minimum, it seems necessary to distinguish between two kinds of international financial crisis. One kind involves a loss of confidence by speculators in a country's currency, provoking capital flight. Since currency crises often lead to imposition of capital controls that interfere with servicing of foreign-currency debt, a loss of confidence in a country's currency will often be accompanied by a collapse of foreign-currency-denominated lending as well. This is the kind of crisis that struck Latin America in 1982: investors feared capital losses on their holdings of Latin currencies, and also feared (correctly) that servicing of Latin foreign-currency debt would be interrupted by exchange controls. The result was the simultaneous emergence of capital flight and the cutoff of hard-currency bank finance.

The important point about this kind of crisis, which I will call for short a *currency* crisis, is that although it originates in international financial markets it need not be international in scope. Or to put it another way, a few countries may be plunged into currency crises at the same time that the rest of the world continues to have both financial and macroeconomic stability.

The other kind of crisis involves not loss of confidence in a currency, but a loss of confidence in real assets (or the equity that those assets back). Suppose that the Japanese real estate market decides that a few square blocks of Tokyo are not really worth more than California, and that the price of Japanese land falls accordingly, with ramifications that reach around the world. This would be a very different kind of crisis, one in which the international aspect arises in the way that developments in one country's financial markets affect other markets in other countries. The global stock market shock of October 1987 is the most dramatic recent example, but of course the worldwide financial and then macroeconomic crisis of 1929–31 is the grand example. This paper will pass lightly over the domestic origins of such crises, leaving that topic for the companion paper by Lawrence Summers, but the process by which national asset shocks become global needs a name; I will call them *contagion* crises. More or less by definition, contagion crises do not affect only one or a few countries.

There are important differences between the study of currency and contagion crises. Currency crises inevitably involve the central bank of the crisis country; contagion crises usually involve acts of commission or at least omission on the part of central banks, but the role is not as essential. Currency crises have been the subject of a reasonably large, if limited, theoretical literature, whereas contagion crises have not. This difference is at least partly because it is possible to imagine currency crises in which individual investors are rational, with the central bank playing the role of naive actor, thereby preserving the standard economic assumption of individual rationality. By contrast, it is essentially impossible to make sense of the asset price crashes that are the starting point of contagion crises without appealing to some kind of investor irrationality.

Finally, the macroeconomics of currency crises and contagion crises are quite different—while both can lead to recession, currency crises are usually associated with inflation in the victims, while contagion crises are associated with worldwide deflation.

2.1.2   Two Classic Examples

Most of macroeconomics draws its stock of experience and analogy from the well-documented business cycles of the post-1947 period rather than from the more extreme but poorer quality data of the interwar period. The literature on crises is an exception, however. Until the emergence of the Latin American debt crisis in 1982, the postwar period had not offered any grand crises to study (leading some economists and all too many bankers to conclude that such things could never happen again); thus the interwar experiences and earlier are all that we have. Also, the relatively low formal level of the study of crises means that the literary tradition, which draws on older historical cases, has remained alive in this field.

The upshot is that when discussing international financial crises we are still influenced strongly, whether we realize it or not, by images generated by a few classic cases from the interwar period. In particular, our image of a currency crisis is largely drawn from the case of the French franc in 1924–26; our image of a contagion crisis from the worldwide spread of the U.S. stock market crash of 1929.

The Franc in the 1920s

France, like all of the major European nations, was forced to allow its currency to float after World War I. Immediately after the end of wartime pegging (backed by U.S. loans), the franc fell to about half its previous value in terms of gold, a fall similar to that experienced by Britain. Unlike Britain, however, France had a persistent fiscal problem, with its domestic revenues inadequate to service the war debt. For several years after the war French leaders continued to insist that German reparations would pay for French expenditures; but as Germany plunged into hyperinflation this became an obvious fantasy. The clear alternative for France was inflation: since the debt was fixed in nominal terms, and the revenues of the French government (largely indirect taxes) were essentially indexed to the price level, it was clear from the beginning that France could solve its fiscal problems by inflating them away and allowing the franc to depreciate on foreign exchange markets.

Evidently this situation invited speculative fluctuations for perfectly rational reasons: any news indicating that the French government was more likely to choose inflation as the answer to its problems would drive the franc down, any news indicating a possible willingness to cut expenditure or raise taxes would cause it to rise. Thus introduction of new taxes and the successful flotation of some new loans led to a rise in the franc from 6.25 U.S. cents to 9.23 cents over the period from April 1920 to April 1922; bad diplomatic news and accelerating chaos in Germany (cutting into prospects for reparations) then precipitated a rapid decline to 6.86 cents by November 1922.

What struck observers at the time, however, was that, at a certain point, these fluctuations seemed to develop a life of their own, driven not by identifiable outside events but rather by seemingly self-fulfilling crises. In January 1924 lack of confidence led to the failure to place a large government debt issue; the news of this failure prompted a fall in the franc that drove it to 3.49 cents by March. Yet when the government responded with a program of tax increases, the franc promptly rebounded to 6.71 cents, inflicting heavy losses on speculators and allowing the French authorities actually to increase their foreign exchange reserves. This rise in the franc also turned out to be an overreaction, and two months later the franc was down to 5 cents.

The final act in the story came in the period from October 1925 to July 1926. As in the 1924 crisis, the immediate precipitating event was the inability of the government to place new debt issues—an event that was itself caused by lack of confidence. The franc fell from 4.7 cents in September to 2.05 in July. The appointment of the fiscally tough-minded Raymond Poincaré as premier and finance minister, however, brought the crisis to an end with only modest further fiscal adjustment; by the end of the year the franc had risen to 3.95 cents, and the French government was actually intervening heavily to hold the franc down, acquiring large reserves of gold and foreign exchange in the process. Subsequently the franc was widely regarded as undervalued, bringing France persistent surpluses in its balance of payments until Britain went off the gold standard in 1931.

The fluctuations of the franc had substantial macroeconomic effects. The depreciation of the franc led to substantial inflation; the subsequent stabilization was followed by a sharp although brief recession.

To observers at the time, the story of the French franc seemed an object lesson in the dangers of destabilizing speculation. They noted that the exchange rate repeatedly and massively overshot the levels at which it eventually paused. They also noted that the fiscal problems of the government were, in the immediate run, as much the result as the cause of speculative attack. Ragnar Nurkse (1942) prepared a classic report for the League of Nations that is widely regarded as a key intellectual underpinning for the Bretton Woods system; in this report the history of the franc plays a central role in the case for pegged as opposed to flexible exchange rates.

Modern revisionist assessments of the franc have downplayed the element of irrationality. They point out that the fiscal problem of the French government, and the incentive to inflate its way out, were real. Thus an exchange rate that made wide swings on the basis of news about the government's fiscal prospects was reasonable. The important point for now is that the case of the franc, with its picture of exchange markets responding to a troubled currency with wide swings and, in particular, large overshooting, still influences the images that economists have about currency crises; in particular, the famous "hard landing" scenario of Marris (1985) is strongly influenced by the history of the franc, as filtered through the writings of Nurkse, Kindleberger, and others.

1929

No economic event has had as much written about it as the crash of 1929 and its aftermath. This paper will not try to add to the literature regarding the causes of the crash, and why it was followed by so large a real contraction of the U.S. economy. All that I will do here is point out some aspects of the international transmission of the crisis.

The popular image of 1929 is of a single, dramatic moment: the U.S. stock market crashes from the heights to near zero in a matter of hours, dragging down all of the rest of the world's financial markets with it, and immediately precipitating the Depression. It is now a familiar argument that the U.S. crisis was not so simple; that the sharp business cycle contraction of 1929–30 would have been only on the order of the slumps of 1920, 1974, or 1982 had the crisis not spread to general banking collapse in 1930–31. It needs to be noted here that the international spread of the crisis was also not quite so neat.

For one thing, the transmission of the immediate financial shock, while by no means absent, was not complete. The first column of table 2.1 shows some comparative changes in stock price indices from September to December of 1929. Stock markets fell around the world; but with the exception of Canada, they fell much less than the U.S. market (so that the 1929 crash was much less global than the 1987 crash, as we will see). Most of the eventual fall in the U.S. stock market took place over the next two years rather than in the initial crash; the second column of the table shows that this decline was generally milder outside the U.S., especially in the United Kingdom.

The spreading slump in real activity presents a similar picture, shown in table 2.2. The U.S. slump was transmitted to the rest of the world, but in general the slump was milder elsewhere—the exceptions are Canada and,

Table 2.1   **Stock Market Declines, 1929–32**

	September– December 1929	December 1929– December 1932
United States	31.9	69.4
Canada	33.5	72.4
France	10.8	47.3
Germany	14.4	44.9
United Kingdom	16.0	24.8

Source: C. P. Kindleberger. 1973. *The World in Depression.* London: Penguin.

Table 2.2   **Real Output Declines after 1929 (trough as % of 1929)**

	Industrial Production (%)	GNP
United States	55	68
Canada	68	76
France	74	83
Germany	58	80
United Kingdom	86	93
Japan	92	no decline

Source: L. B. Yeager. 1976. *International Monetary Relations: Theory, History, and Policy.*

more interesting, Germany. The United Kingdom experienced a notably milder slump than the other major nations, and Japan experienced only a more or less normal cyclical downturn.

In spite of the unevenness of the spread of both financial crisis and real slump in 1929–32, the events of those years still serve as a model for international transmission of a financial crisis.

2.2 Currency Crises

Currency crises occur when investors lose confidence in the currency of a particular country, and seek to escape both assets denominated in that currency and other assets whose income might be affected by exchange controls. There have been a few currency crises among advanced countries in the postwar period—arguably the attack on the dollar that shattered the Smithsonian system in 1973 qualifies, as does the attack on sterling in 1975, and the attack on the franc in 1982. Among developing countries, currency crises have been common, and since 1982 most of Latin America and a number of other countries have suffered from what may be described as a coordinated currency crisis.

Currency crises have been the subject of considerable theoretical and some empirical analysis, because the interplay between central banks and private investors provides an easier game to model than the kind of amorphous irrationality that underlies common descriptions of other kinds of financial crises. So it is useful to review the concepts of this literature briefly.

2.2.1 Origins of Crisis: Rational Models

The first question we need to ask is, Why should currency problems turn into a currency *crisis?* That is, why should large-scale capital flight or a sudden drop in the exchange rate materialize suddenly, instead of building gradually over time? Most popular discussions of financial crisis emphasize the irrational aspect, the herd instinct that leads to a stampede (Kindleberger uses the German word *Torschlusspanik*—"gate-shut-panic"). In currency crises, however, a number of authors have pointed out that given certain plausible kinds of central bank behavior, sudden crises may represent fully rational behavior on the part of investors.

Rational Speculative Attacks

The most studied case is that of speculative attacks on a central bank that is trying to maintain an ultimately unsustainable fixed rate. The speculative attack concept was first introduced by Salant and Henderson (1978) in a model of the gold market; it was first applied to currency crises by Krugman (1979) and has been the subject of a large literature, including in particular papers by Flood and Garber (1984) and Obstfeld (1986).

The basic idea of the speculative attack may be conveyed by a simple example. Imagine a country that has a persistent budget deficit that it finances by borrowing from the central bank; in the long run the central bank will have to cover these loans by printing money, so that eventually the country will have to experience persistent inflation and a continuously depreciating currency. For the time being, however, the central bank is pegging the exchange rate—say to the U.S. dollar—using a dwindling stock of foreign exchange. This allows the country to keep its inflation rate temporarily at the U.S. rate of inflation rather than the (much) higher rate that the country will have once its reserves are exhausted and it must allow its currency to float.

When the country runs out of reserves, it will be forced to abandon its policy of pegging the exchange rate. As a result the rate of inflation will sharply accelerate, and the real demand for money will suddenly drop.

How will this reduction in money demand be accommodated? If speculators did not anticipate the collapse of the fixed exchange rate, that rate would survive until reserves had been exhausted; then the sudden drop in money demand would have as its counterpart a sudden step depreciation of the currency. Informed speculators will try to anticipate such an event, however, since it yields large capital losses. They will therefore try to get out of the currency before the collapse. Efforts to get out would, however, themselves accelerate the loss of reserves, provoking an earlier collapse; speculators would therefore try to get out still earlier; and so on. The upshot is that if speculators are fully informed, there will be no step drop in the exchange rate at all. Instead, when reserves fall to some critical level there will be a sudden attack on the currency that exhausts all of these reserves at a single blow, shrinking the money supply and simultaneously forcing a transition to floating rates that produces a validating reduction in money demand.

The appeal of this story of speculative attack is that it shows that abrupt surges of capital flight need not represent irrational behavior; it thereby allows economists to use their preferred tools, which assume rational behavior, to approach the subject. However, the rational speculative attack model as usually stated applies only to a fixed exchange rate or at best to a crawling peg.

Only recently have models been suggested that allow for "rational" crises when the exchange rate is in a managed float.

Target Zones and Credibility

Even when the exchange rate is not formally pegged, governments are rarely indifferent to its value; explicit or implicit targets for the exchange rate are the rule rather than the exception. Recent theoretical literature has shed some light on how the presence of exchange-rate targets should influence the exchange rate's behavior even when no active intervention is in progress; papers include Krugman (1991), Flood and Garber (1988), Miller and Weller (1988), and Froot and Obstfeld (1991a, 1991b). One point that becomes clear in these models is that "news" that influences the exchange rate need not arise from large exogenous events. Instead, relatively small fluctuations in exchange rates can, by the response they elicit (or fail to elicit) from monetary authorities, convey information that leads to large subsequent exchange rate changes.

Suppose, for example, that it is widely believed that the Japanese government will act to keep the dollar from rising above 150 yen—but that nobody is really sure whether they will or not. Then the strong possibility that there is a ceiling on the dollar will tend to hold the dollar down, but not as much as an unambiguous ceiling would. Now suppose that outside events lead the dollar to rise in spite of the possible ceiling, until it reaches 150 yen. Then, whatever the Japanese government does will represent news, because 150 is regarded by the market as a line in the sand that Japan has told it not to cross. If Japan does in fact act strongly to defend the yen at this point, its credibility is enhanced, and the dollar will suddenly drop back—say to 142. If Japan does not act, its credibility will be lost, and the effects of anticipated action in holding the dollar down will disappear; so the dollar will surge, say to 158.

There are two important points here. One is that the market need not have been irrational in failing to anticipate a sudden jump in the dollar, because the dollar could jump *either way*. So there is not a one-way option that creates a certain profit opportunity. The other point is that when the exchange rate jumps, there will have been no identifiable large piece of news arising outside the exchange market; the news is generated endogenously by the fact the market itself tested the authorities' resolve.

The new target zone literature has helped show that sudden crises under floating rates need not represent investor irrationality—a useful caution against Kindleberger-style stories that place complete emphasis on manias and panics. One would not want to deny, however, that irrational crises are also possible.

2.2.2 Origins of Crisis: Irrational Markets

There are an infinite number of ways for markets to be irrational and no way to choose among them on the basis of rigorous economics. There are several popular stories, however, that can serve as useful metaphors for how crises might occur.

Destabilizing Speculation

The traditional explanation for volatility in foreign exchange markets, which goes back to Aftalion's (1927) "psychological" theory of foreign exchange, relies on bandwagon effects. When a currency is rising, investors conclude after a while that it will continue to rise; they buy on that basis, and in so doing they generate an accelerated rise. When for whatever reason the rise slows or stops, the process runs in reverse. Thus the exchange rate engages in fluctuations that at best exaggerate the swings in underlying fundamentals and at worst generate completely pointless variability.

The most recent alleged example of this phenomenon at work would be the ups and downs of the dollar. What is particularly notable in recent experience is the tendency of experts to produce arguments to rationalize whatever trend the dollar is currently following, *after* the trend has become visible. Most notably, the rising dollar in the spring of 1989 was followed, not led, by changes of opinion about sustainable dollar levels by such respected currency experts as David Morrison at Goldman, Sachs (London). This kind of ex post rationalization is part of the process by which cycles get exaggerated and perhaps created.

The Minsky theory of financial crisis is clearly related to the destabilizing speculation view, although it contains elements of our second story, trigger points.

Trigger Points

This is a neologism. I use it to refer to situations in which some group of investors has either explicitly or implicitly precommitted itself to buy or sell a currency when the price reaches a particular level. Examples would include situations in which futures contracts will automatically be liquidated when the investor's margin is eliminated and situations in which speculators follow stop-loss strategies designed to limit their risk. Portfolio insurance schemes in stock markets are of the same kind and will be returned to later.

Suppose that a large number of investors have, de facto, precommitted themselves to sell a currency when the price falls below some level. Then if other events push the currency down to that level, it will trigger a selling wave that quickly pushes the currency considerably lower.

Reputedly, something like this happened to the yen in April 1989. It is reported by financial sources that many Japanese investors in the United States had covered their positions by buying yen futures. When the dollar rose above 140 or so yen, these contracts were automatically liquidated, quickly pushing the dollar to 150.

There are two useful points to make about trigger point crisis stories. First, it is not necessary that all of the relevant investors have exactly the same trigger point; a sudden crisis can result even if they are somewhat dispersed, provided that there are enough of them and they are bunched closely enough. To see this, imagine that there was one group of Japanese investors whose futures would be sold at 140, another at 141, and so on. Now suppose that when the yen rose above 140 it triggered only enough selling to drive the rate to 141.5. This rise in the dollar would, however, trigger selling by the second group; this could in turn trigger selling by the third group; and the cascading effect could lead to a very fast rise from 140 to 150.

On the other hand, existence of even a very large group of investors with trigger points need not create a crisis if other investors know they are there. Had the rest of the market known that many Japanese investors would, in effect, sell yen if the dollar rose above 140, this knowledge would have supported the dollar earlier; then, when the selling was triggered, yen would have been bought by other investors, who would know that the risk of future sudden declines in the yen would be reduced by the cleaning out of these trigger-strategy investors. (For a formal discussion, see Krugman 1987). The possibility of sudden financial crises therefore comes from the fact that the market does not know how much selling will actually be triggered when the price reaches some critical level. (Sanford Grossman made this point with regard to portfolio insurance, somewhat in advance of the October crash.)

Sustainability

A particular source of potential crisis that has attracted widespread attention in discussions of the dollar is the problem of "sustainability." Briefly, this position argues that sometimes currencies rise to levels that are clearly unjustified, in the following sense: they can only be rationalized by expectations about the future path of the currency that would involve an explosive accumulation of foreign debt. Presumably the currency rises this high because of an absence of sufficiently far-sighted investors. The sustainability argument says that at some point, perhaps when the accumulation of debt has risen sufficiently to draw attention to itself, the market notices that the exchange rate is unsustainable, and there is a crash. In 1985, when the dollar was near its peak, Marris (1985) and, more formally, Krugman (1985) argued that the dollar was unsustainable in this sense and got some probably unjustified credit when in fact it came down.

2.2.3   Macroeconomic Effects of Currency Crises

The macroeconomics of currency crises are fairly straightforward in practice, but rather messy in theory. That is, in practice currency crises typically lead to recessions in the affected countries. In standard theoretical models, however, it is easy to get the reverse result, an *expansionary* effect from a speculative attack on a currency. So a key question regarding currency crises is, Why do they usually turn out to be contractionary in practice?

Standard Theoretical Arguments

In thinking about the macroeconomic effects of a currency crisis, it is useful to represent the crisis in some simplified way. At the risk of missing some key elements, I will think of the effect of the financial crisis as being to lead investors to require a risk premium to hold the affected country's assets. Thus, for example, if before the onset of the crisis investors were willing to hold a country's interest-bearing liabilities at an interest rate of 10 percent, when the crisis hits they now demand 20.

The impact of such a risk premium should, in terms of standard models, depend crucially on whether the country has a fixed or a flexible exchange rate. If the rate is fixed, the effect is normally contractionary; if the rate is flexible, it could easily be expansionary.

Consider first what happens with a fixed rate. In standard models the imposition of a risk premium will lead to capital flight that reduces the country's money supply; this induced monetary tightening will lead to higher interest rates, and thus to a fall in demand and a contraction in output.[1]

With a flexible rate, however, the risk premium will be reflected not in capital flight but in a depreciation of the country's currency. Instead of a monetary squeeze, this depreciation will produce an improvement in competitiveness that will increase net exports and thus have an *expansionary* effect on the domestic economy.[2]

This contrast creates a puzzle. Why are the normal results of currency crisis contractionary when the model is ambiguous? And why is it that countries in crisis do not simply float their currencies as a way to avoid recession?

Reasons for Contraction

The reasons for contraction as a result of currency crisis probably lie principally in the policy response, which is typically a combination of very tight money and fiscal austerity. It is this policy response, rather than the direct impact of the financial crisis, that generates the recession.

Why do countries engage in contractionary policies when their currencies are under attack? The main reason is fear of inflation. Without contractionary policies, a financial attack would lead to a sudden currency depreciation that would directly raise import prices and, possibly, indirectly feed into other prices through explicit or implicit wage indexation.

---

1. Strictly speaking, even this contractionary effect is not necessary. If the risk premium wholly reflects expected inflation, then the rise in nominal interest rates will reflect no change in real interest rates and hence might not reduce demand. In practice, we can probably discount this; the risk premium will not be pure inflation expectations, and even a purely nominal interest rise will typically reduce demand when some agents are liquidity constrained.

2. One might wonder whether higher interest rates might not offset the expansionary effect of higher net exports. The answer is no: the economy must expand, so that increased money demand raises the interest rate to offset the required risk premium. The result is similar to the standard result of perverse transmission of monetary shocks under floating rates, described below.

Contractionary domestic policies help counter this inflationary impact of currency crisis in at least three, and perhaps four, ways. First, tight money and high domestic interest rates directly help discourage capital flight and limit the depreciation of the currency. Second, reduced domestic demand reduces demand for imports as well, which also helps reduce the required currency depreciation. Third, a domestic recession helps dampen the inflationary impacts of a declining currency.

The fourth possible channel for helpful results from austerity is that such austerity may help restore investor confidence. To the extent that the crisis represented a more or less rational assessment of the fiscal and monetary stability of the country, a change in policy may be helpful as much for its effect on expectations as for its direct economic impact.

The point that contractionary policies are forced by fears of inflation may perhaps best be illustrated by counterexample. In 1985, Brazil attempted a reversal of the contractionary policies it had imposed in response to the debt crisis.[3] The initial results seemed to show that the contractionary effects of the financial crisis were not inevitable: growth accelerated. The Brazilian trade surplus began to shrink rapidly, however, and eventually an accelerated rate of currency depreciation spilled over into a rapid acceleration of domestic inflation; the experiment in expansionary policies was then reined in.

2.2.4 Latin America

The debt crisis in Latin America provides an extreme example of currency crisis in action—so extreme as to pose some serious puzzles. While the origins of the crisis are understandable at least in hindsight, the severity and persistence of the effects of the crisis remain something of a mystery.

Financial Origins of the Latin Crisis

The deep roots of the debt crisis are outside the scope of this paper. The only point to be made here is that the Latin crisis began as a more or less conventional currency crisis, and only then developed into a "debt" crisis.

Initially, what happened was that a deterioration in the world economic environment led to growing expectations that Latin currencies would be devalued; expecting this devaluation, investors began a flight from Latin currencies. At first, however, hard-currency borrowing continued unaffected, and even accelerated, because lenders thought that the risk was purely currency-related. Only after a considerable length of time—and a substantial increase in hard-currency debt—did lenders apparently realize that the difficulties of the countries could affect their servicing of debt as well as their exchange rates, precipitating a cutoff of lending.

---

3. The Brazilian policy change included a currency reform, a moratorium on debt service, and wage-price controls; obviously these were very important, but the failure of the Brazilian expansion in spite of these additional policies only reinforces the point.

Table 2.3   **Capital Inflow and Capital Flight in Mexico (billion $U.S.)**

Year	Hard Currency Loans Plus Direct Investment	Capital Flight
1978	3.74	.07
1979	6.34	.23
1980	12.69	− .68
1981	30.62	9.73
1982	10.58	8.23
1983	2.27	2.42
1984	1.94	2.33
1985	− .18	1.92

Source: E. Zedillo. 1987. "Mexico." In *Capital Flight and Third World Debt,* ed. D. Lessard and J. Williamson. Washington, D.C.: Institute for International Economics.

Table 2.3 illustrates the point for Mexico. The left column shows "non-peso" capital inflows—hard-currency lending plus direct investment—while the right column shows capital flight. At first these rose together: 1981 was the peak year for both capital inflow and capital flight. Only after the spring of 1982 did lending dry up.

The flight of private capital from Mexico fits rather nicely into the rational speculative attack framework described above. On the other hand, this story poses some questions about the rationality of the hard-currency lenders, principally commercial banks. Was the news about Mexico in 1981 sufficiently clear that it simultaneously made sense for individuals to pull their money out at unprecedented rates while banks poured money in at equally unprecedented rates? One doubts this; so there is at least a strong presumption that the most dramatic of all currency crises involved a considerable element of market irrationality.

It is worth noting that as late as early 1982 most economists and bankers denied that Latin America's debt burden was excessive and regarded a debt crisis as unlikely. This is a useful caution against overconfidence now: even if we find little reason to fear an international financial crisis for the advanced countries, we should remember that the crisis of the developing countries was almost entirely unforseen.

Macroeconomics

The sad tale of the macroeconomic consequences of the Latin crisis is familiar; table 2.4 offers a few representative numbers. The *qualitative* combination of accelerated inflation and reduced growth is what our theoretical discussion led us to expect. However, the sheer size of the consequences is surprising, even given the large shock.

The shock was substantial. As a consequence of the cutoff of lending coupled with capital flight, Latin America shifted from receiving a net inward resource transfer of about 1 percent per year in 1981 to a net outward transfer

Table 2.4   Macroeconomic Performance in Latin America (growth rates)

Year	GNP Per Capita	Consumer Prices
1971–80	3.1	39.8
1981	− 2.6	60.8
1982	− 3.1	66.8
1983	− 4.8	108.6
1984	1.4	133.0
1985	1.4	144.9
1986	1.9	87.8
1987	.4	130.0
1988	− 1.3	277.6

Source: International Monetary Fund. 1989. *World Economic Outlook* (April). Washington, D.C.: IMF.

of about 4 percent in 1984; this outward transfer then diminished somewhat, to about 2.5 percent of GNP in recent years. There was also a deterioration in the terms of trade of some Latin American debtors, notably the oil exporters.

One might have expected this large shock to generate a temporary severe recession, followed by recovery; perhaps a pessimistic forecaster might have surmised that output would remain on a permanently lower track, never making up the ground lost in the initial slump. What one would probably not have forecast is that the several years of severe output decline would be followed by more or less permanent stagnation of real output per capita. If the growth rate from 1971–80 is taken as a norm, the apparent shortfall in output relative to trend is about 30 percent. This huge multiplier is hard to justify in any existing macroeconomic models.

2.3   Contagion Crises

A contagion crisis happens when a financial crash in one country—typically a stock crash—precipitates financial crashes in other countries as well, generating a worldwide recession. Prior to World War II such contagion crises were common. Since then there have been no clear-cut examples. The two large recessions of 1974–75 and 1979–82, although internationally synchronized, originated in oil price shocks (themselves due to political turmoil) and the simultaneous efforts of industrial nations to curb inflation through tight monetary policies rather than in financial panics. The stock market crash of 1987 was very coordinated internationally but did not lead to any economic contraction. So the study of contagion crises necessarily focuses on fairly distant economic history, primarily on the events of 1929–32.

2.3.1   Origins of Crisis

There is not much to be said here about the reasons for initial asset market crashes in any given country. Unlike the case of currency crises, there is no easy way to rationalize sudden events in the stock market by appealing to the interaction of market participants with a central bank. Thus analysis of stock market crashes almost inevitably assumes irrational behavior, or at best some serious market failure.

Two of the stories (one hesitates to call them models) about irrational crises described in the currency crisis section are also widely used to analyze stock market crashes. First, bandwagon behavior can clearly lead to exaggerated fluctuations in stock prices; in particular, if investors are drawn into a rising market but flee from a falling one, sudden declines without any major news can obviously occur.

The alternative trigger point story can also apply. In its more primitive form, we can imagine that large numbers of investors choose to follow stop-loss strategies, planning to sell if stock prices drop below some predetermined level, so as to cap their possible losses. As in the currency case, this means that a small random event that pushes the price below some critical level can set in motion a cascade of selling. Also as in the currency case, the step drop in the price depends on investors not following this stop-loss strategy being imperfectly informed about how many investors will bail out if the price drops.

In the 1987 crash there was, of course, a high technology wrinkle in this story: the widespread use of computerized portfolio insurance, which essentially implemented a completely automatic stop-loss strategy. It is now apparent that the number of portfolio insurers was underestimated by the market, so that everyone was taken by surprise by the volume of automatic selling provoked by the initial stock decline. Even in 1987, however, it seems likely that old-fashioned manual stop-loss selling was more important than the computers, and the historical record shows that crashes can occur perfectly well without computers.

In the widely cited Minsky (1972) crisis model, there are elements of both destabilizing speculation and trigger points: the fall in prices is started by a bandwagon effect, but perpetuated in part by forced sales by illiquid investors.

2.3.2   The Transmission of Crisis

Suppose that, for whatever reason, the stock market in a major country crashes. How does this crash get transmitted to the asset markets and eventually the real economies of other advanced nations? This is an issue that is on somewhat firmer theoretical ground than the analysis of stock crashes themselves. There are three main channels through which the crisis might be transmitted. First, to the extent that equity markets are linked, there could simply be a direct comovement of stock prices; this could then generate a coordinated recession through whatever mechanism equity crashes cause recessions (if they do). Second, by generating a recession in one country, an equity market crash could generate global recession through a conventional multiplier process. Third, if asset crash leads to monetary crisis, this monetary crisis could then propagate worldwide.

Equity Market Linkages

It is not completely obvious that a crash in one national equity market need lead to price declines in other markets. Suppose that next week the world suddenly decides that Japanese stocks are grossly overpriced. One possibility would be that the investors would try to shift their funds into other stock markets, so that the Japanese crash would be matched by price *rises* elsewhere.

To rationalize the simultaneity of price falls seen in 1929, and even more so in 1987, it is necessary to invoke one of two explanations. One is purely psychological: fears about one country's stock market generalize to fears about others, leading to a general rout. The other explanation draws on a hypothetical distinction between insider and outsider investors. The outsiders have been drawn into one country's market by bandwagon effects, and at a certain point the outsiders have come to regard the stocks as overvalued and have withdrawn. When the market crashes, the outsiders leave and the insiders come back—pulling out of other markets, which then fall.

One might also want to note the possibility that investors understand that a stock market crash in one country will generate a worldwide recession through other channels, and drive down stock prices around the world in anticipation.

Foreign Trade Multiplier Effects

Suppose that a stock market crash in one country leads to a conventional recession—say by reducing wealth and precipitating a decline in consumption. This recession will then reduce imports by the contracting economy. The fall in imports will induce a contraction in other countries. The recessions in these countries, in turn, will start a second round of contraction in the initiating country; we will thus have the foreign trade multiplier process that has been familiar since the work of Romney Robinson (1954).

While this story is clear and well-understood analytically, it is questionable how important it can be in practice. Most empirical estimates of international multiplier effects are fairly small—so small, in fact, that they have been an embarrassment in attempts to justify macroeconomic policy coordination. It will be argued shortly that the conventional multiplier story has very little explanatory power for the 1929–32 contraction.

Monetary Repercussions

It is now widely accepted that the Great Depression happened in part because a sharp but conventional business cycle downturn, aggravated by the stock market crash, precipitated a banking crisis beginning in late 1930. The macroeconomic effects of this bank crisis may then have operated through several channels. The conventional channel emphasized by Friedman and Schwartz (1963) was the contraction in the money supply: as individuals increased their cash holdings and vulnerable banks increased their reserve ratios, the money multiplier fell; given a roughly constant stock of high powered money in the US economy, broader measures of the money supply fell considerably.

Bernanke (1983) has argued that the effects were broader than this; that the closure of many banks and the shaken state of those that remained led to much more severe credit rationing than before, so that the shadow price of funds to many firms rose relative to the interest rate.

If we accept that a stock market crash can lead indirectly to a monetary contraction, plain or fancy, the next question is how such a contraction is transmitted internationally. Here, as in the case of currency crises, the standard theoretical literature is surprisingly ambiguous. Under fixed rates, the standard Mundell-Fleming model predicts a worldwide contraction resulting from monetary contraction in any one country; indeed, with perfect capital mobility the Mundell-Fleming model essentially denies that there is such a thing as a purely national monetary shock. Under flexible rates, however, the simple Mundell-Fleming model actually predicts that monetary shocks will be transmitted *perversely:* a monetary contraction in one country will produce expansion elsewhere.

The reason for this result is that in the simple Mundell-Fleming model, interest rates must be equalized. A monetary contraction in one country, which raises interest rates in that country, must be matched by an equal rise in rates elsewhere. The only way this can happen is through a depreciation of other currencies against the contracting country that stimulates exports abroad (at the contracting country's expense), which then generates, through a multiplier process, an expansion in output that raises money demand. (For an exposition, see Dornbusch 1980). The resemblance between this result and the perverse effect of a currency crisis under floating rates is apparent.[4]

The perverse transmission of monetary shocks is a result that may be softened or even reversed in more complex models. For example, regressive expectations on the exchange rate, by dampening the appreciation of the contracting country's currency, can allow positive transmission. This is especially true if one adds a realistic lag in the response of trade to the exchange rate. Frankel (1988), in a survey of a number of empirical macroeconomic models, has found that by and large they predicted mildly positive transmission.

Realistically, however, the best argument for positive international transmission of monetary shocks, like that for contractionary effects of currency crises, lies in endogenous policy response. Because a passive monetary policy would involve a large depreciation of the affected country's currency, fears of inflation will tend to induce monetary authorities to match monetary contraction abroad.

---

4. Notice also that this argument implies that the trade balance of the contracting country worsens rather than improving.

We should also note that while the standard result that with a floating rate monetary contraction in one country is expansionary abroad may not be robust, a weaker proposition can still be maintained. This is that a country can insulate itself from much if not all of foreign monetary shocks by allowing its currency to float.

2.3.3 The Spread of the Great Depression

Now that we have some basic concepts, we can turn briefly to the events of the Great Depression. In tables 2.1 and 2.2 we have already seen some key statistics about the financial and real spread of the crisis. There was a clear linkage of equity markets, although the fall outside North America was considerably smaller than inside. Since most accounts give even the U.S. stock market crash only an auxiliary role in bringing on the Depression, this must a fortiori have been true elsewhere.

Many discussions of the Great Depression have placed strong emphasis on the trade multiplier, often associated with assertions that protectionism played a key role. Kindleberger's famous "spiderweb" diagram, showing the contraction of U.S. trade from 1929 to 1932, has become a staple of crisis literature. Even a rough look at the numbers, however, makes it clear that *trade linkages cannot have been a major factor in the Depression.*

Table 2.5 presents some basic numbers; it shows U.S. national product, exports, and imports in constant dollars for 1929 and 1932, and compares percentage changes. The use of constant dollars is not crucial but helps maintain perspective; much of the contraction of trade pointed to by Kindleberger represents deflation rather than a decline in trade volumes (though the decline in volumes was certainly impressive enough in percentage terms).[5]

There are three key points to be gained from examination of table 2.5. First, the United States was a relatively closed economy in 1929, with imports and exports about 6 percent of GNP.[6] Since the United States probably accounted for no more than 40 percent of the gross product of market economies at that point, exports to the United States were less than 4 percent of the rest of the world's GNP. Second, the fall in U.S. imports in real terms was less than 40 percent, implying a negative demand shock to the rest of the world of less than 1.5 percent of output—too little, even with a generous multiplier, to account for more than a fraction of the observed decline in output. Third, a little noted fact is that during 1929–32 U.S. net exports actually fell—some-

---

5. Worldwide, the decline in trade volumes was about the same as the decline in industrial production. Both were larger than the fall in gross product; but this is not surprising. Typical modern estimates suggest that both trade volumes and industrial production have cyclical income elasticities of about 2. The point is that in spite of Smoot-Hawley, the decline in trade was only about what one might expect given the Depression.

6. For readers worried about deflators, this statement is true when 1929 dollars are used as well as 1982 dollars.

Table 2.5   U.S. Output and Trade, 1929–32 (billions of 1982 $U.S.)

	1929	1932	Percent Change
GNP	709.6	509.2	− 28.2
Exports	42.1	23.2	− 44.9
Imports	37.4	23.7	− 36.6
Net exports	4.7	− .5	

Source: Department of Commerce. Various years. *The National Income and Product Accounts of the United States, 1929–82.*

thing that is very difficult to reconcile with the view that the United States exported its Depression through a decline in imports.

This suggests that emphasis should be placed on the third channel, monetary linkages. Unfortunately it is difficult to unravel the chain of events here, partly because the contagion crisis was intermingled with local currency crises. In particular, first Austria, then Germany suffered from speculative attacks and bank runs, driven partly by concern over financial stability, partly by concerns over political events.

What is fairly clear from the record is that the standard argument that floating provides insulation from monetary shocks is borne out quite well. The two countries that allowed their currencies to float—Britain and Japan—did relatively well compared with the countries that doggedly defended their parities, France and Germany. And of the two relatively successful economies, Japan did better, and also allowed its currency to depreciate more.

2.4   Two Crises That Did Not Happen

In contrast to what did happen to the world as a whole in 1929–32 and what happened to Latin America after 1982, what has *not* happened is the key observation with regard to crisis in the industrial world since 1985. Many observers have warned, in recent years, of the potential for international financial crisis, in particular, of the risks of a free-falling dollar. And there have been major financial shocks: a fairly rapid decline of the dollar from early 1985 to late 1986 and the spectacular stock market crash of 1987. Yet the predicted "hard landing" for the U.S. economy has not so far occurred, and the stock market crash was followed by a year of strong economic growth throughout the OECD. So the question is, Why have these financial events not had more real consequences?

2.4.1   The Dollar and the Hard Landing

In a highly influential work, Stephen Marris (1985) crystallized the fears of many observers about the strong dollar. Marris argued, correctly in retrospect, that the very strong dollar of late 1984 and early 1985 could not be sustained.

He also argued, so far quite incorrectly, that a falling dollar would produce a severe macroeconomic crisis in the United States.

Why did the "hard landing" not materialize? It was not because the exchange rate adjustment turned out to be gradual. The dollar fell essentially all the way back to its 1980s level in less than two years, losing roughly half its value against the German mark and the Japanese yen from February 1985 to December 1986. What failed to materialize were the real consequences of that decline.

In the Marris scenario the declining dollar was expected to have a strong and immediate inflationary impact on the U.S. economy. In order to contain this impact, the Federal Reserve would be obliged to impose very tight money, leading to a deep recession; Marris assumed that while the monetary tightening would reduce imports and thereby ease the necessary depreciation of the dollar, it would not succeed in attracting capital once a full-scale speculative flight from the dollar was underway. Instead, foreign investors would insist on pushing the dollar down sufficiently to quickly eliminate the U.S. current account deficit. Indeed, in his hard landing scenario, Marris assumed that the U.S. would be forced by capital flight to run a current account *surplus* of 1.5 percent of GNP.

In practice, this scenario has broken down at two points. First, dollar decline has not produced the dramatic inflationary impact Marris expected. Second, foreign investors have not so far demanded the kind of radical trade adjustment he described.

The reasons for the limited inflationary impact of dollar decline have been the subject of considerable study. Part of the explanation lies in energy and commodity prices, which declined worldwide during much of the period of dollar decline. Another part of the explanation lies in the "pricing to market" strategies followed by many foreign firms, especially in Japan: these firms did not raise their dollar export prices nearly as much as the rise in their dollar production costs. This strategy was possible partly because of inflated profit margins during the previous period of dollar strength, but the magnitude of the absorption of exchange rate changes has still been startling.

It is also true that the actual adjustment forced on the United States has still been quite modest: the current account deficit, which peaked at 3.6 percent of GNP in 1987, is expected to be about 2.5 percent of GNP this year. Had the markets insisted on an adjustment of the magnitude Marris envisaged, the required fall in the dollar would have been a great deal larger, and the inflationary impact would have been correspondingly larger as well. This could presumably still happen, although the story recently has been one of a surging rather than a crashing dollar (which was of course true in early 1985 as well).

Finally, it should be noted that the case made by Marris for the necessity of a severe recession is not too clear. The presumed reason is the need to contain inflation. However, a close reading of Marris reveals that the size of the required recession is never derived; indeed, the explicit model used to construct the scenarios has an exogenous base rate of inflation so that in the model's own terms no recession is necessary. Marris simply assumes that a recession roughly the same size as the 1974–75 and 1979–82 slumps would be needed, on the basis that the dollar shock would be analogous to an oil shock.

2.4.2   The Stock Market Crash

Table 2.6 presents some summary data on the October 1987 stock market crash and its aftermath. In its opening phase the crash was comparable in size to the 1929 shock and considerably more globalized. There, however, the parallel ends. Instead of continuing to decline, stock prices generally recovered. As for real effects, the year following the crash was marked by generally stronger growth than the year previous.

Why did one of the great financial panics of history not have any second act? The most important reason was probably monetary policy: the Federal Reserve and its counterparts abroad promptly loosened money when the markets fell, giving prevention of a spreading crisis temporary priority over inflation control (and in the case of the United States over defense of the dollar).

This fits in with the general sense that the 1929–32 crash should have been rather easy to prevent. It has always seemed to macroeconomists that an expansionary monetary policy by the Federal Reserve plus a willingness by governments to abandon fixed rates if necessary could easily have prevented the market crash from producing a major slump. The events of 1987 were hardly a controlled experiment, but they provided a clear demonstration of the power of sensible policy.

2.5   Risks of Future Crisis

Given this survey of the problem of international financial crises, what can we say about the risks of future crises and the policies to prevent them?

The answer depends on whether contagion or currency crises are at issue. After the experience of 1987–88, it is difficult to get too worried about contagion crises. Stock market crashes may occur again; however, 1988 showed that such crashes need not turn into global contractions, as long as sensible

Table 2.6   **The 1987 Crash** (percentage changes)

	Stock prices, October 13–20	Stock prices, 20 October 1989 through 5 January 1989	Industrial production, Year Following
United States	− 26.6	+ 16.5	+ 5.0
Germany	− 13.8	+ .9	+ 3.2
Japan	− 17.0	+ 37.6	+ 9.4
United Kingdom	− 22.1	+ 23.9	+ 2.2

Source: The Economist.

monetary policies are followed. In 1929–32 monetary policy was persistently, almost mysteriously, wrongheaded—both in the United States and in other countries, particularly Germany. Without that wrongheadedness it is hard to see how an equity market shock could produce catastrophic consequences.

Suppose, for example, that Japanese stock prices were to collapse. Then Japan could prevent a severe recession with an offsetting monetary expansion. If Japan failed to do this, the rest of the OECD could still manage to insulate itself from much of the crisis by allowing the dollar and the European currency unit (ECU) to decline against the yen. It is hard to see any reason why these straightforward policy responses should fail to do the job.

The problem of currency crises, on the other hand, is more uncertain. The U.S. success so far in avoiding a hard landing is partly due to the fact that financial markets have not actually forced a large adjustment of the U.S. current account. If they did, the inflationary consequences of the required exchange rate change would be much larger than anything that has happened so far.

The example of Latin America is also worrying. Unlike the example of the Great Depression, the debt crisis is a recent case whose effects are still strongly felt. It is still not clear what should have been done to prevent or mitigate the crisis: What advice would we have given the finance minister of a typical debtor in 1979, knowing that the crisis was coming? And there is something we do not fully understand about the macroeconomic impacts of the currency crisis in Latin America.

So if there is a type of international financial crisis to worry about, it is probably a currency crisis—the United States as a giant Latin-style debtor—rather than a replay of 1929.

References

Aftalion, A. 1927. *Monnaie, prix, et change.* Paris: Sirey.

Bernanke, B. 1983. Nonmonetary effects of the financial crisis in the propagation of the Great Depression. *American Economic Review* 73 (June): 257–76.

Dornbusch, R. 1980. *Open Economy Macroeconomics.* New York: Basic Books.

Flood, R., and P. Garber. 1984. Collapsing exchange rate regimes: Some linear examples, *Journal of International Economics.*

———. 1988. The linkage between speculative attack and target zone models of exchange rates. Mimeograph.

Frankel, Jeffrey. 1988. Ambiguous macroeconomic policy multipliers in theory and in twelve econometric models. In *Empirical Macroeconomics for Interdependent Economies,* ed. Ralph Bryant. Washington, D.C.: Brookings Institution.

Friedman, M., and A. Schwartz. 1963. *A Monetary History of the United States.* Princeton, N.J.: Princeton University Press

Froot, Kenneth, and Maurice Obstfeld. 1991a. Exchange rate dynamics under stochastic regime shifts: A unified approach. *Journal of International Economics,* forthcoming.

———. 1991b. Stochastic process switching: Some simple solutions. *Econometrica* 59, no. 1 (January): 241–50.

Kindleberger, C. P. 1978. *Manias, Panics, and Crashes*. New York: Basic Books.

———. 1984. *A Financial History of Western Europe*. London: Allen & Unwin.

Krugman, P. 1979. A model of balance of payments crises. *Journal of Money, Credit, and Banking*.

———. 1985. Is the strong dollar sustainable? In *The U.S. dollar: Prospects and policy options*. Kansas City: Federal Reserve Bank of Kansas City.

———. 1987. Trigger strategies and price dynamics in equity and foreign exchange markets, NBER Working Paper 2459 (December). Cambridge, Mass.

———. 1991. Target zones and exchange rate dynamics. *Quarterly Journal of Economics*, forthcoming.

Marris, S. 1985. *Deficits and the dollar: The world economy at risk*. Washington, D.C.: Institute for International Economics.

Miller, M., and P. Weller. 1988. Solving stochastic saddlepoint models: A qualitative approach. Mimeographed.

Minsky, H. 1972. Financial stability revisited: The economics of disaster. In *Reappraisal of the Federal Reserve discount system*. Washington, D.C.: Federal Reserve Board.

Nurkse, R. 1942. *International Currency Experience*. Geneva: League of Nations.

Obstfeld, M. 1986. Rational and self-fulfilling balance of payments crises. *American Economic Review* 76.

Robinson, R. 1954. A graphical exposition of the foreign trade multiplier. *Quarterly Journal of Economics*.

Salant, S., and Henderson, D. 1978. Market anticipations of government policies and the price of gold. *Journal of Political Economy* 86 (August): 627–48.

---

2. C. Fred Bergsten

The Hard-Landing Scenario

The Anatomy of the "Hard Landing"

In his background paper for this conference, Paul Krugman refers to the hard landing as the "crisis that did not happen . . . so far." He adds that it "could presumably still happen." I believe that the risk remains acute and is in fact both the most likely source of crisis for the American and world economies and the most likely trigger for ending the current expansion.

My focus is *not* the type of "hard landing" hypothesized by Larry Summers in the crisis scenario that makes his background paper so lively. There the international dimension arises at the end of a sequence of financial disturbances whose roots are domestic. To be sure, the Summers pattern is also conceivable and further underlines the importance of the globalization of markets in this context. But I will emphasize the risk of a crisis whose causality is opposite to that of Summers, one that is generated initially by the external sector of the economy with rapid and painful transmission to the domestic side.

The hard-landing scenario is simply the typical "stabilization crisis" that has been observed throughout history in a number of countries. Private investors stop (in an ex ante sense) providing the $10 billion of net capital inflow needed by the United States each month and perhaps withdraw some of their $1 trillion of previously accumulated liquid assets. Foreign central banks decline to fill the gap. (I will shortly suggest why such developments could occur.) The dollar plummets, perhaps by 20–30 percent (or even more, as overshooting is to be expected in such a situation).

Expectations are generated that prices will rise in response by 3–5 percentage points, and nominal interest rates begin to rise by a likely amount.[1] The Federal Reserve feels compelled to try to stop the process, and roll back the fear of increases in the price level, by raising real interest rates—thereby pushing nominal rates into the 15 percent range. The twin deficits are a sufficiently important component of the problem that restoration of market confidence requires a credible multiyear program of substantial fiscal tightening, at least on the Gramm-Rudman-Hollings schedule without gimmicks.

The impact on the economy emerges in a straightforward manner. Inflation rises as a direct effect of dollar depreciation, especially if the economy is near full employment and full capacity utilization (as at present). The combination of sharply higher interest rates and fiscal tightening pushes the economy into recession—the more rapidly and sharply, the more vigorously the Fed moves to counter the accelerated inflationary threat.

Since the new policy stance might have to be maintained for a year or so to restore full confidence in the currency and the stability of the economy, the turndown might be unusually prolonged by normal U.S. standards. The subsequent improvement in the current account, generated by both the lower dollar and the domestic turndown, would be substantial but would take a year or so to eventuate and to begin restoring a modicum of growth. (This would be especially true at present because, as already noted, the economy as a whole—and the tradeables sector in particular—are running so close to full capacity.[2])

The Summers analysis becomes exceedingly relevant at this point. The sharp rise in interest rates could trigger substantial financial turmoil in light of the high leveraging of American corporations and the uncertain loan portfo-

1. Stephen Marris, *Deficits and the Dollar Revisited* (Washington, D.C.: Institute for International Economics, August 1987), 44. A fall of 10 percent in the trade-weighted dollar typically produces a rise of about 1.5 percentage points in the CPI, though the ratio could presumably be higher if the economy were already at full employment and full capacity utilization.

2. It should be noted that the portion of the trade improvement generated by the economic downturn would only be temporary. Imports rise sharply during normal U.S. recovery periods of rapid "catch-up growth" and return to the baseline level. Hence only the further dollar decline, to the extent it persists, would produce lasting trade gains.

lios (including Third World loans) of some financial institutions. Hence the Fed would face the Summers dilemma: the higher interest rates needed to stop the currency crisis would further intensify the risk of financial disruption, while any substantial injection of additional liquidity as lender of last resort could increase the inflationary spiral and precipitate more dollar depreciation. In such a situation, there would almost certainly have to be even greater fiscal tightening even though it would exacerbate the turndown. Fiscal as well as monetary policy would face a true dilemma, from which there is no pleasant escape. Thus the "hard landing" would arrive.

Why Hasn't It Happened?

The crucial economic relationship that creates the "hard landing" is the juxtaposition of dollar depreciation and higher interest rates. From early 1985 through late 1987, the real effective exchange rate of the dollar declined by about 40 percent. But long-term real interest rates, despite some major bumps in 1987 (to which I return below), fell by about 2.5 percentage points during this period. Hence there was no hard landing for the economy.

Krugman (in this volume) suggests two reasons for this outcome, both related to the failure of the dollar's decline to produce a substantial run-up in inflation: the contemporary fall in energy and other commodity prices, and the unexpectedly low pass-through of dollar depreciation to export prices by Japanese and perhaps other foreign firms. The first was sheer luck. The second may or may not prove to be sustainable.

Other authors, including Krugman elsewhere, have suggested a third reason: that foreigners are increasingly providing the financing needed by the United States through investment in real dollar assets, notably direct investment in plants and real estate, that are viewed as largely indexed against inflation and dollar depreciation and thus would not lose much of their value even in a hard landing. The United States clearly *is* getting into asset settlement of its external deficit to a substantial degree. However, well over half the inflow of private foreign capital in 1988 ($143 billion) still moved into liquid assets—an amount that about equalled the total increase in our net liabilities to foreigners.

I believe there are three other reasons why the hard landing has not yet occurred. First, the dollar decline occurred while the US economy "enjoyed" a substantial margin of unused capacity. Unemployment fell from 7.4 percent at the start of 1985 to 5.8 percent at the end of 1987, and capacity utilization of industry rose from 81.1 percent to 82.4 percent. But the availability of resources throughout the period, especially in the tradeable goods sector that had remained depressed throughout the general recovery of 1983–84 because of dollar overvaluation, meant that the lower dollar could translate readily into trade improvement rather than higher prices.

Second, as the hard landing began to threaten in early 1987, the U.S. government and the central banks of the G-7 reversed course and began opposing rather than fostering dollar depreciation. They did not achieve full market credibility, and hence halt the dollar's slide, until the bear squeeze in the first week of 1988. But they apparently supported the dollar to the tune of about $120 billion during 1987 and made clear their determination to continue doing so in 1988 because of the futility of expecting U.S. fiscal action during the Presidential election year.

Third, the U.S. current account deficit began to decline in real terms from the middle of 1986 and in nominal terms from the middle of 1987. The budget deficit dropped sharply in fiscal year 1987. Both have continued to fall as a share of GNP. We know from studies of unemployment that the voting public tends to react more to trends than to levels of that key economic variable. I would conjecture that markets frequently follow the same pattern. Hence the steady reduction in the twin deficits, though both have remained quite high by U.S. historical standards, may have promoted stability (and subsequent strength) in the dollar.

Despite these mitigating factors, I believe that we came fairly close to a hard landing in 1987. Treasury once again began to talk down the dollar in early January. Inflows of private capital dried up and there were repatriations by some large Japanese investors. The exchange rate fell sharply. Interest rates jumped. The crucial juxtaposition that characterizes a hard landing was at hand.

Two factors intervened to avoid substantial repercussions on the real economy. The clearcut element is that the central banks stepped into the breach with massive intervention and the Louvre Accord. The more conjectural is the reputed indirect intervention of the Japanese Ministry of Finance via some of the largest Japanese financial institutions, despite the huge losses which they took as a result.[3] Absent these developments, the hard landing could well have occurred despite the anti-inflationary impact of lower oil prices, the continued existence of considerable spare capacity in the economy, the beginning of some reduction in the twin deficits, and the lower-than-expected price pass-through. And we still experienced Black Monday in the fall as well as the sharp drop in the bond market in the spring.

It should also be noted that the United Kingdom may now be in the early phase of a hard landing. The pound is falling sharply despite steady increases (to very high levels) in British interest rates, after having risen for some time when "uncapped" by the authorities. To be sure, the British current account deficit is considerably larger than our own as a share of GNP and inflation is much higher. Sterling is not the dollar. But Britain almost certainly will experience a sharp recession along with rapid inflation for a while, reminding us that hard landings do occur.

3. Richard Koo, "Japanese Investment in Dollar Securities after the Plaza Accord," in U.S. Foreign Debt, Hearing before the Joint Economic Committee, U.S. Congress (13 September 1988).

Could It Happen Now?

I believe that the risk of a hard landing for the United States will be greater over the next year or two than at any time to date. A series of foreseeable events suggests that private capital inflow may again dry up, as in 1987, and that the foreign central banks may not come to the rescue.

First, the trade and current account deficits are likely to turn up again in 1990. The IMF expects an increase in the current account deficit to about $140 billion from about $125 billion this year.[4] My colleague William Cline projects a steady increase, on current policies and exchange rates, to over $200 billion by 1992.[5] Nor can one, on current readings, be very optimistic about the outlook for the budget deficit.

Such a trend reversal would signal a growing and perhaps indefinite external borrowing requirement for the United States. The needed capital inflow would rise from the present level of $10 billion per month to $15–$20 billion per month. Our net international investment position, already at minus $533 billion at the end of 1988, would rise past $1 trillion in the early 1990s and move onto an explosive path.[6] Since markets may be affected by trends more than levels, as noted, such a shift could at a minimum remove a key underpinning from the dollar stability/strength of the last two years—and even trigger its reversal.

Second, interest rate differentials will almost certainly continue to move against the dollar. Slower growth and modest inflation (and perhaps election-year politics) will probably push interest rates lower here. Continued rapid growth and rising inflation concerns abroad will clearly drive up interest rates there. The real dollar-DM differential has already shifted in favor of the DM in absolute terms, and the real dollar-yen differential now favors the dollar by less than one percentage point.

Political instability or other unpredictable factors could of course offset such developments and keep the dollar high or even rising. But a reduction of the "safe haven" effect is just as likely as the opposite, especially if East-West tensions continue to thaw and the LDP clearly retains power in Japan.

There is thus a significant risk that private foreign investors will stop, or sharply curtail, their dollar investments at some point in the foreseeable future. I would not argue that they will forever forgo new investments in the United States, but only that—like any investors—they may decide that they can make those investments at a considerably better price if they withdraw for a while and come back later. We know that there are plenty of alternative

4. International Monetary Fund, *World Economic Outlook* (April 1989).

5. William R. Cline, *United States External Adjustment and the World Economy* (Washington, D.C.: Institute for International Economics, March 1989); "Impact of the Strong Dollar on US Trade," June 1989.

6. As developed in Paul Krugman, *Exchange-Rate Stability* (Cambridge, Mass.: MIT Press, 1989) 106–7.

investment vehicles for fairly sustained periods of time and that the view the "the money has no place else to go" is absurd over any short-term or ever medium-run period.

Nor would I argue that the markets are behaving "irrationally." Most market participants maintain an extremely short-run focus, and many have made money by buying dollars over the past two years. The trend *has* been their friend. But "market rationality" and "sustainability" are very different concepts, and my focus of course is on the latter.

The crucial actors then become the central banks, and there are several reasons to believe that they may not be willing to bail out the dollar again. First, most of their economies are now experiencing domestic-led growth, and they no longer need undervalued currencies to support expansion. Second, as already noted, most of them are increasingly concerned about inflation and may prove unwilling to undermine the credibility (and perhaps effectiveness) of their monetary policies by buying huge amounts of dollars. Their current efforts to avoid further depreciation of their currencies support this view, and they well remember that the two periods of double-digit inflation in the 1970s were associated with such intervention.

Third, in an environment of renewed increases in America's external (and perhaps internal) deficit, foreign central banks may simply prove unwilling to underwrite a seemingly unending process of excess domestic expenditure by the United States—which all of them believe is due almost entirely to the policies of the United States itself. In 1987, they could see progress on both deficits and were waiting for more to eventuate from their own Plaza initiative. In 1988, they knew that further U.S. fiscal action was unlikely and memories of Black Monday were still fresh.

But the outlook for the international imbalances, and the domestic economic circumstances of the key countries abroad, suggest that their attitudes may be very different in 1990 and beyond. This would be particularly likely if, as in 1977–78, they had to finance substantial outflows of private capital from the United States as well as gargantuan current account deficits.[7]

To be sure, foreign central banks have no interest in contributing to financial panic or a global crisis. They are unlikely to want to see the dollar enter a totally free fall. But neither can we count on their pouring in the level of resources needed to offset an investment strike by private foreigners, or even the amounts they provided in 1987. Indeed, depending on the magnitude of private dollar selling, the monetary authorities might not be *able* to defend the dollar by intervention alone even if they wanted to—especially in light of the recent loss of their credibility in failing to preserve the upper bands of their reference ranges.

7. In 1977–78, dollar purchases by foreign central banks were about twice as large as America's current account deficits (of $15 billion annually). A similar ratio today would require purchases of $250-$300 billion.

The final link in the chain is the most crucial: the impact of a sharp fall in the dollar on the U.S. economy. Here too the situation is very different than in 1985–87. We are near full employment and full capacity utilization, especially in several of the leading export industries, so the impact on inflation and interest rates would be much more severe.[8] There is no prospect of another sharp fall in energy or commodity prices; the contrary may be more likely, and would intensify both the inflation and current account risks. To maintain its credibility in fighting inflation, including with respect to its response to administration preferences in an election year, the Fed would have no choice but to respond aggressively.

I am afraid that conditions are thus in place that raise again the risk of a hard landing.[9] At a minimum, we would be foolish to dismiss the possibility in light of the enormous costs it could levy on the country (and on the world economy). I will turn finally to how best to prevent it.

How to Prevent It

The underlying cause of America's external imbalance remains its low rate of domestic saving.[10] Unfortunately, there are no policy tools that we can rely on with much confidence to raise private saving. Thus the policy focus must remain on reducing, and hopefully eliminating, the deficit in the federal budget on the timetable currently set by Gramm-Rudman-Hollings.

The only other defense mechanism against the risk of a hard landing is a willingness to raise interest rates as needed to defend the dollar. This could, of course, lead to excessively tight money from the standpoint of domestic growth. Over time, moreover, it would lead to even higher budget deficits and—unless private saving responded exogenously in a positive direction— to even larger external deficits and thus an unstable spiral.

Induced dollar depreciation would help if domestic demand growth slowed to a pace which no longer fully utilized all domestic resources. A "second Plaza agreement," which would focus solely on further exchange rate changes, would therefore be desirable, even in the absence of further fiscal or

8. From the second quarter of 1987 to the second quarter of 1989, capacity utilization for industry as a whole rose from 79.9 percent to 83.8 percent; for manufacturing, the increase was from 80.5 percent to 84.1 percent.

9. Marris (n. 1 above), xlvii, foresaw the current situation very nicely: "If nothing is done about the budget deficit, growing confidence that central banks had put a floor under the dollar could push the dollar up again. . . . But the political realities are such that nothing much may be done about the budget deficit until the electorate really feels the pinch. Thus . . . the world's central banks may actually facilitate inaction on the budget. . . . Equally, if the dollar remained too strong and the U.S. trade position began to deteriorate again, the markets would eventually lose confidence in the authorities' ability to defend the dollar and the stage would be set for an even harder landing."

10. C. Fred Bergsten, "The Domestic and International Consequences of America's Low Saving Rate," paper presented to the conference, "Saving: The Challenge for the U.S. Economy," sponsored by the American Council on Capital Formation (Washington, D.C., 12 October 1989).

monetary steps, if the growth of domestic demand were to slow exogenously. (Of course, monetary policy changes might be needed to effectively implement such an agreement.)

An alternative suggested by some is the issuance of foreign currency bonds by the U.S. Treasury. Foreign demand for such bonds might indeed be heavy for a while and buy more time for U.S. adjustment to occur. But the history of this idea, from the Roosa bonds of the early 1960s through the Carter bonds of the late 1970s, shows that they work only in the context of an effective adjustment program (as in 1978–79) and subject the United States to substantial costs otherwise (as with the Swiss franc bonds of the early 1960s, which were not redeemed until the mid-1970s). They are no substitute, except in the short run, for dealing with the problem at its source.

It is thus essential, if tedious, to reiterate the standard remedy for eliminating the current account deficit to stop the buildup of America's foreign debt and thus avoid the risk of a hard landing:[11]

- budget correction on the Gramm-Rudman-Hollings timetable;
- continued rapid growth of domestic demand in the major surplus countries (Japan and the EC);
- effective resolution of the Third World debt problem inter alia to permit renewed import growth there;
- further dollar depreciation against the currencies of the surplus countries, *in the context of a freeing of U.S. resources through budget correction or exogenous slowdown of domestic demand,* to about 100 yen and 1.50 DM (assuming no intra-EMS realignment);
- adoption of target zones, or similar improvements in international monetary arrangements, to *keep* exchange rates at their new equilibrium levels so that American exporting and import-competing firms will exploit their renewed price competitiveness by expanding capacity in the United States; and
- a successful Uruguay Round of trade negotiations to help head off more protectionism and assure the United States of market access for the trade improvement that it must achieve.

3. *Rudiger Dornbusch*

International Financial Crises

I would like to join those speakers who have expressed wariness; I do not think we have learned where financial crises come from, and our increased ability to apply emergency treatment does not comfort me. It is true that,

---

11. The details are in C. Fred Bergsten, *America in the World Economy: A Strategy for the 1990s* (Washington, D.C.: Institute for International Economics, November 1988).

unlike the case in the 1930s, the Federal Reserve and the central banks of all industrialized countries have done an exceptional job already twice in the past two years, but that gives me only so much comfort.

Walter Bagehot's view was that crises result when authors, rectors, and grandmothers become greedy. "At intervals, from causes which are not to the present purpose, the money from these people—the blind capital, as we call it, of the country—is particularly craving; it seeks for some one to devour it, and there is 'plethora'; it finds some one, and there is 'speculation'; it is devoured, and there is 'panic' " (as quoted in Burton [1902] 1971, 311).

Other interpretations have placed professionals rather than amateurs at the center. Neither view helps put the finger on the necessary conditions and the decisive trigger.

What Happens in a Crisis?

There are three essential ingredients for a crisis: vulnerability, awareness, and fear. None of these terms is a standard economic expression and that is conscious; they are meant to describe a state of mind.

Vulnerability can arise from an overexpansion of credit relative to debt-service ability. The trigger event would be a decline in debt-service ability— higher interest rates or a decline in earnings from a recession or a commodity price decline. Figure 2.1 shows the expansion in nonfinancial sector debt relative to GNP in the United States. There is no obvious criterion of what is too much. In fact, preceding a crisis the rationalization of why too much is not really too much is an essential part of the game. But there is also little doubt that were a crisis to occur, excessive accumulation of debt would be blamed.

Shiller (1988) has pointed to "awareness" as a decisive element in the stock market crash. Market participants felt that a crash could happen. Awareness is the state of mind where market participants are trigger happy; they are will-

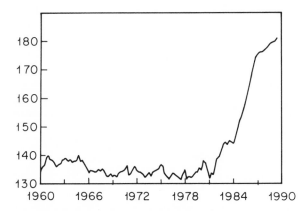

Fig. 2.1   The debt-GNP ratio in the United States

ing to interpret events in terms of a scenario of decline and even of major adjustment. Perhaps one can go a step further to say that the average market participant is waiting for a good time to get out and only few are waiting to get in. Rational expectations do not allow such a situation, but they seem to occur. For example, in fall 1989, on a Friday afternoon, the dollar declined against the Deutsche Mark by 7 pfennigs in 15 minutes—the general comment was that the dollar had reached a peak where everybody wanted to unload. Awareness thus represents a peculiar imbalance of opinion where prices are out of line with assessments, but where the attempt to unload has been postponed.

The third essential ingredient in producing a crisis is fear that unless a position is liquidated *now* major losses will result. The fear thus reflects the fact that investors are willing to reassess dramatically their market evaluation and that they are willing to take major losses on the face value to reach safe ground. The fear is undoubtedly promoted by two facts, rapidly falling asset prices and the sharp widening of bid-ask spreads or the actual disappearance of markets. During the sterling crisis of 1976, for example, bid-ask spreads increased vastly on several occasions, as figure 2.2 shows. There is useful research to be done on the linkages between spreads, the rate of movement of asset prices, and asset holders' eagerness to liquidate.

A rereading of crisis literature (or, more properly, "panic" literature) suggests that more emphasis should be given to the psychological element—How do asset market participants perceive or "frame" the events around them and how do they react when "reality" rapidly changes? The *sauve qui peut* mentality is not fruitfully explored with traditional rational expectation models.

The Lender of Last Resort

The part about crisis that is well understood has to do with the credit system and contamination effects. Market participants understand that *anyone* is vul-

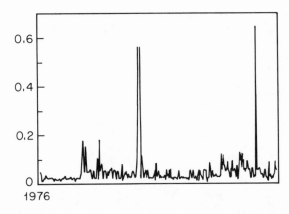

Fig. 2.2   The bid-ask spread for spot exchange (% of average rate)

nerable in a crisis because they may have lent to someone who has in turn lent to someone, and so on. There is no time to find out and the safest strategy is to hold on to cash, postpone payments, and, above all, call in loans as fast as possible. The only remedy of the authorities is to follow the Bagehot principle—during crisis discount freely. But Bagehot recommended lending at high interest rates; the novelty of the 1980s is to push rates down. At high rates the vulnerability from debt burdens would amplify the crisis.

The accepted wisdom is that the central bank is the lender of last resort. Here I must register my doubt. What is at stake today is no longer liquidity in the sense of high-powered money or gold. In the crisis of 1847, for example, bank notes were the issue: "The chancellor of the exchequer states that the tenor of the remarks by those who applied to him was 'Let us have notes . . .' 'We don't mean indeed to take the notes, because we shall not want them; only tell us that we can get them, and this will at once restore confidence' " (Palgrave 1894, 461).

Today, guarantees by the Treasury would do just the same as guarantees by the Fed. The issue is really whether, unlike in the nineteenth century, proper crisis management requires an expansion in the monetary base.

International Aspects

Now let me go to the international aspect of the assignment for this panel. The first question is: Is there something in the world economy that produces crises, or country problems, that may or not spread? Krugman's excellent paper has introduced the useful distinction between country problems and world problems. All crises start off as country problems, not system problems, and then they may or not spread out. This is what the bank literature calls contamination (see Saunders 1988). When they do spread, one would like to think it has to be a large country problem to get a really good world crisis going, but that is not true. Poor little Austria produced the Great Depression if we can believe Charlie Kindleberger, and Argentina produced a crisis in Great Britain in the 1890s. Thus the contagion mechanisms do deserve attention.

But the other way around is certainly true: when a big problem happens in a big country then the little countries have problems. When the U.S. stock market crashes, stock markets decline worldwide, and investors in small countries like Mexico seek security in U.S. Treasury bills, not in their own. In the end, the small, poor countries suffer disproportionately because in the flight to safe assets they may be the poorest provider.

We understand, in fact, very little about the systemwide propagation of crises. The way we could go most wrong is to take one of our macroeconometric models, ask what it tells us about linkages, conclude that those linkages are really very small, and therefore be persuaded that international crises are not a big deal. However, the Great Depression did happen. Macroeconometric models say that a 1 percent decline in U.S. demand has an impact on Europe that is within a rounding error of zero, and that suggests we ought not worry about spillover effects, but that implication is wrong.

Why should we not become comfortable? We must not become comfortable because the international transmission takes place not only and in the first place through demand (if that were all, then we would probably be talking about hiccups, not crises) but rather through asset markets and through expectations. In asset markets transmission might occur through credit rationing, and that is, then, primarily a country problem, or through the comovements of stock markets, and from stock markets' affecting investment. Credit rationing was one mechanism by which Latin America was pulled into the Great Depression—falling commodity prices were the other. Neither of these play any role in our macro models. And we have also a linkage from stock markets and confidence to investment and consumer spending. Long before the transmission takes place through trade we can have a highly synchronized decline in world demand.

A highly synchronized decline in world demand is not studied with macro models because we only feed them small and sympathetic shocks; we do not feed them crisis scenarios in which everybody says, "Oh no, the world is going down, bad idea to invest today."

My second point concerns the speed with which a world decline in demand can take place. Before policy coordination could be discussed, if there were a fast decline in world demand there were two ways countries could go: they could meet and resolve what to do about it, or they could immediately pursue some policies that try to isolate the problem. Krugman argued in his background paper that flexible exchange rates work to isolate countries, but then of course we have to ask whether they aggravate the problems wherever they started by isolating that country to eat its own disturbances. You have to ask whether countries actually pursue flexible rate policies to isolate them or whether they rather opt for trade restrictions.

In the 1930s the understanding was that flexible exchange rates might help a bit, but a quota could do the work much better. Quotas were invented precisely to provide a very safe way of sheltering countries from external shocks. And, with quotas, came the invention of trading blocks—imperial preferences, things like that, to isolate entire blocks from external shocks. If countries by themselves, or as groups, try to shelter themselves, then one easily gets into a depression spiral from which it is difficult to escape.

I am skeptical about the possibility of avoiding crises because we are not very good at coordination. Research by Jeffrey Frankel suggests that it is not even clear what countries should be doing. If one's trading partner has a different model in mind, and if there is not strong agreement on what should be done, decentralized decision making takes over. Things could easily get out of hand. Certainly today, at the world level there is no coordination of views on what should be done in the case of a decline in world demand. I do not see Europe hastily going to fiscal expansion; I do not see Europe hastily going to money creation.

Policymakers are good at short-run coordination, that is, what to do on a Monday morning if the stock market goes down. Particularly, they are good at what to announce—perhaps even what not to do. There is much less agreement on what to do in the next three-, four-, or five-month period if we were to have the onset of a major decline in world demand.

Latin America: After the Crisis

Next I want to focus on currency or country crises, specifically on Latin American experiences (see table 2.7). The issue that concerns me is that entire countries, much like the stock market, can go on sale, and the puzzle is, why? Imagine that, for some reason, a country goes on sale, and the real wage is 30% less than it was a year ago. This is in fact what happened in Britain in 1976, as figure 2.3 shows, and in Mexico in the 1980s.

In a case such as Mexico's, one has to ask if there is any sense in which a mispricing occurs and, if it is a mispricing, what to do about it and who should take action. There is, in fact, a coordination problem in getting the country back into the credit market, and the coordination problem has to do with irreversible investments and the option value of waiting. In the aftermath of stabilization there is a lack of confidence and, as a result, no stabilizing capital

Table 2.7   **Estimates of Capital Flight (cumulative, billion $U.S.)**

	Argentina	Brazil	Mexico	Peru	Venezuela
1979–82	22.4	5.8	25.3	n.a.	20.7
1983–87	6.8	24.8	35.3	3.3	18.9

Source: Cumby and Levich (1987); updated by the author.

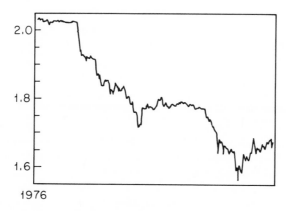

Fig. 2.3   **The dollar-sterling exchange rate**

reflow.[1] Foreign direct investment is slow to come, and Latin America's own assets are even slower.

Investors have an option to postpone the return of flight capital, and they will wait until the *front loading* of investment returns is sufficient to compensate for the risk of relinquishing the liquidity option of a wait-and-see position. How can governments reassure investors? The common answer is to bring about a "credible" stabilization. Credibility is the buzz word, used to explain vacuously why programs fail or succeed. In practice, credibility comes down to high interest rates and an exchange rate so competitive that expected further depreciation is unlikely. But high interest rates are counterproductive from a point of view of growth because they lead to holding of paper assets rather than real investment. A low real exchange rate cuts the standard of living and thus reduces domestic demand and profitability for all investments except in the traded-goods sector.

If real depreciation is not sufficient to bring about investment the government faces a very awkward position: income has been shifted from labor to capital, but because the real depreciation is not sufficient, the increased profits are taken out as capital flight. Labor will obviously insist that the policy be reversed. This uncertainty is an important feature in understanding the real exchange rate–capital flight relationships and the poststabilization difficulties.

Stabilization by itself is not enough to trigger a virtuous circle. There is a need for a coordination mechanism that overcomes the competitive market tendency to wait. What markets consider a sufficient policy action may be beyond the political scope of democratic governments. In fact, if governments went far enough to create the incentives that would motivate a return of capital and the resumption of investment on an exclusive economic calculation, the implied size of real wage cuts might be so extreme that now, on political grounds, asset holders consider the country too perilous a location.

In the aftermath of major macroeconomic shock there may simply be no equilibrium that is politically safe and economically rewarding on a scale that induces the return of growth as the response of competitive markets. Without the leverage afforded by external capital—1920s style or in the form of the Marshall Plan—there may be little prospect of reconstruction.

New Weak Linkages

I want to conclude with a remark of where the next crises are being generated. My impression is that financial deregulation in developing countries may be doing just that. There is great enthusiasm underway to take Korea and give it a modern, healthy financial system, where the Korean savings can be taken to London to put into junk bonds.

---

1. In Dornbusch (1989) this topic is modeled in detail.

This is a really very potent source of financial instability. Why? Because at the pace at which liberalization is taking place and capital markets are opened, regulation in no way is allowed to catch up with the reality of actual liberalization. And the same may well be happening in Europe in 1992 in the fringe countries—perhaps in Greece, perhaps in Spain.

Financial regulation should be way ahead of the unlocking of very, very repressed financial markets because the disequilibrium that evolves is the tendency to do in most countries the kind of business investors are not allowed to do anywhere else. The weakest link in the chain will give, and financial deregulation is a predictable way of creating more weak linkages in the world system.

References

Burton, T. (1902) 1971. *Financial Crises.* Freeport, N.Y.: Books for Libraries. (Reprint.)

Cumby, R., and R. Levich. 1987. Definitions and Magnitudes. In *Capital Flight and Third World Debt,* ed. D. Lessard and J. Williamson. Washington, D.C.: Institute for International Economics

Diamond, D., and P. Dybvig 1983. Bank Runs, Deposit Insurance and Liquidity. *Journal of Political Economy* 91, no. 3 (June): 401–19.

Dornbusch, R. From Stabilization to Growth. Typescript. MIT.

Palgrave, R. H. I., ed. 1894. *Dictionary of Economics.* London: Macmillan & Co.

Saunders, A. 1987. The Interbank Market, Contagion Effects and International Financial Crises. In *Threats to International Financial Stability,* ed., R. Portes and A. Swoboda. New York: Cambridge University Press.

Shiller, R. 1988. Portfolio Insurance and Other Investor Fashions as Factors in the 1987 Stock Market Crash. In *NBER Macroeconomics Annual 1988,* ed. S. Fischer, 277–97. Cambridge, Mass.: MIT Press.

4. Jacob A. Frenkel

Intervention, Coordination, and Crises

In contrast with earlier speakers on this panel, I shall not venture to evaluate the likelihood of a soft or hard landing in the wake of recent events. Instead, I shall try to respond to Martin Feldstein's request to discuss some more general aspects of policymaking that bear on the issues raised by Paul Krugman.

To set the stage, I would like to tell you about some of the surprises I encountered when I moved from the University of Chicago to Washington. One surprise came from having spent many years looking at exchange rate equations where the most prominent independent variables were the money supply or expected money supply of the domestic and foreign economies. I found that these variables—monetary aggregates—play a much less prominent role in policy discussions, at least among the industrial countries, than in the theoretical and econometric models. A second surprise also arose from my thinking that exchange rate policies are most closely linked to monetary policy: it was to find representatives only from the ministries of finance rather than from the central banks at the meetings of the G-7 deputies. A third surprise was that, in this context, an economist seems to be expected to be primarily a good forecaster. Fourth, I thought that academic research had raised significant doubts on the effectiveness of intervention as the main instrument of exchange rate policy (especially if the intervention is not concerted), but I found much greater willingness to rely on intervention. Fifth, I found a much greater focus on nominal exchange rates than on real exchange rates, and sixth, I found greater focus on flows (like budget deficits) than on stocks (like government debt).

With all this in mind I would like to discuss briefly the issues that Paul Krugman raised in his paper. I like very much the distinction between a so-called currency crisis and a contagion crisis. Krugman concludes that a contagion crisis is probably a historical anachronism because simple policymaking can now deal with it. But I believe that this is the kind of crisis we should all still be afraid of. I shall say more on this as I proceed, but at this point I want to emphasize a point about the international transmission of crises. I think it is important that we include protectionism as one of the known dangers because extended protectionism has implications beyond just trade flows. It makes the difference between an inward and outward orientation and between open and closed capital markets.

Let me now turn to the questions that Martin Feldstein has raised in this context. First, what are the sources of crisis? Second, and more important, can institutional arrangements be altered in order to prevent a crisis? I have a long list of points to make; they are not in any particular order of priority.

Exchange Rates, Intervention and Sustainability

First, we all know that what matters for economic behavior is real exchange rates. We also know that what makes the headlines are nominal exchange rates. This is a distinction that we should keep in mind all the time, because when we speak about the need for an exchange rate change of 5 or 10 percent in real terms, it is a much bigger change in nominal terms.

Second, why is there so much focus on intervention? There are basically two possible explanations. One possibility is that there is a serious belief that intervention is an effective instrument. In fact, at a meeting organized by Gerald Corrigan at the Federal Reserve Bank of New York in early October 1989, there was a general appeal from the audience to the central bankers around the table to reexamine the findings of the Jurgenson report, that is to reexamine whether sterilized intervention has any effectiveness. The second possibility, which is more likely to be correct in my view, is that policymakers view sterilized intervention not as the *essence* of policy, but rather as one *element* of policy. And as always when some elements of policy are more difficult to implement than others, one ends up with the elements that are easiest to implement.

A third subject that I wish to mention is the notion of sustainability. The concept of sustainability is elusive because it depends on the expected future evolution of many variables. Thus we all see current account imbalances, but we have different views about their future evolution and financing, and hence about their sustainability. One often sits around a table and confronts the question "Why are you crying wolf?" after predicting "seven of the past five" crises arising from supposed unsustainability. As one of the governors of the International Monetary Fund has said, it took many years to accumulate these deficits, and it is likely that it will take many years to run them down. By definition, something that is not sustainable will resolve itself, but the real issue is, at what cost? That is what makes sustainability a policy issue.

Coordination and Cooperation

A fourth issue is the role of policy coordination. When I first became involved in the discussions of policy coordination a few years ago, I was not very sensitive to such distinctions as that between "coordination" and "cooperation." I saw a good intellectual case for coordination (which I did not distinguish from cooperation) because we are, after all, an interdependent world. If one country performs an action that affects the rest of the world, there are externalities, and cooperation or coordination seems a good way of internalizing those externalities. As one becomes more sensitive to the distinction between cooperation and coordination, however, one recognizes that there are different priorities among countries, different constraints, different institutions, different assessments of reality, different readings of the record of the past, different philosophies, and different jurisdictions of who can do what. Some people argue that the Bonn Summit of 1978 was the most successful summit of all, while some view it, in retrospect, as regrettable. There are different readings even of the Louvre Accord as well as of many other agreements. In view of all this, I think that what one should advocate is nearer to the cooperation end of the coordination-cooperation spectrum.

Let me highlight some of the stumbling blocks that tend to appear in discussions around the table. These are not secret: they are all in the public record. First, the G-7 representatives may disagree about where we are. For instance, is it true that external adjustment has stalled, or is it not true? Before any action can be taken, the group must resolve such basic disagreements.

Second, suppose everyone agrees on "where we are"—say, that adjustment has stalled. There remains the question of what, if anything, should be done about it; and that again gives much scope for dispute. For example, Mr. Lawson, as chancellor of the exchequer of the United Kingdom, argued that since the increase in his country's external deficit in recent years is a result of private-sector behavior, it does not in itself constitute a problem. But we heard similar remarks—that one should not interfere with the actions of two consenting adults—in the early days of the debt crisis, and they make me a little nervous. I think we should be careful to identify the externalities that may be involved. Still, it is of course a valid question to ask whether anything should be done in such a situation.

Third, assuming agreement that there is a problem, there may be another source of difficulty in determining which international group should be concerned about and considered responsible for the situation. Is it a global, systemic problem, or a regional problem? Is it a G-7 problem, or is it an EMS problem, a European issue? Thus some would argue that the German external surplus is primarily an intra-European matter, rather than an issue for the system at large—as if macroeconomic corrections of surpluses and deficits are regional in their nature.

Fourth, what sort of action should be taken by the coordinating group? Should the arrangement be such that the actions of some countries offset those of others—what I call the "tango principle?" Thus the United States might contract domestic demand, while other countries would expand, one-for-one: when one leg moves back, the other leg moves forward. That was the aim two years ago, but now the situation has changed. It is now recognized that the global situation matters a lot. If, for example, the world economy is near full capacity then it makes less sense for the surplus countries to stimulate demand than would be the case if there was large excess capacity. In sum, the kind of coordinated actions that are needed will obviously depend on the circumstances.

When we think of how problems such as these are tackled, I think it is important to remember that the G-7 is not the only forum. There is in fact a number of organizations, including the OECD, the Bank of International Settlements, the European Community, and the International Monetary Fund itself, where countries' macroeconomic policies are discussed regularly in the context of the broader world economy. In many cases, it is the same individuals who meet in the different forums, and I think that element of personal contact may help a consensus to jell. By the same token, though, the existence of the various forums provides potential for conflict. Thus, suppose there is a meeting on Monday of the finance ministers of the European Community, and on Friday a meeting of the G-7, where a subset of the European Community participates together with Japan, the United States, and Canada. How can we calibrate the various agreements that have been made in one forum with the agreements, commitments, and understandings that have been made in another, and ensure their consistency? I think it is in the nature of the beast that we shall always have parallel forums that cover different areas with partially overlapping sets of participants. One issue is to determine how these groups are going to coexist.

Finally in this context, let me note that there are several issues that seem very clear in theory but are much less clear in the policy arena. For example, one frequently hears in policy discussions that either the budget deficit in the United States must fall or there will have to be some movement in the exchange rate, as if those possibilities are substitutes rather than (as theory tells us) complements. Similarly, when we talk about fiscal policies, what is the relevant measure of the fiscal balance? In Japan there is a strong belief that the relevant measure is that of the "central government" rather than the "general government" since social security should be excluded, but in the United States the usual measure is the general government balance, which includes social security. This kind of difference obviously gives rise to problems in the assessment of relative fiscal stance.

Conclusion

Let me conclude with a few final remarks. First, Martin Feldstein asked me whether the G-7 representatives focus at all on the long run. Recently, in fact, there has been increased interest in and discussion of savings, demography, and other long-term issues. Nevertheless, I think it is fair to say that what claims most attention in these forums are problems of a current nature, how to solve them, and how to prevent them from occurring in the future.

Second, I want to emphasize the importance of the issue of "overinsurance" that has already been raised. We can all predict the outcome of an insurance system that does not charge an appropriate premium or where the premium is not closely related to the insurance that one gets. Indeed, when the public sector provides such insurance, or when it is expected to provide it, it is likely that the private sector will undertake excessively risky actions and thereby raise the likelihood of crises.

Third, it might have been useful to ask around this table, What is the value of the fundamental equilibrium exchange rate between any pair of the major currencies? I am sure that the variance of the response would be huge. I think this tells us two things. First, any international monetary system must accommodate the fact that we are not sure what the equilibrium exchange rate is. Second, if you are thinking about the possibility of target zones for exchange rates, be sure not to make exchange rates the only focus for policymaking. After all, exchange rates are not the fundamentals, and there is a danger of diverting attention from the true fundamentals unless one sees target zones in a broader context that includes those fundamentals. In addition, I have difficulties with any proposed system that relies heavily on active and frequent use of fiscal policy, because I do not believe that fiscal policy is a sufficiently flexible instrument. In a way I consider this to be fortunate, because otherwise there would have been a temptation to overuse fiscal policy in attempts at finetuning.

Finally, let me make one remark about overburdening monetary policy. Paul Krugman concluded his paper by saying that contagion crises can be avoided as long as sensible policy is undertaken. By "sensible policy" he means "sensible monetary policy," and correctly so. However, this adds another task to monetary policy, the overburdening of which has been the story of the 1980s. Before the mild financial crash of Friday, the 13th of October 1989, we said that monetary policy was already overburdened because it was expected to deal with exchange rates, interest rates, inflation, growth, and so on. But since that Friday, we have added another task: we now expect policymakers to withdraw the excess liquidity, which they provided to the system, in a very skillful way to avoid the inflation that might otherwise come "the morning after." There is indeed a great danger that we come to expect too much from monetary policy. Even the most skillful conducting of monetary policy cannot remove the dangers of crises. Monetary policy must be supported by appropriate regulatory and supervisory systems as well as by budget policy that is viewed as being sustainable.

5. Charles P. Kindleberger

International (and Interregional) Aspects of Financial Crises

My usual role in a conference of this sort is the opening paper entitled "Blank-Blank-Blank Financial Crises, the Rise of Financial Centers, Capital Flight—whatever—A Historical Perspective." It is pleasant to be relegated to the role of clean-up, although I recognize that the last paper of a conference in the afternoon tends to find the audience diminished as some conferees head for the airport to get home for dinner.

Instead of history, I choose to start with some theory. Connections between national (and regional) economies run through many channels. Most theorists think of their specialty as the most important of these connections and sometimes as the only significant one. The list includes money (initially gold and silver, later short-term capital); other capital movements, including those through securities (bonds, shares, and, most recently, securitized mortgages), direct investment and real estate; trade mostly in goods rather than services and associated largely with income changes of the Keynesian variety; foreign-exchange rates; prices; and psychology. A Milton Friedman looks mainly at money flows, especially of high-powered money in 1921 and 1929 gold, asserting that the case for the United States initiating the depressions starting in those years was that the gold flows were to this country. In his 1989 Robbins lectures, Peter Temin pointed to income changes brought about by the deflationary policies of Hoover, Baldwin, Laval, and Bruning, who were clinging to the gold standard; in his earlier volume, *Did Monetary Forces Cause the Great Depression?* (New York: Norton, 1976), he points to shifts in consumer spending on automobiles and housing, somehow brought about. Those who blame the Hawley-Smoot tariff for the depression of the 1930s focus on trade and the blow to it of tariff increases and retaliation. Few join me in thinking that the start of a recession can come from cutting off a flow of capital that then forces the recipients to cut investment and imports. One current fear, however, is that West Germany, Japan, and, to a lesser extent Taiwan and Switzerland, may stop supporting the U.S. bond, stock, and real estate markets, putting pressure on investment here.

Another of my pet views about 1929 is that the decline in share prices communicated itself rapidly to commodities, especially raw-material imports, normally then shipped to New York on consignment and bought on arrival by brokers on bank credit. When New York banks seized up because of the troubles in brokers' loans, this credit was cut off, making commodity prices plunge. The decline in New York prices spread worldwide through arbitrage and instantaneous markdowns, without the necessity for slow-moving trade changes, though the volume of U.S. imports fell. The debt-deflation model of Irving Fisher is still relevant, despite the propensity of some theorists to say that it smacks of money illusion, which their analysis does not allow. My answer is that producers facing falling prices know they have lost income, as do their banks, whereas producers are slow recognize their increase in real income and unlikely to found new banks.

One important channel of communicating price changes is through changes in exchange rates. There are some, such as McCloskey and Zecher, who think that the exchange rate is always at the purchasing-power-parity level, and hence neutral. This seems to me to misread the history of 1931 when a downward ratchet operated in a buyer's market, with depreciation leaving domestic prices unchanged and appreciation depressing them. In a seller's market, the ratchet may work the other way, as in the 1970s. In the uneasy balance between buyer's and seller's markets, an exchange-rate change lowers prices part way in the appreciating country and raises them part way in the depreciating one—a matter of considerable assistance to the world economy in the 1980s.

The psychological connection among markets is brilliantly revealed at the end of each quarter in the chart in the contemporary *New York Times,* which traces out the profiles of share prices in a dozen countries for the previous three months. They run along broadly similar lines, despite the fact that only a handful of securities are traded in several markets. Similarly, the implosion of 19 October 1987 was echoed in equity markets worldwide.

Now I would like to make a methodological point that I have been belaboring for a number of years. Most theorists seize one of these connections among international markets—money, goods and the income changes behind them, securities, prices inclusive of exchange-rate changes, and psychology—and run with it, whereas in my judgment, the situation changes from time to time and calls for a change in model. In 1929, the stock market crash spread to commodities and, through them, to the banking system. A flight to quality in 1930 hit hard at institutions with low-grade securities and today hovers over the low-grade bond market. Deflation in stocks may also spread to real estate, in 1987 also hurt by the decline in oil prices, especially in the southwestern United States. The patterns among markets may differ. If deflation spreads from stocks to commodities, the effect is almost instantaneous. The impact on real estate is slower. Homer Hoyt's neglected classic, *One Hundred Years of Land Values in Chicago* (University of Chicago Press), written in 1933 and recapitulating five cycles in Chicago real estate prices, underscores the differences on the upside, speculation in stocks spreads easily and quickly to real estate. On the downside, when stock prices collapse, real estate speculators congratulate themselves that they have claims on tangible assets and term debts, as opposed to day-to-day brokers loans. Over time, this consolation proves limited. Demand for real estate turns down sharply as buyers wait for prices to decline, but interest and tax payments stay up. Supplies of houses and other buildings continue to emerge from the long pipeline. Whereas a crash in securities is over in months, attrition in real estate, according to Hoyt, may take three, four, sometimes as many as eight years. A similar prolonged attrition takes place in sovereign debt where default has been avoided thus far, since the crisis began in 1982, because earlier defaults interrupted capital flows to developing countries for periods as long as 30 years.

The international propagation of booms and crashes occurs readily in markets for money, bonds, stocks, commodities, and direct investment. It has not operated in the past through real estate, although increasing integration of the U.S. real estate market into the world may produce a similar synchronization in the future as securitization of mortgages and foreign investment in hotels, office buildings, apartments, and the like occur. The 1925 Florida land crash and the 1974 Arab-induced bubble in London real estate were both localized, though psychological contagion today may link the extended real estate market in Japan to other national markets, including the one in the United States. Or it may work the other way. I know of one operator who is reacting to the troubles in Boston real estate by assembling a fund in London to pick up bargains.

We know from the days of Henry Thornton and Walter Bagehot that national financial crises may be halted by a lender of last resort who props up markets by making money available to hard-pressed debtors with illiquid assets. (There are other devices, such as the guarantee of liabilities of institutions threatened with failure, but I restrict the analysis to last-resort lending.)

International "lending" at last resort is less well understood but has occurred historically in a variety of forms: exchanges of gold for silver, discounting of foreign bills of exchange, promises not to draw on foreign deposits, forward purchases of oil for cash, bridging loans, and swaps under the Basle Agreement of March 1961. These are invoked when financial crisis in one country threatens to spread abroad. Last-resort lending is short-term therapy. What happens next?

In Bagehot's formulation, last-resort lending should be undertaken only on good collateral. In English financial history, this proviso has been honored in the breach as well as in the observance, and for all kinds of reasons. The Bank of England acquired titles to a copper works, a coal mine, a West Indian plantation, and, in 1836, the assets of three American "W" banks that it was able to liquidate only in 1848. In its various "salvage" operations, the Bank of Italy acquired the problem loans of various Italian banks to prevent them failing in 1907, 1922, 1926, and 1930–33, finally consolidating them into the Istituto Ricostruzione Industriale (IRI) in 1933 to hold more or less in perpetuity. The Reconstruction Finance Corporation in the United States at the end of 1932 saved a number of banks, though it failed to forestall the collapse of the banking system in March 1933. Its assets were safely liquidated in the wartime expansion after 1940. Swaps used to halt foreign-exchange crises that are not undone by a return flow of capital after a stipulated period, such as six months, are funded into long-term obligations of the IMF or between central banks or governments.

The initial lender with bad loans faces an agonizing choice between write-off or workout. In Third World debt, American banks first sought to work out their nonperforming loans, but ended up writing off substantial portions of them. It is seldom recognized that the lender of last resort has the same problem. Unreversed swaps may get funded, but central banks that hold foreign exchange that declines in price keep it on the books at cost until sold, rather than "mark to market," which is the conservative banking rule. This is tolerable since central banks with power to create money cannot fail. If they lose money from buying high and selling low, it reduces the profit they normally pay to government, shifting the loss to the nation at large. The contrast between the successful workout of the RFC and the unsuccessful one of the IRI has been mentioned. The Resolution Trust Corporation set up under the 1989 legislation in the United States to rescue the thrift institutions in trouble is expected to liquidate a substantial portion of the bad debts taken over and to write off other amounts estimated as high as $190 billion. The liquidation process—the working out—is likely to prevent the recovery of the real estate market in this country, or depress it further, except in the event of a vigorous, unexpected continuation of the 1982–89 boom.

As therapy for financial crises, last-resort lending has the difficulties of moral hazard on the one hand and liquidation of the acquired assets on the other. There is a third possibility: that the function will get caught up in politics and thereby be prevented from effecting the necessary and salubrious work of rescue. In 1931, France refused to come to the aid of Austria, after the first feeble step, on foreign policy grounds. The legislation to assist the thrifts in the United States almost became entangled in political questions that divided the parties after the highly partisan political campaign of 1988: how much to put on the 1990 budget; whether to raise any of the loss repayment by taxation, a step the president refused to consider; and whether the taxpayer should bail out the bank officials guilty of bad judgment and in some cases malfeasance and fraud. The great benefit of central banks as lenders of last resort is that they are mostly not immediately subject to political debate and decision. Crises must be handled with dispatch, which is why a voting body such as the IMF is more successful in cleaning up arrears than in mounting the barricades in moments of crises.

In the series of financial crises since 1979, this country and the world have been fortunate in that the lender-of-last-resort process has escaped being caught up in political disputes. At the domestic level, some of these escapes have been narrow. Internationally, while the U.S. role as leader of the world economy has slipped, there is no challenger that refuses to cooperate in crisis management or offers competing solutions that might stalemate decision. If a new economic world leader is called for in the interest of stability and the United States tries to hold on to its position as number one, the transition may give rise to difficulty as occurred in the 1930s when Britain proved unable to provide stability and the United States was unwilling to.

Summary of Discussion

Krugman began by expressing his agreement with most of the panelists' statements and by reiterating the key point of his paper, that currency, or country, crises are more to be feared than contagion crises because we know what to do about the latter. He went on to discuss alternative views about the future path of the dollar. Because the interest rate differential between the United States and other leading countries is almost zero, the financial markets seem to think that the current level of the dollar is sustainable. In contrast, international trade modelers estimate that, at the current value of the dollar, U.S. external debt is on an explosive path. The consequences of a possible sharp fall in the dollar are unclear—the United States experienced virtually no harmful effects from the 1985–87 dollar decline, but Latin American countries have been hurt badly by the decline in their currencies.

Krugman continued that Dornbusch's story about the effect of capital flight in Latin America is not persuasive quantitatively, as real physical capital has not flown fast enough to cause the 30 percent drop in real wages. The explanation of these countries' poor economic performance is especially puzzling as the debt crisis has been handled by fast, focused, and sustained international coordination.

Robert J. Gordon disputed the idea that an exchange rate crisis would be accompanied by either massive U.S. inflation or deflation. Bergsten's views are based on an aggregate supply curve, which is flat where the economy has excess capacity and is quite steep to the right of that. There is no evidence of such a nonlinearity in the United States in the last 40 years. Also, the likely response of monetary policy to a currency crisis reduces the probability of a hard landing. Since Alan Greenspan and the Federal Reserve can disentangle inflation in food and energy prices from core inflation, they can also disentangle import price effects. And if they are de facto targeting nominal GNP, then it is movements in the GNP deflator, which excludes imports, that matter, not movements in the Consumer Price Index (CPI). For a dollar crash to cause a recession, there would have to be a big effect on the prices of import substitutes, not just imports, which would take a long time. The successful U.S. experience in 1985–87 is relevant to any future falls in the dollar.

Bergsten responded that his conclusions do not rely on nonlinearity nearly as much as Gordon suggested: a 10 percent decline in the value of the dollar can increase the CPI by up to 2 percentage points, according to Federal Reserve analyses of the 1970s and Jeffrey Sachs's work in the mid-1980s. This is because import price increases do tend to pass through to other prices in the economy and the Federal Reserve will have to respond to that—increasing rather than dampening the prospect for a hard landing of the economy. And it is clear that the Federal Reserve does not in fact ignore movements in the CPI or any of the other major inflation indicators and that a currency crisis could in any event force it to abandon its normal aim of targeting nominal GNP.

Minsky stated that the likelihood of a hard landing was reduced by the potential role of Japan and Germany in Eastern Europe. Debt-financed exports from the United States, Japan, and Europe to Eastern Europe can be a driving force for those economies, even while Japanese and European exports *to* the United States can decrease. This can improve our trade balance quite quickly.

Robert J. Shiller addressed Kindleberger's comments on psychological contagion. The evidence of international contagion in stock markets must lie in positively correlated price forecast errors, not positively correlated prices themselves. There is evidence of this correlation, but there is surprisingly little contagion between real estate markets and stock markets and between real estate markets in different geographic areas. *Krugman* noted that real estate markets do not clear in the short run, so the "declared" prices should not be compared to prices in other asset markets.

Jeffrey Frankel agreed with Frenkel's call for renewed attention to the effects of sterilized foreign exchange intervention. He reported results obtained with Kathryn Dominguez concerning such intervention by the German Bundesbank. They find strong effects of actual intervention, as well as an additional effect through expectations, when the intervention is publicly reported.

This induced a comment by *Michael Mussa* that the best prescription for creating an international crisis was to foster a belief that sterilized intervention can be a potent policy tool.

Ralph C. Bryant began discussion of the international aspects of financial regulation, deposit insurance, and lender-of-last-resort policies. He stressed the problem of "regulatory arbitrage" across national borders and the policy issues it raised. For example, in a world environment in which national financial markets are increasingly integrated, to what degree is it possible for the bank regulation and deposit insurance regimes in the United States to continue to coexist with the significantly different regimes prevailing in other industrial countries? As another illustration, the enhanced integration of financial markets makes it somewhat more difficult to reach lender-of-last-resort decisions in times of crisis, in part because the division of responsibilities among central banks could be unclear. For example, how would the Bank of Japan and the Federal Reserve share responsibility in the event of a crisis in the dollar-clearing payments system in Tokyo managed by the Chase Manhattan Bank?

Feldstein agreed that more stringent U.S. banking regulation will increase U.S. banks' cost of funds and drive customers to foreign banks. The question is whether we want to have foreign imports of banking services or distorted prices through subsidized deposit insurance.

Minsky added that raising the capital asset requirements for banks implies a bigger markup of lending rates over the cost of funds in order to maintain a given rate of profit on equity.

Edward J. Kane believed that the recent "risk-based capital agreement" is a toothless international compromise that continues "competition for regulatory business" across countries.

Richard F. Syron was very concerned about the impact of regulatory arbitrage, but he felt that the international capital agreement was at least a beginning. For example, Japanese banks will have to raise their capital ratios, which they will be able to do fairly easily, but with potential impact on the rate of return on equity. These types of international regulations are difficult to put into place but are very important.

William S. Haraf noted that although recent U.S. concerns about deposit insurance have led to more interest in the "narrow bank" concept, where insured banks must invest in only safe assets, Europe is moving in the opposite direction toward full universal banking. He concluded that this is not such a bad idea if institutions are adequately capitalized and market discipline is ensured, but the contrast with current U.S. thinking will stimulate future conflict.

3   Macroeconomic Consequences of Financial Crises

1. Lawrence H. Summers
2. Hyman P. Minsky
3. Paul A. Samuelson
4. William Poole
5. Paul A. Volcker

1. Lawrence H. Summers

Planning for the Next Financial Crisis

It used to be said that a repeat of the depression of the 1930s was inconceivable now that governments better understood how to manage their economies. Yet, both Latin America and Europe have suffered economic downturns during the 1980s on a scale comparable to the 1930s. And, in 1987, the world's stock markets suffered the greatest one-day drop in their history. It is little wonder that the possibility of financial crisis with major economic consequences has again emerged as a major cause for concern.

The problem of planning for financial crisis has much in common with the problem of planning for war. We are fortunate in that the worst disasters we can contemplate are much worse than those with which we have had experience. While certain principles may be robust, technological changes reduce the relevance of historical experience and create new threats. With financial crisis as with war, prevention is much better than cure. But in neither case can prevention and cure be cleanly separated. Credible government commitments to defend financial institutions can deter speculative attack just as credible threats of reprisal can discourage military attack. But, policies that deter attack also encourage reckless behavior. Thus critics argue that excessively strong military force breeds adventurism and that excessively generous de-

The author is indebted to David Cutler for research assistance and to J. Bradford De Long for useful discussions.

135

posit insurance leads financial institutions to take unwarranted and dangerous gambles.

Because of their inability to do experiments, and the paucity of relevant precedent, military planners make extensive use of war games. By following out the logic of various constructed scenarios, they evaluate the efficacy of alternative strategies. I use a similar mode of analysis here in considering appropriate government policy once financial crisis comes. For the most part, I ignore issues of maintaining a stable and sustainable policy environment and issues relating to the prudential regulation of financial institutions. Instead, I concentrate primarily on lender-of-last-resort strategies. Only in so far as commitments made by lenders of last resort affect the likelihood of crisis do I touch on the issue of crisis prevention as opposed to crisis cure.

The paper is organized as follows. Section 3.1 describes and tries to dramatize the three stages of the canonical "Kindleberger" (1978) crisis and considers its relevance in the current environment. I conclude that technological and financial innovation have probably operated to make speculative bubbles which ultimately burst more likely today than has been the case historically. However, other institutional changes have made it less likely that financial disturbances will be transmitted to the real economy. The most important are the presence of automatic stabilizers and deposit insurance, and the Federal Reserve's recognition of the potentially disastrous consequences of a major decline in the money stock.

Section 3.2 takes up the critical issue of lender-of-last-resort policy. I distinguish four positions on the appropriate behavior of public lenders of last resort. The first *laissez-faire* position, which has enjoyed a mild revival in recent years, holds that there is no reason for public intervention in financial markets, that private institutions could and would perform the lender-of-last-resort function if there was no public interference. The second, *monetarist* position holds that the only appropriate role of the government is to insulate the money stock from developments in asset markets. In large part, this can be done through open market operations directed at maintaining a stable money stock without any need for the authorities to intervene on behalf of specific institutions. The third, *classical* position follows Bagehot (1873) in seeing a clear but limited role for a public lender of last resort. On the classical view, last-resort lending is appropriate only to solvent banks, at a penalty rate, for short time periods according to a preannounced plan.

The fourth, *pragmatic* position is the one embraced implicitly if not explicitly by policymakers in most major economies. It holds that central banks must always do whatever is necessary to preserve the integrity of the financial system regardless of whether those who receive support are solvent or can safely pay a penalty rate. This position concedes that some institutions may become too large to fail. While lender-of-last-resort insurance, like any other type of insurance, will have moral hazard effects, I argue that these may be small when contrasted with the benefits of protecting the real economy from financial disturbances.

Section 3.3 asks how a financial crisis could affect the real economy in the presence of a sufficiently aggressive lender of last resort. This would be most likely if the provision of liquidity was itself destabilizing. Suppose foreigners lose confidence and rush to get out of dollar assets in U.S. financial institutions. Such a situation would be difficult for the authorities because the actions necessary to preserve the health of financial institutions would conflict with the goal of preventing a currency collapse. Conversely, the high interest rates necessary to avert a collapsing currency would tend to create financial distress.

Section 3.4 concludes by assessing the magnitude of the crisis risk and by suggesting steps that might make financial crisis less likely.

3.1 The Canonical Crisis

Perhaps the best definition of a financial crisis is the one offered by Goldsmith (1982) in commenting on Minsky (1982). He defines a financial crisis as "a sharp, brief, ultra-cyclical deterioration of all or most of a group of financial indicators—short term interest rates, asset prices, (stock, real estate, land) prices, commercial insolvencies and failures of financial institutions." On this definition, even very sharp declines in asset values such as the two-thirds decline in U.S. real stock prices between the beginning of 1973 and summer of 1974 does not represent a financial crisis. Nor do widespread financial institution failures such as the S&L crisis unless they occur suddenly and lead to widespread failures of financial institutions.

On a narrow definition, the incidence of financial crisis has surely diminished over time. After noting that "a disinflation or a deflation may be long drawn out. Nominal wealth may decline, real debts may rise, but these are not financial crisis," Anna Schwartz (1986) goes so far as to claim that "no financial crisis has occurred in the United States since 1933, and none has occurred in the United Kingdom since 1866. All the phenomena of recent years that have been characterised as financial crisis—a decline in asset prices of equity stocks, real estate, commodities; depreciation of the exchange value of a national currency; financial distress of a large non-financial firm, a large municipality, a financial industry, or sovereign debtors—are pseudo-financial crisis."

The issue of what constitutes a financial crisis is semantic. But Schwartz is clearly correct in her implication that the financial stresses of recent years have had relatively little effect on real economic activity. The situation is very different than that of a century ago, when financial panics and sharp declines in economic activity often coincided. Perhaps the critical question about financial crises is whether financial instability no longer affects the real economy in the way that it once did, or whether in fact there is a risk that the next financial disturbance will turn out to have a major impact on the real economy. One way of trying to get some insight into this question is to try to construct a scenario where financial crisis leads to disaster and then to evaluate its plausibility. This should either lead to a rejection of Schwartz's view or to the identification of the crucial differences that make crises less likely today than they were in an earlier era.

3.1.1 Prelude to Crisis

Here is a scenario that poses many of the issues that come up in historical discussions of the onset of financial crisis. In this section, I use this scenario as a vehicle for expositing Kindleberger's model of the canonical crisis and considering its current relevance. Then in the next section, I use it as a vehicle for considering various positions about the appropriate behavior of the lender of last resort. Finally, in the third section, I consider possible new genres of financial crisis. It goes without saying that the scenario presented here is employed as an analytic device and does *not* represent a forecast of the future in either broad outline or detailed particular.

The year was 1991. The world economy had been growing for 9 consecutive years. Widespread fears that the U.S. economy would land hard after the twin deficits of the Reagan years had proven false. The notion that recessions were a thing of the past took hold. Analysts explained that because of the increasing diversity and internationalization of economic activity, poor performance in a single sector of the economy was no longer enough to drag the whole economy down. They also argued that the market itself had supplanted the Fed as a controller of inflation. Whenever inflation loomed, interest rates rose automatically, slowing growth down to a sustainable level. The competitive problems of the 1980s and the Reagan administration's anti-union policies exerted a continuous restraining influence on wage demands, allowing corporate profit rates to rise to levels not seen since the 1960s.

Reduced concern about inflation and strong earnings were good news for the stock market. Three other fundamental factors also buoyed the market. First, with the Nikkei index at 55000, Japanese investors began to diversify on a large scale. At last, the Tokyo offices of major American financial institutions began to pay off. Predictions that the flow of Japanese money into the American stock market would rise from $75 billion a year to $250 billion a year by 2000 became commonplace. Second, junk bond investors who were fortunate enough to buy during the fall 1989 slump earned spectacular returns. With a vindicated Michael Milken back in business, the pace of corporate restructuring increased. Nearly $200 billion in equity was withdrawn from the market during 1990. Third, reduced capital gains taxes, lower taxes on dividend income through adoption of Treasury Secretary Brady's corporate tax integration program, and newly enacted IRA accounts also contributed to the demand for stocks.

With the Dow Jones average above 4000 by 1990, the small investor returned to the market. The argument that, over a 15-year period including the crash up to the end of 1990, investors in stocks had earned an average real return of 11 percent, and that, with a reduced cyclical element, the future would be even brighter, proved persuasive. With the baby bust of the 1980s, fewer families needed to invest in purchasing a larger second home. Instead, the money went into stock market. Mini-stock-market future contracts invented by a major brokerage firm that enabled individuals to put up just $2,000 and control $35,000 worth of stock were approved by the CFTC and proved to be a major hit. A distinguished group of economists and financial experts convened early in 1990 and recommended that, given new economic realities, universities and other nonprofit institutions should hold 75 percent of their endowments in equity, since over the long term if not the short term, the stock market provided an extremely attractive risk return ratio.

During the first half of 1991, the Dow Jones average rose from 4000 to 4800. Investors in mini-stock-market futures saw their initial $2,000 stake rise to $9,000. Most reinvested their proceeds. Lawyers and dentists explained to one another that investing without margin was a mistake, since using margin enabled one to double one's return, and the risks were small given that one could always sell out if it looked like the market would decline. By mid-September, the Dow had reached 5400.

This account has the three major elements that Kindleberger stresses in his account of the prelude to crisis.[1] First, there is a displacement, a change in fundamental values that leads to a fully justified increase in asset prices. Here it is an increase in earnings, and there is an appropriate expectation that the variability of economic performance may have decreased. Further arguments, (the Japanese, the tax cuts), lend support to the idea that an asset price increase is justified.

Second, the increase in asset prices and the confidence it brings about leads to an increased use of leverage. This takes place both at the firm level, as firms lever themselves much more highly, and at the individual level, as the use of the futures markets permits individuals to lever their purchases of stock. In one description, this increased demand for credit pushes interest rates up, leading to an increase in the velocity of money. In another, a proper definition of money should include the credit extended by brokerage firms to individuals and so the money supply has increased. Either conception suggests that the increase in asset values leads to increased liquidity, which in turn increases the demand for goods and services and leads to economic expansion.

---

1. Kindleberger's account places more emphasis than this one on the presence of fraud and corruption. Perhaps this deserves to be treated as a separate major element.

Third, the boom is fueled by the *positive feedback behavior* of some investors.[2] Individuals who emulate the strategies that have fared well in the recent past, and so buy stock following price increases and sell following price declines, are displaying positive feedback behavior. So are the institutions who use recent history to set their investment strategy. Investors who rush to sell out when they get margin calls, or to cover short positions when the market moves up are also positive feedback investors. By increasing the demand for shares when prices are rising and reducing it when prices are falling, positive feedback behavior increases market volatility.

Kindleberger is not entirely clear on what determines when good news is followed by enough use of leverage and enough positive feedback behavior to create a mania or a bubble. Surely institutional factors matter. If may also be that it takes a long run of good news to create enough confidence for conventional inhibitions about leverage to erode, and for sluggish households and institutions to get the word that a new era has begun. The accident of what catches the public's fancy is relevant as well.

Has anything happened to make this sort of prelude to crisis less likely now than it might have been in earlier times? It seems unlikely. First, financial innovation has greatly increased the use of leverage in the economy. This may be seen in many ways. At the broadest level, the ratio of high-powered money (currency plus bank reserves) to GNP has fallen from 6.9 percent in the 1920s to 5.7 percent today, and much of today's high-powered money is held outside the country. The ratio of household debt to disposable income has risen from 36 percent to 92 percent today. The ratio of corporate debt to corporate equity has risen sharply, especially in recent years. And the importance of cross-border lending and borrowing on both a net and gross basis has increased spectacularly.

Second, the Depression and even the sharp stock market declines of 1973–75 recede from memory. There was of course the crash in 1987, but the recent performance of the American market and, even more strikingly, several foreign markets, suggest that its lesson may have been double-edged. Some were scared away. But others concluded that a market that could prosper following the crash was basically sound and safe. While portfolio insurance strategies of the type that were popular before the crash have become less fashionable, little else has changed, and other types of market-timing strategies have taken their place. Recall that markets crashed in other countries where portfolio insurance was not in widespread use.

Third, the steady decline in transaction costs and the increase in trading volumes has surely increased the perception of liquidity in asset markets. The perception is a valid one in normal times. As long as one's desire is not uni-

---

2. This type of behavior may be even more important in real estate markets than in the stock market. Kindleberger cites evidence suggesting that at the height of the Boston real estate boom, nearly two-thirds of condominiums purchased were intended for resale.

versally shared, it is easier to liquidate a position than it would have been in the past. Of course, when everyone wants to move in the same direction, no technological improvement in the organization of the market can increase liquidity.

The view that bubbles could again emerge in asset markets is supported by statistical evidence on speculative prices. Cutler, Poterba, and Summers (1989) document that in the markets for stocks, bonds, foreign exchange, and precious metals there is positive serial correlation over periods of weeks and months. This implies that there is logic to short-term, positive feedback trading, which seeks to catch and ride trends. On one estimate (*The Economist* 1989), almost four-fifths of foreign exchange trading is driven by technical systems that give rise to positive feedback. A different sort of evidence comes from the work of Barsky and De Long (1989) who, in studying the American stock market, find clear evidence that stock prices rise much more than proportionately with dividends, as would be predicted by any theory emphasizing the market's eventual overreaction to good news.

Can anything be done to make the type of prelude to crisis described here less likely? There is the problem that bursting a balloon is much easier than gradually letting the air out. Seeking to talk the market down will not work if the government's statements are not credible and may work too well if its statements are too fully credible. Perhaps there is scope for regulation to combat the growth of leverage or the illusion of general liquidity. Suggestions range from increased margin requirements to taxes that would disproportionately fall on short-term traders.[3] All such regulatory approaches are probably becoming more difficult for any nation to implement unilaterally because of the ease with which financial activity can be relocated.

If financial crisis is less likely today than it once was, the reason is probably not a reduction in the likelihood of a bubble starting. I turn next to the bubble's burst and its consequences for the real economy.

3.1.2   The Panic Begins

Here is how the scenario described in the preceding subsection might continue:

In October of 1991, problems began to surface. The widely admired 1990 leveraged buy out (LBO) of a Fortune 20 company got into serious trouble and the price of the publicly traded 'stub equity' fell by 75 percent. One major Wall Street firm was forced to merge with another after a poorly supervised trader lost $500 million by failing to properly hedge a complex position in the newly developed foreign-mortgage-backed securities market. Economic forecasters were confounded by a drop in the demand for

---

3. For a discussion suggesting that transactions taxes would probably not have large effects on volatility one way or the other but might increase economic efficiency in other ways, see Summers and Summers (1989).

durable goods as both consumers and businesses were saturated after a decade of strong demand. Yet another hot summer reduced the wheat crop. At
the same time, the U.S. government had reluctantly concluded that making
a substantial amount of wheat available to the Soviet Union was necessary
in order to reduce the risk of Stalinist backlash against Mikhail Gorbachev.
Investors got jittery even as the 1.3 percent Consumer Price Index (CPI)
increase in September was dismissed as an aberration due largely to agri-
cultural prices.

These jitters were compounded when trade frictions between the United
States and Japan heated up. Recognizing that a large bilateral trade surplus
would, as a matter of arithmetic, continue for as long as Japanese investors
invested heavily in the United States, MOF quietly offered administrative
guidance calling for reduced investment in American stocks. Given
congressional pressure for new withholding taxes on capital gains received
by foreigners, this guidance was effective. Confronting problems of both
unemployment and inflation, American policy-makers made it clear that
monetary policy would be used to try to keep the economy growing steadily
not to support any particular level of the dollar exchange rate.

Articles urging the proposition that no one had gone broke and many had
prospered selling out too soon became ubiquitous. The realization that the
Japanese had shifted from being net buyers of stock to being net sellers
gradually spread. On the Wednesday before Thanksgiving, the Dow fell
172 points. Experts cautioned that this was a decline of 3 percent, and that
there had been several dozen previous occasions when the market had fallen
as much. But the markets in London and Tokyo were off almost 10 percent
on Thursday and Friday, with American securities declining the most.

On Monday morning the floodgates opened as a huge number of individuals and institutions decided that the market had become too risky for them.
During the day, selling pressure was increased as the intraday margin systems instituted after the crash of 1987 forced many traders in both Chicago
and New York to liquidate their positions. An effort to get firms to prop up
the market by buying their own shares failed, as firms complained to the
authorities that they were so levered already, that they could not part with
any cash or take on new debt. Institutions learned from the experience of
the 1987 crash and avoided making margin payments to customers until
they had received the cash their customers were owed, putting pressure on
the payments system. Circuit breakers kicked in when the market was down
200 points and again when it was down 400. But as rumors swept the floor,
that, off the floor, large blocks were being sold at large discounts to past
market prices, the panic only increased. By the end of the day, over 1.3
billion shares had changed hands as the Dow Jones average declined by
1153 points.

Again, the main elements in Kindleberger's model are present. First, at
some point, an event occurs that raises doubts about the future. Some insiders

decide to take their profits and get out. Second, the market hesitates. The pool of new speculators dries up. The possibility of a panic becomes real. Third, the prophecy becomes self-fulfilling as investors rush to get out while they still can. As always in troubled times, there is a flight to quality.

As with the first stage of Kindleberger's crisis model, there is little reason to believe that this second stage has become less likely over time. Mutatis mutandis. The scenario here is very much like the one played out on 19 October 1987. In the wake of that event, a vast effort has gone into seeking regulatory changes that would make market meltdowns less likely or at least less violent. It is doubtful that much has been accomplished. The observation that the market had a 66-hour circuit breaker before the Monday crash raises questions about the efficacy of closing the market during a panic. So does the experience of Hong Kong, where the market was closed and not permitted to reopen.

Raising margin requirements may well help stop bubbles from starting but it is unlikely to be helpful in controlling bubbles once they start. Indeed, it creates positive feedback by accelerating the selling out of positions of those caught by price declines. As Garcia and Plautz (1988) note, this is what happened during the 1980 silver episode. Raising margin requirements also makes it more difficult for venturesome speculators who want to buy at what they regard as low prices.

Increasing capital requirements for specialists or broker dealers may, as discussed below, protect the integrity of the payments system, but it is unlikely to do much to stabilize prices in a rapidly falling market. Specialists can create liquidity but they cannot stabilize a market where everyone wants to sell. The reality is that little has happened to make the second stage of a Kindleberger crisis less likely than it was historically. Nor are there plausible regulatory actions that would achieve this objective.

3.1.3   Crashes and the Real Economy

So far, the scenario that I have constructed represents what Schwartz labels a "pseudo crisis." The disturbance has not yet affected the health of financial institutions or been transmitted to the real economy. The important institutional and attitudinal changes that have taken place in the last 50 years have been directed much more at containing the damage that financial problems might cause than at preventing speculative bubbles from starting. As I argue in the next section, which is directed at the appropriate behavior of lenders of last resort, this makes a very big difference. In order to illustrate the importance of these changes, I complete my scenario by assuming the authorities behave in the way they did in the 1930s. Needless to say, this is not what I would anticipate.

One major brokerage house had been very eager for business. As a consequence, it treated the investor suitability requirements for trading futures and writing options as a formality. When the market fell more than 1000 points, many of its customers could not meet their obligations. Those who could heard the rumors that the firm might fail and decided to delay making their payment. Worried about the firm's continued ability to function, one of the major clearing houses did not make its payment but instead held on to it as collateral. By the end of the day, it was clear that the brokerage firm would not survive.

Once rumors that a major brokerage house might fail looked right, suspicion fell on the clearing house of which it was a major part and on the banks with which the clearing house did business. One major Chicago bank was rumored to have lent very heavily to purchasers of stock and options. On Tuesday morning a queue formed outside its door before it opened. Seeing the line outside the bank on "Good Morning America," many other people decided they were better off taking money out of their banks. Many foreign holders of American bank assets remembered what had happened to the dollar after the crash of 1987 and worried about the health of the American banking system and did not roll over their CDs.

With the chairman of the FDIC at his side, the president went on TV and announced that the small depositors had nothing to fear, since deposits of up to $100,000 were fully insured by the FDIC, which would surely meet all its obligations. The chairman of the Federal Reserve announced that the Federal Reserve would not allow liquidity problems to bring down any major bank. The effect was not the intended one. Holders of large CDs, both foreign and domestic, as well as those who were owed money by securities companies, interpreted the announcement as saying that the government would not necessarily meet their obligation if the institution holding their obligation was not solvent.

As credit contracted, the level of M2 declined by 4 percent in a two-week period, even though the stock of base money increased slightly. Forecasters called for recession and for a sharp decline in the rate of inflation. With inflation expectations way down, real interest rates rose sharply. Banks froze loans to builders until they had a chance to see which way the economy would head. Businesses held out on new plant and equipment spending until they saw how the situation shook out. Firms whose bank had been liquidated had an especially difficult time getting credit of any kind, because no one knew them. Fearful that the political pressures caused by recession would generate legislation that would make it more difficult for them to lay off workers, they rapidly downsized their work forces.

Those who had warned about budget deficits claimed that the wolf was here at last. Political leaders extracted the message that increases in budget deficits would have disastrous consequences for business confidence. As a consequence, the provision allowing the repeal of the Gramm-Rudman targets if the economy went into recession was suspended. Spending was cut, and even some minor taxes were increased, in an effort to prevent the budgetary situation from deteriorating.

The result was the worst recession since the Depression. Unemployment rose to 11 percent and real GNP declined by 7 percent. For the first time since the war, there was a decline from year to year in the consumption of nondurable goods.

Could this really happen? For the most part, it depends on how the government carries out its lender-of-last-resort responsibility, an issue discussed in the next section. Here I comment on two other aspects of the scenario. Both address the macroeconomic policy response to a weakening economy.

As table 3.1 demonstrates, a major difference between the pre-and post-World War II economies is the presence of *automatic stabilizers* in the postwar economy. Before World War II, a $1-drop in GNP translated into a $.95 decline in disposable income. Since the war, less each $1 change in GNP has translated into a drop of only $.39 in GNP. This change is largely the result of the expansion of government's role in the economy. When the economy slumps, government tax collections decline and government transfer payments increase, both of which cushion the decline in disposable income. The mirror image of stability in disposable income is instability in the government deficit. Hence, automatic stabilizers cannot work if the government seeks to maintain a constant budget deficit in the face of changing economic conditions.

The other fundamentally important change over the past 50 years regards monetary policy. Quite apart from whatever it does or does not do to back up financial institutions that get in trouble, the Federal Reserve has the ability to alter the money stock through open market operations. In the face of a deflationary crisis like the one described above, it is hard to see why it would not be appropriate to pursue an expansionary monetary policy that would prevent the expectation of deflation from pushing real interest rates way up. The use of such a policy would at least limit the spillover consequences of financial

Table 3.1   **Relation between National Income and Disposable Income**

Period	Effect of $1 Change in National Income on Disposable Income	$\bar{R}^2$
1898–1916	.76	.54
	(.16)	
1923–40	.95	.61
	(.24)	
1949–82	.39	.59
	(.06)	

Source: J. Bradford De Long and Lawrence H. Summers. 1986. The changing cyclical variability of economic activity in the United States. In *The American business cycle: Continuity and change*, ed. Robert J. Gordon, 679–719. Chicago: University of Chicago Press.
Note: The table shows regressions of the change in annual disposable income on the change in national income. Standard errors are in parentheses.

institution failures. Whether it would be enough to fully contain the damage is the issue of whether a lender of last resort is necessary, the subject of the next section.

3.2 The Lender-of-Last-Resort Function

Most treatments of financial crisis assign a central role to what is or is not done by the lender of last resort. In its 1984 submission to the Bush Commission on Financial Deregulation, the Federal Reserve highlighted the primacy of its lender-of-last-resort function:

> A basic continuing responsibility of any central bank—and the principal reason for the founding of the Federal Reserve—is to assure stable and smoothly functioning financial and payments systems. These are the prerequisites for, and complementary to, the central bank's responsibility for conducting monetary policy as it is more narrowly conceived. . . . What has not changed, and is not likely to change, is the idea that a central bank must, to the extent possible, head off and deal with financial disturbances and crises.
>
> To these ends the Congress has over the last 70 years, authorized the Federal Reserve (*a*) to be a major participant in the nation's payments mechanism, (*b*) to lend at the discount window as the ultimate source of liquidity for the economy, and (*c*) to regulate and supervise key sectors of the financial markets, both domestic and international. These functions are in addition to, and largely predate, the more purely "monetary" functions of engaging in open market and foreign exchange operations and setting reserve requirements.

Accepting Congress's goal of maintaining a smoothly functioning payments and financial system, there remains the question of what public actions can best achieve this objective. I consider here four positions regarding the appropriate behavior of the lender of last resort, each of which has received substantial support in the history of thought on this subject.

3.2.1 Free Banking

The case for free banking, without a public lender of last resort, has undergone something of an intellectual revival in recent years. But as Goodhart (1985) stresses, it goes back to Bagehot (1873) and before. While Bagehot is remembered for his views on how a central bank should carry out the lender-of-last-resort function, he actually preferred a system of free banking. Thus he wrote:

> A large number of banks, each feeling that its credit was at stake in keeping a good reserve, probably would keep one; if anyone did not, it would be criticized constantly, and would soon lose its standing and in the end disappear. And such banks would meet an incipient panic freely and generously. They would advance out of their reserve boldly and know at such periods, it must show strength, if at such times it wishes to be thought to

have strength. Such a system reduces to a minimum the risk that is caused by the deposit. If the national money can safely be deposited in banks in any way, this is the way to make it safe. (Bagehot 1873, 104)

There is considerable controversy as to how well free banking worked during the historical periods in which it was tried. It is a fact, though, that the institution has not endured. A number of market failures associated with a free banking system may suggest the reasons why. Each ultimately relates back to problems of information asymmetry that call banking institutions into existence in the first place. The niche of the banker is his ability to assess creditworthiness, an ability borne of general experience and experience with particular borrowers. If a bank's assets could readily be evaluated by the public, there would be little need for banks as institutions.

The fact that the value of a bank's loan portfolio is private information has two important implications. First, it means that the bank cannot mark its portfolio to market continuously. This means that it must offer depositors fixed dollar repayments, creating the possibility of runs. Whenever a bank gets into trouble, the depositors who get their money out first do best. The situation is very different from that of equity holders in a company, who gain no advantage from moving quickly when public information suggests that their company is in trouble. Second, it means that bank assets are illiquid. If all bank assets could readily be traded on a secondary market, the need for banks would be greatly reduced. Firms could simply sell securities to the public without the need for an intermediary.

As the model of Diamond and Dybvig (1983) suggests, these two features of banking institutions are likely to lead to instability in the absence of public actions. More precisely, prophecies about a bank's health are likely to be self-fulfilling. A bank may be perfectly healthy as long as it is expected to remain perfectly healthy. But if it is expected to fail, depositors will demand their money. If the bank is forced to liquidate its asset portfolio at distress prices, because of the difficulty outsiders have in evaluating its components, the bank may become insolvent.

The instability associated with self-fulfilling prophecies is magnified by three further considerations. First, there may be "reputational externalities," where one bank's failure affects the public perception of the health of other banks.[4] This might be because of concern about the consequences of the failed bank's default, because of a perception that other banks hold portfolios similar to the portfolio of the bank that just failed, or because of concern about the macroeconomic ramifications of bank failures.

Second, bank failures will have an adverse impact on the firms that depend on them. To the extent that established relationships represent a kind of capital, beneficially owned by both borrower and creditor, both will suffer losses when a bank fails. To some extent, firms can avoid this problem by forming

---

4. I owe this term to Richard Zeckhauser.

relationships with a number of banks, but this obviously imposes costs of its own.

Third, bank failures and failures of the firms that depend on banks may have a pronounced impact on the level of aggregate demand. As banks contract credit, the supply of money declines. Especially if the price level does not react immediately, the result will be higher real interest rates, which will tend to discourage spending as well as increase the pressure on financially fragile institutions. This transmission mechanism figures prominently in many accounts of the onset of the Depression (e.g., Friedman and Schwartz 1963).

All of these factors suggest that economists' traditional presumption in favor of free and unregulated markets cannot be reflexively applied to financial institutions. This is especially the case when there are already substantial interventions in the market, through deposit insurance and through the tendency of market actors rightly or wrongly to suppose that the government is likely to bail out institutions that get into trouble. However, establishing that the market's functioning will be impaired by information problems does not demonstrate that improvements are possible, given that governments also lack complete information. I turn next to the consideration of possible active lender-of-last-resort strategies.

3.2.2   A Monetarist Lender of Last Resort

Historical accounts of panics always emphasize the effect of failing financial institutions on the money supply and the adverse effects of a falling money stock on economic performance. A minimalist view of the function of the central bank would hold that, in the face of a major disturbance, it should use open market operations to make sure that the money stock, somehow defined, is not allowed to decline precipitously; a more activist view would seek to insure that it rises rapidly enough to offset any decline in velocity associated with financial panic. On this monetarist view, there is no need for the Fed to make use of the discount window or moral suasion in the face of crisis. It suffices to make enough liquidity available.

Goodfriend and King (1988) argue that "banking" policy as distinct from monetary policy is unnecessary. Providing emergency loans to institutions suffering liquidity problems is similar to the line-of-credit service that the private sector already provides. It is not obvious why the Fed is more efficient than the private sector at the monitoring and supervision that is required. A policy of maintaining liquidity but not helping out specific institutions has the virtue of avoiding political pressures to bail out insolvent institutions and of making it more difficult for institutions that are in trouble to exploit the protection provided by deposit insurance in order to take on excessive risks.[5] These features help ex post, ex ante; they also discourage risk taking.

---

5. This could be done by pledging a bank's best collateral to the Fed, and then using the proceeds to pay off uninsured depositors.

Is this approach sufficient to contain the damage that financial crisis might otherwise cause? Relevant experience is scarce, since the modern Federal Reserve has taken a more active role in times of crisis, and crises in earlier times usually coincided with sharp declines in the money stock. But the analysis of the potential difficulties with a free banking system suggests that support of specific institutions, rather than just the money stock, may be desirable. Declines in the money stock are just one of the potential adverse impacts of bank failures. Bank failures, or the failure of financial institutions more generally imposes external costs on firms with whom they do business and through the damage they do to the reputations of other banks. Private lenders have no incentive to take account of these external benefits, and so there is a presumption that they will lend too little.

The point here may be put in a different way. Because of the relationship-specific capital each has accumulated, reserves at one bank are an imperfect substitute for reserves at another. Maintaining a given aggregate level of lending is not sufficient to avoid the losses associated with a financial disturbance.

There is one reasonably clear lesson from the crash period. It would not have been sufficient for the Fed to keep the money stock growing steadily. As table 3.2 illustrates, their successful action, involved rapid money growth. By almost any measure, monetary policy turned highly expansionary during the crash period. Had there been no market break, it is extremely unlikely that monetary policy would have been so expansionary. In this sense, the Fed did more than avoid the transmission of the financial disturbance to the real economy through a declining money stock.

Table 3.2   **Federal Reserve Activity and the Crash of 1987**

A. Money Supply

Monetary Measure	% Growth Rate (Annualized)	
	October 1987	Average 1987
Monetary Base	11.9	7.0
M1	15.2	3.1
M2	7.0	3.3
M3	7.8	4.8
L	10.1	5.0

B. Federal Reserve Credit (Billion $US)

Measure	October 7	October 14	October 21	October 28	November 4	November 11	November 18
Credit	237.9	239.5	243.5	251.3	236.1	240.4	237.9
Loans	1.4	.9	3.2	.8	.6	.5	.7
Float	1.3	2.1	1.1	2.0	.6	.6	1.5

Source: Federal Reserve Board. Various issues. *Federal Reserve Bulletin.*

Journalistic accounts (e.g., Metz 1988) leave the impression that, in addition to the provision of liquidity, moral suasion (arm twisting?) was a major element of the Fed's response to the crash as it sought to convince major banks to support other financial institutions. Evaluating its importance for the ultimate outcome is difficult. However, an alternative elaboration of the scenario developed in the previous section makes it plausible that it might have been quite important.

Stung by continuing criticisms of policies that had led the government to incur a $400 billion dollar S&L bailout, policymakers were skittish about standing behind ailing institutions of any kind. Following the advice of the Shadow Open Market Committee, who issued a report in 1990 urging that the Federal Reserve confine its lender-of-last-resort role to preventing the money stock from falling below its 'normal growth path' and avoiding any sharp run-up in real interest rates, the Fed announced its intention to provide liquidity to the system, but made it clear that the choice of what banks did with their increased reserves was entirely up to them.

Bankers considered the risk-return ratio on short-term loans to several major firms caught out by differences in the settlement periods between different markets. They realized that it did not take much of a risk that their loans would somehow go bad, to offset the opportunity to earn premium interest rates over a period of days or weeks. There were limits on the interest rates banks could charge, since the willingness of a customer to pay a high interest rate indicated the depth of its problems. After rumors began to circulate that one major investment house had failed to properly hedge a major underwriting commitment, the banks pulled in their lines of credit. While the Federal funds rate fell by 350 basis points overnight, several major securities firms had difficulty getting credit, and one went under, bringing down a major clearing house.

The markets were closed for a day as the damage was sorted out. When an attempt was made to reopen them, it was impossible to find buyers. Fearing that the markets might close again, locking them in, no major buyers came forward even as prices fell. The panic continued . . .

The crucial point here is that driving down the federal funds rate is not likely to be sufficient to stop prophecies that predict the failure of banks or securities firms from proving to be self-fulfilling. A more ambitious set of lender-of-last-resort policies would seem to be necessary.

3.2.3 The Classical Lender of Last Resort

The classical view of proper behavior of the lender-of-last-resort dates back at least to Bagehot (1873). It may be stated briefly as follows: central banks should adopt, announce, and follow a policy of lending freely and aggressively but at a penalty rate to all sound but no unsound borrowers in time of crisis. Thus Bagehot writes "in wild periods of alarm, one failure makes many and the best way to prevent the derivative failures is to arrest the primary failure which causes them" (25). He continues, "If people could be convinced that utter ruin is not coming, most likely they would cease to run in such a mad way for money" (64). And he recognizes that "the way to cause alarm is to refuse someone who has good security to offer" (97).

Bagehot was well aware of the potential adverse incentive effects of providing insurance. This awareness accounted for his admonition that the lender of last resort should "never lend to unsound people" (97). He also insisted that loans in time of crisis be made at a penalty rate. This was intended to discourage regular reliance on the lender of last resort, to discourage risk taking by financial institutions, and to enable the Bank of England to make profits. Bagehot regarded it as critically important that a lender-of-last-resort policy be preannounced in writing: "Until we have on this point what loans will be made in times of crisis, a clear understanding with the Bank of England, both our liability for crisis and our terror at crisis will always be greater than they would otherwise be" (101).

Bagehot's approach is appealing. It offers the promise that panics will be controlled, but that excessive risk taking will be penalized. His admonitions amount to asserting that the central bank should be wise and should prevent panics but not interfere when institutions are on the verge of failing for fundamental reasons. But, they beg the fundamental question of how liquidity and solvency problems are to be distinguished in the very short time in which a lender of last resort must act. If no one doubted an institution's solvency, it is hard to see how it could experience liquidity problems.

As the scenario developed in the previous subsection suggests, the steps that Bagehot recommends the central bank take to avoid encouraging excessive risk taking also compromise its effectiveness in time of crisis. The reputation externalities, loss of relationship-specific capital, and the macroeconomic fallout of the bank failure do not depend on whether it failed for liquidity reasons or because it was fundamentally insolvent. High interest rates on government loans make it more difficult for banks to meet their other obligations. And banks that pay them send signals that they are in serious trouble, signals that will be destabilizing in times of panic.

3.2.4   The Modern Pragmatic View

Garcia and Plautz (1988) carefully compare the behavior of the American Federal Reserve with the classic lender-of-last-resort concept. Four important differences stand out. First, current practice is to make loans only to depository institutions and only indirectly to other financial institutions. During the crash, the Fed did not make direct loans to clearing houses or to investment banks that experienced liquidity problems, but instead encouraged banks to loan to them while maintaining their prudential standards. Depending on just how hard arms are twisted, the distinction may be immaterial. But as other institutions take on more and more of the attributes of banks, the risk that they too will face runs increases.

Second, the extent of the government safety net has not been explicitly spelled out. It is clear that deposit insurance extends de facto more widely than it extends de jure, but its exact extent has never been made clear. This probably reflects concerns about moral hazard. Preserving the possibility that the government will not step in encourages depositors to scrutinize financial institutions and institutions to reduce their risk taking. This virtue of ambiguity must be traded off against the increase in the risk of panic that it creates. It is noteworthy that the Fed waited until Tuesday morning, 20 October, to reaffirm its commitment to providing liquidity.

Third, the Federal Reserve under some circumstances does support institutions that are insolvent, as the Cleveland District Bank explicitly recognized in its 1985 report. This practice obviously runs the risk made all too real by the S&L experience of encouraging excessive risk taking. But it may be necessary if stability is to be preserved. The definition of solvency in a situation where the value of bank assets depends on how rapidly they must be liquidated is ambiguous.

There is one additional aspect of the problem, a detailed discussion of which is beyond the scope of this paper. Instantly closing insolvent institutions may wreak havoc with the payments mechanism. As a Federal Reserve memorandum of May 1985, quoted in Humphrey (1986) notes: "Total daylight overdrafts average $110 to $120 billion per day. . . . On any given day about 1600 to 1700 institutions are in overdraft." Humphrey contemplates the possible impact of the failure of a single institution. He shows what would happen if a randomly selected large participant in the CHIPS system failed on a random day. In his simulation, the consequence would be that 24 other institutions would then be unable to meet their commitments. This in turn would lead to the failure of another 26 institutions.

Fourth, the Federal Reserve has in the past provided support at below rather than above market rates. When it supports nondepository institutions indirectly by making funds available to the banking system as it did during the crash, it does not charge a penalty rate. Even in the Bank of New York episode described by Volcker (1986) when the Fed made a $23 billion loan because of a computer problem the bank was experiencing, assistance was extended at a rate well below the Federal funds rate. Again, the conflict between the goal of discouraging risk taking and resolving the crisis is apparent.

The modern pragmatic approach has the very substantial virtue of having prevented the financial disruptions of recent years from having had substantial consequences for the real economy. It is difficult to gauge the price of this success. Almost certainly, the subsidy provided by the presence of a lender of last resort has led to some wasteful investments and to excessive risk taking. I am not aware of serious estimates of the magnitude of these costs. Estimates of the cost of bailouts, which represent transfers, surely greatly overestimate the ex ante costs of inappropriate investments. If the presence of an active lender of last resort has avoided even one percentage point in unemployment sustained for one year, it has raised U.S. income by more than $100 billion. It would be surprising if any resulting misallocation of investment were to prove nearly this large.

Lender-of-last-resort policy is probably an area where James Tobin's insight that "it take a heap of Harberger triangles to fill an Okun gap" is relevant. It may well be that the moral hazard associated with lender-of-last-resort insurance is better controlled by prudential regulation than by scaling the insurance back. This at least is the modern pragmatic view that has worked so far.

3.3   How Might Crisis Come?

The primary adverse side effects associated with an aggressive lender-of-last-resort policy like the one advocated in the previous section involve moral hazard. In the presence of a Federal safety net, depositors will not scrutinize the loan portfolios of financial institutions. This will encourage excess risk taking. The problem is magnified because a few aggressive institutions can put pressure on the rest by offering premium interest rates. Safe institutions that do not desire to take unfair advantage of lender-of-last-resort protection then must choose between raising the rates they offer and accepting fewer deposits. Just as bad money drives out good, there is a tendency for bad financial institutions to drive out good ones.

The question of how best to manage the moral hazard effects of lender-of-last-resort activity is beyond the scope of this paper. Raising bank capital requirements would seem to be an obvious approach. In this section I ask a different question. Are there any circumstances in which excessively aggressive lender-of-last-resort behavior could exacerbate rather than mitigate financial crisis? Here is a continuation of the scenario developed above that may be instructive in considering this question.

As the market declined sharply and the Federal Reserve promised to provide all necessary liquidity to the system, the Federal funds rate dropped very sharply. Market participants thought back to the experience of the crash of 1987. They recalled that between October of 1987 and the end of the year, the dollar fell by almost 15 percent against the yen and other major currencies. Given that, the financial distress was greater this time around than it had been in 1987, the U.S. external debt and underlying inflation rates were greater than they had been in 1987, and that experience in the late 1980s suggested that exchange rate intervention was both less efficacious and less frequently practiced than it had been earlier, speculators concluded that the dollar was likely to drop further than it had after the October 1987 crash.

The dollar dropped 4 percent as daily volume in the foreign exchange market approached $1 trillion. As the dollar fell, technical trading systems, which by some estimates drove 80 percent of all trading activity, picked up the downward momentum and sent signals that the dollar was to be sold. Recognizing the possibility of a dollar collapse, many firms rushed to hedge their holding of dollar assets by purchasing long-term dollar puts. As the issuers of these puts moved to hedge their position, the dollar came under further selling pressure.

No one doubted that the U.S. government would meet its obligations on Treasury bills. But a rumor started in Tokyo that the FDIC and the Federal Reserve Bank were looking at ways of standing behind Americans but not foreigners in troubled American banks. The realization spread that foreigners accounted for more than half of deposits at several major American banks, just as they had at Continental Illinois. Many foreign investors rushed to sell dollar assets. The remainder refused to roll over CDs issued by heavily exposed American banks and instead purchased Treasury bills. Banks that depended on foreign deposits started experiencing very heavy withdrawals.

The Federal Reserve received conflicting advice. Some argued that the generous provision of liquidity was exacerbating the crisis. They argued that by driving down U.S. interest rates and by suggesting that the Fed was not concerned about the exchange rate, the policy of generously providing liquidity to financial institutions was actually counterproductive. Capital outflows caused by the expectation of a rapidly falling dollar actually were exceeding government capital infusions. Others claimed that, without a clear lender-of-last-resort commitment, the payments system would collapse and, at that point, flight from the dollar would accelerate.

Both arguments were correct. With a single instrument—the provision of liquidity—at its disposal, the Federal Reserve was unable to hit both a liquidity and an exchange rate target. American officials frantically sought international cooperation to reduce interest rates, so that U.S. rates could be reduced without causing a dollar panic. But they were refused. The Germans feared that inflationary consequences of the ongoing pre-1992 investment boom. The Japanese were not eager to help out and were especially reluctant to reduce interest rates at a time when the ratio of their land value to GNP was at an all time high.

After several weeks of chaos, an emergency monetary summit was convened. It was agreed that the major nations would fix the dollar exchange rate at a new parity level of 80 yen and 1.3 marks. U.S. monetary policy sought to maintain interest rates at a level consistent with these targets. Several large banks, but none of the largest banks, failed. Consumer confidence reached a record low. Nervous about the future, businesses curtailed their investment plans. Inflation increased sharply as import price increases fed through the system creating doubts about the Federal Reserve's ability to defend the 80 yen exchange rate. The economy sank into a deep recession . . .

The crucial point here is that the international dimension greatly complicates the problem of the lender of last resort. While sufficiently activist lender-of-last-resort policies can always contain a liquidity crisis, there is the risk that they will set off a currency crisis. Kindleberger (1973) suggests that this is what occurred during the Austrian Credit Anstalt crisis in 1971. In the face of crisis, the authorities need a second instrument so that a measure of stability can be maintained in both the foreign exchange market and the banking system.

There are two related strands in the argument that a combined liquidity-currency crisis could handcuff the monetary authority. First, if foreigners lose confidence in U.S. financial institutions at the same time they lose confidence in the dollar, simultaneous crises will occur. Beyond the possibility of a loss of confidence, they may simply, at some point, stop being willing to prop up a financial system in which they have already lost confidence. Koo (1989) makes a persuasive case that Japanese support for the dollar in 1987 was politically motivated at least in part and cost in real terms as much as the Marshall Plan. Second, apart from any fears foreigners may have about U.S. institutions, there is the risk that the lower interest rates that are part of the response to a domestic financial crisis will bring on a currency crisis.

One possible additional instrument for the authorities in time of crisis is fiscal policy. But it is hard to see what could be accomplished beyond some stabilization if aggregate demand started to decline. Excessive deficit increases are not likely to reassure foreigners who are fleeing from dollar assets. Nor are the higher interest rates that would result likely to reduce pressure on financial institutions. Reducing the deficit in the face of a major downturn is hardly the right response to crisis either. Realistically, changes in budget policy are not likely to be made or implemented quickly enough to have an immediate impact in time of crisis.

Yet another possibility is direct intervention to prop up asset prices. If this is possible, it will serve to increase confidence in the financial system and reduce the need for reductions in interest rates that would otherwise lead to a currency collapse. Journalistic accounts such as Stewart and Hertzberg (1987) suggest that manipulation of a minor but crucial futures market played an important role in preventing a further meltdown on Tuesday, 20 October 1987. They also assign a prominent role to orchestrated equity repurchases by major companies. Hale (1988) argues that the primary thrust of Japanese securities regulation in general, and especially in the aftermath of the crash, is raising the value of stocks rather than maintaining a "fair" marketplace in the American mode.

The difficulty here is that it is very uncertain whether interventions to prop up the market will work. Accounts of the crash period all suggest that the point of greatest danger was at midday on Tuesday, 20 October, after the Federal Reserve had made it clear that it would provide all necessary liquidity, and after a significant market rally. The situation was turned around, but if a misstep had been made, or if the MMI contract had not mysteriously rallied by the equivalent of over 300 Dow points within a few minutes, the market might have fallen much further.

The scenario alluded to a final possible additional instrument—foreign monetary policy. If it can be dedicated to the foreign exchange market, then domestic policy can concentrate on the domestic objective of providing liquidity. In a sense though, this just pushes the problem back one stage. If other nations dedicate their monetary policy to achieving a foreign exchange target, they lose the ability to conduct monetary policy with a view to domestic objectives. They may therefore be unable or unwilling to cooperate when crisis comes. Perhaps this is an argument for fixing exchange rates or at least institutionalizing the principle of cooperation to insure that they do not move too rapidly.

Notice that the argument in this section strongly supports the conclusion of the last one that there is a case for direct lender-of-last-resort policies beyond the general provision of liquidity. Targeted assistance can presumably restore confidence in financial institutions with less of a reduction in interest rates than would be necessary with general monetary policies.

3.4 Conclusions

Could the United States again experience a financial crisis like those that so frequently disrupted the real economy before World War II? As with the problem of assessing the risk of major war, one is fortunate that there is not enough relevant experience to permit an accurate judgment. But there is cause for concern.

Kindleberger's preconditions for crisis are as likely to be satisfied today as they ever have been in the past. It is probably now easier to lever assets than ever before and the combination of reduced transactions costs and new markets in derivative securities make it easier than it has been in the past for the illusion of universal liquidity to take hold. Asset price bubbles are now as likely as they have ever been. Bubbles eventually burst. The increased speed with which information diffuses and the increased use of quantitative-rule-based trading strategies make it likely that they will burst more quickly today than they have in the past.

The suggestion is sometimes made that the 1987 experience may have encouraged more prudent behavior and so made bubbles less likely. There is little concrete evidence to support this hope. There have been only minor regulatory changes since the crash. While the usage of portfolio insurance has declined since the crash, various dynamic trading strategies, some of which rely on momentum and so give rise to positive feedback, continue to be widely used. Offsetting these stabilizing responses is the reality that the payments system has probably become more fragile than before as institutions have recognized the risks that their normal procedures exposed them to in times of crisis.

If financial crisis is less likely now than it used to be, the reason is the firewalls now in place that insulate the real economy from the effects of financial disruptions. Most important in this regard is the federal government's acceptance of the responsibility for stabilizing the economy. Automatic stabilizers that are now in place cushion the response of the economy to changes in demand conditions. At the same time, it is now nearly inconceivable that there would be no active lender of last resort in time of crisis. This makes crisis caused by contagious bank failures much less likely than in the past. It also means that whatever happens to financial institutions, the money stock will not be allowed to collapse.

These factors must be balanced against the difficulty of providing liquidity in time of crisis when exchange rates are flexible and expectations are extrapolative. Because the risk of a currency collapse is now greater than it was when exchange rates were fixed and the world's capital markets are tightly interconnected, the monetary authority's scope to act as a lender of last resort has surely been reduced.

References

Bagehot, W. 1873. *Lombard Street.* London.

Barsky, R., and J. B. De Long. 1989. Dividend growth and stock prices. Harvard University. Mimeograph.

Cutler, D., J. Poterba, and L. Summers. 1989. Speculative dynamics. Mimeograph.

Diamond, D., and P. Dybvig. 1983. Bank runs, deposit insurance, and liquidity. *Journal of Political Economy* 91, no. 3 (June):401–19.

Friedman, M., and A. Schwartz. 1963. *A monetary history of the United States.* Princeton, N.J.: Princeton University Press.

Garcia, G., and E. Plautz. 1988. *The Federal Reserve: Lender of last resort.* Cambridge, Mass.: Ballinger.

Goodfriend, M., and R. King. 1988. Financial deregulation, monetary policy, and central banking. In *Restructuring banking and financial services in America,* ed. W. S. Haraf and R. M. Kushmeider. Washington, D.C.: American Enterprise Institute.

Goodhart, C. 1985. *The evolution of central banking.* London: London School of Economics and Political Science.

Goldsmith, R. 1982. Comment on Minsky. In *Financial crises: Theory, history and Policy,* ed. C. Kindleberger and J-P. Laffargue. New York: Cambridge University Press.

Hale, D. 1988. Market regulation and the crash. In Kansas City Federal Reserve Board Conference on Financial Market Volatility.

Humphrey, David. 1986. Payments finality and the risk of settlement failure. In *Technology and the Regulation of Financial Markets,* ed. Anthony Saunders and Lawrence J. White. Lexington, Mass.: Lexington Books.

Kindleberger, C. 1973. *The world in depression, 1929–1939.* Berkeley: University of California Press.

————. 1978. *Manias, panics, and crashes: A history of financial crisis.* Basic Books. (Rev. ed., 1989).

Koo, R. 1989. Testimony before the Joint Economic Committee.

Metz, Tim. 1988. *Black Monday.* New York: Morrow.

Minsky, H. 1982. The financial instability hypothesis: Capitalist production and the behavior of the economy. In *Financial crises: Theory, history and policy,* ed. C. Kindleberger and J-P. Laffargue. New York: Cambridge University Press.

Schwartz, A. 1986. Real and pseudo-financial crises. In *Financial crises and the world banking system,* ed. F. Capie and G. Wood. New York: St. Martin's.

Stewart, J., and Hertzberg, D. 1987. How the stock market almost disintegrated a day after the crash. *Wall Street Journal* (November 20), 1.

Summers, L., and V. Summers. 1989. When markets work too well: A cautious case for securities transactions taxes. *Journal of Financial Services Research.*

Volcker, P. 1986. Statement before the Subcommittee on Domestic Monetary Policy, House Committee on Banking, Finance, and Urban Affairs. Reprinted in *Federal Reserve Bulletin.*

2. Hyman P. Minsky

The Financial Instability Hypothesis: A Clarification

The background papers refer to Minsky's financial instability hypothesis without filling in the details. I thought that we might as well hear about the hypothesis from the horse's mouth, although we all know that an author is not necessarily an authentic interpreter of a work.

The financial instability hypothesis was advanced as an interpretation of Keynes's General Theory when issues of interpretation were deemed important (Minsky 1975, 1982, 1986). The conceit is that Keynes was aware of the great contraction and wholesale collapse of the financial and economic system of 1929–33 as he was developing the General Theory. In particular, I assumed that Fisher's debt-deflation theory of great depressions (Fisher 1933) was known to Keynes.

The financial instability hypothesis is addressed to this economy rather than to an abstract economy. Our economy is taken to be a capital-using capitalist economy with complex, sophisticated, and ever-evolving financial institutions and usages. The model focuses on the relations between finance, asset values, and investment. It can be characterized as a Wall Street view of the world: the principal players are profit-seeking bankers and businessmen.

I will briefly examine how the financial instability hypothesis addresses five issues: asset pricing, financial flows, the relation between financial and economic crises, why it has not yet happened, and what it might take for it to happen.

Asset Pricing

In chapter 17 of the *General Theory*, in the rebuttal to Viner's incisive review (Viner 1936; Keynes 1937a) and in the contribution to the Fisher festschrift (Keynes 1937b), Keynes treated liquidity preference as determining the price level of capital and financial assets.[1]

I take Keynes's fundamental insight to be that there are two price levels in a capitalist economy and that the proximate determinants of these price levels are quite different. One is of current wages and output, which, when combined with financing conditions, yields the supply conditions for investment output. The other is of capital and financial assets, which, when combined with financing conditions, yields the demand for investment output. The supply prices of investment output can best be viewed as a markup on labor costs, whereas the prices of capital and financial assets are capitalizations of future expected cash flows, of future gross profits in an uncertain world.

For a skeletal no-government capitalist economy to be prosperous, the price of a large enough set of capital assets needs to be greater than the price at which similar assets can be produced by a large enough margin so that an investment large enough to sustain an acceptable level of profits and thus of employment and output takes place.[2] Financial mechanisms enter into determining investment by affecting the prices of capital assets, production costs of investment output, and the leverage on internal finance.

Following Keynes, each asset yields expected, though uncertain, cash flows through time, q, has expected carrying costs, c, and has a liquidity premium, I, which will vary as institutions and circumstances change.[3] The I of a particular asset reflects the ease with which it can be turned into money either by being pledged for loans or by being sold: this I depends upon the structure and performance of markets and institutions. Developments that have an impact on the way markets and institutions function change the I embodied in an asset.

Money is the asset that is transferred when financial commitments are fulfilled. In this construct money does not yield a cash flow, has minimal carrying costs, and has the maximum liquidity. The price per unit of money is always 1. Money prices of other assets are such that the utility of the expected cash flows net of the carrying costs plus the utility of the liquidity of the asset, as conditioned by the ever-evolving financial system, are equal on the margin to the utility of the liquidity embodied in money.

---

1. Jan Kregel (1987) traces Keynes's treatment of money as determining capital asset prices to Sraffa's (1932a, 1932b) discussion of own rates of interest in his refutation of Hayek's natural-rate-of-interest argument.

2. In a complex big-government capitalist economy, investment can be supplemented by a government deficit to yield an acceptable level of profits.

3. The q's that capital assets, as collected in firms, yield are gross profits. The q's that financial instruments yield are stated in the contracts. What are c-carrying costs to debtors are q-expected cash receipts to creditors.

An increase in the quantity of money lowers, on the margin, the utility of a dollar. In order to lower on the margin the utility of a dollar invested in assets whose value is derived mainly from the expected q's, the dollar price of such q-yielding assets needs to rise. As assets possess different mixes of q, c, and I, a change in the quantity of money will change the relative prices of assets and the price levels of assets and investment output: both the amount and the composition of investment will be affected. In this construct money is never a mere veil, it is never neutral.

For the purposes of the financial instability hypothesis, the c's, the carrying costs, incorporate the cash costs imposed by the liabilities that are used to finance positions in capital and financial assets. As the liabilities of a unit are financial assets of other units, the prices of the c-yielding instruments that are used to finance positions are determined by the same expected cash flows, carrying costs, and liquidity concerns that determine the values of q-yielding instruments. A rise in the subjective valuation of liquidity, a fall in the expected profit flows, or a rise in the carrying costs of capital and financial assets will lower the prices of capital and financial assets.

Financial Flows

Liabilities are commitments to pay money at some date, on demand, or if specified contingencies occur. These payment commitments are for both the repayment of principal and income. Cash to meet these payment commitments is obtained either as: (1) income due to contributions to production (gross profits, or profits, wages, and taxes when the model is opened), (2) the fulfillment by some other agent of contractual commitments; (3) the result of borrowing or selling assets, or, trivially, (4) initial cash on hand.

Liabilities in a balance sheet can be read as generating a time series of cash payments, and assets can be read as generating a time series of expected receipts. I classified the structure of these time series as hedge, speculative, and Ponzi finance.[4]

A unit is hedge financing if the expected cash flows from operations or from contract fulfillment over the relevant horizon always exceed, with some margin of safety, the expected contractual, demand, and contingent payments. A firm whose liability structure is heavily weighted by equities is almost always hedge financing. Only if a large shortfall of income below expected income occurs will a hedge unit have difficulty meeting its payment commitments.

A unit is engaged in speculative finance when its expected cash receipts on income account and contract fulfillments exceed the income (interest) payments, but it is not able to pay all of the principal due on its debts. A specu-

---

4. I have been criticized for this terminology, especially for the use of the label "Ponzi" for a financing posture that can be the result of honest error.

lative unit needs to roll over some of its debts, to issue new debts in order to repay maturing debts. Speculative financing units have a position that they have to refinance periodically. A bank has to continually refinance its position.

A Ponzi financing unit does not earn enough on its income account to fulfill its income account payments and so issues debts to meet these payments: its deficit is capitalized. A Ponzi financing unit debits its equity account even as it increases its indebtedness. As recent experience with S&L's has shown, sharp increases in financing charges can transform speculative units into Ponzi units. The present budget position of the United States can be interpreted as an example of Ponzi financing.

Ponzi financing can be accepted as long as it is believed that the situation is transitory and that projected incomes will make the present value of the entire stream of earnings positive. Ponzi units are vulnerable to changes in what is believed about future income prospects and to increases in the cost of funds.

Financial and Economic Crises

This meeting is a roundtable on reducing the risks of economic crisis. The three background papers are on financial, not economic, crisis; furthermore, the papers are not clear on how financial and economic crises are related. The financial instability hypothesis is designed to throw light on the relation between financial and economic crises.

The financial instability hypothesis relates finance and aggregate demand through the impact of financial market events upon investment and the impact of investment upon income and on the flows that are capitalized into the price level of capital and financial assets and that are used to fulfill payment commitments.[5] One way financial market events affect investment is by affecting the subjective valuation placed upon I. A rise in the subjective value of I leads to a decline in the money price of capital and financial assets, which are valued mainly for their q's, the money income they yield. A fall in these prices lowers the difference between the prices of capital assets and the supply prices of investment output. This will tend to lower investment. Furthermore, a fall in the price of financial assets means that investing units will have to pledge larger future payments in order to obtain a given amount of investment financing. Such a change in the terms of financing tends to constrain investment.

There are two sources of liquidity: (1) the cash flows from operations or the fulfillment of contracts and (2) the cash flows that can be generated by selling or pledging assets—those assets which it is believed can be readily sold or pledged to raise cash in case the need arises carry lower interest rates.

5. In the version I prefer, investment leads to an aggregate of profits and the competition of firms for profits leads to output, employment, and the wage bill. Alternatively output and wage and profit incomes can be considered as the result of a multiplier process upon investment and other autonomous spending.

When the successful performance of the economy increases the subjective assuredness of the cash flows from operations, the felt need by businessmen and bankers for liquidity through asset holdings decreases. A lower valuation of liquidity in assets leads to a rise in the price of assets that are valued for the q's they yield. Similarly, if the felt "unsuredness" of the flow of q's increases, bankers and businessmen will move to increase the assets they hold that are valued for the I they yield.

A special proposition of the financial instability hypothesis is that over a protracted period of good times, when the aggregate of the cash flows from operations (aggregate profits) continuously increases, the value of portfolio liquidity declines. Both borrowers and lenders feel that they can safely decrease their holdings of assets that are valued for their liquidity through marketability. In particular, if hedge financing dominates then, as good times roll along, financing costs become such that profit-seeking units that were hedge financing will introduce speculative or rollover financing into their liability structures. The mix of hedge and speculative financing shifts over protracted periods of good times so that the weight of hedge financing decreases and the weight of speculative financing increases. Income shortfalls and interest rate increases transform speculative financing units into Ponzi financing units. In addition, the "euphoria" induced by protracted good times leads to de nova Ponzi financing arrangements that can be validated only if rather optimistic prices can be obtained for assets. As a result the vulnerability of the financial structure to rising interest rates and to shortfalls in gross profits increases with protracted good times.[6]

A concept worth introducing is the making of position by selling out position. When a unit has payment commitments and has been stripped of the assets that can readily be sold or pledged to acquire cash, a shortfall of income from operations or a rise in market interest rates can lead to an attempt to make position by selling or pledging assets that are not usually sold or pledged. The making of position by selling position may be feasible as an isolated incident, but any generalized attempt to make position by selling out position leads to a collapse of asset values. A financial crisis occurs when there is a generalized need to make position by selling out position, which results in a wide and large fall in asset values. As a result, the solvency, on a mark-to-market valuation, of a wide array of financial institutions is compromised. This leads to a spread of refinancing problems.

A financial crisis leads into an economic crisis when investment declines so that a decline in profits as well as output, employment, and wages takes place. The decline in profits leads to both a further fall in asset values (the numerators in the capitalization relation fall) and a further decline in the ability of

---

6. In early versions I had a "nice" accelerator-multiplier process always working. When the financial structure was robust the normal cyclical pattern took place. As the time without a deep and long depression increased, the financial system evolved and became fragile so that a normal downturn was amplified by financial repercussions.

units to meet their financial commitments. In such an environment a sharp fall in commitments for the financing of investment takes place. Further declines in employment, output, wage incomes, and profits follow.

With a lag, unemployment and idle capacity lead to a fall in wages and the prices of investment output. But in a world where debts denominated in money are large, declines in wages and prices may make things worse, not better (Caskey and Fazzari 1987).

Why "It" Hasn't Happened Yet

Apt intervention can abort the process I have sketched at two points. One is that units can be refinanced, so they have no need to try to make position by selling out position. This prevents a sharp and generalized fall in asset prices. The spread of mark-to-market insolvency to units that are not in an immediate need for refinancing will not take place. Refinancing banks and key financial market players that are having trouble making position is the basic central bank lender-of-last-resort operation. Presumably such refinancing takes place when dire systemwide repercussions are believed to be imminent if refinancing is not undertaken.

In various embryonic financial crises since the 1960s the Federal Reserve, specialized agencies such as FDIC and FSLIC, and the U.S. Treasury have refinanced units that otherwise would have had to make position by selling position. Furthermore, in the incipient crises the Federal Reserve has furnished reserves on a generous scale to markets. (Giordano 1987). Because of these measures no generalized or long-lasting interactive process that led to a wide and deep decline of asset prices has taken place during the postwar period.

The second intervention point is profit flows, the aggregate of the q's that come from the income generating and production system. The model for aggregate profits that I use is derived from Kalecki. In the simple heroically abstract version, aggregate profits equal investment; in a version that is a bit less heroic, aggregate profits equal investment plus the government deficit.

The federal government was some 3% of GNP in 1929. The federal government is say 25% of GNP now. The 1929 government was not large enough to run a deficit that would offset the impact that the massive decline of investment between 1929 and 1933 had upon aggregate profits.[7] Today's government is large enough that the automatic and policy response increases in deficits that occur when income decreases sustain aggregate profits.

The combination of lender-of-last-resort interventions, which abort the development of debt-deflation processes, the generalized increase in liquidity as the Federal Reserve reacts to an embryonic crisis, and the deficits that big government runs when income turns down explains why a serious, long-

---

7. It is worth noting that, because of the fall in nominal GNP, the relative size of government doubled between 1929 and 1933.

lasting and deep depression has not taken place up until now. Big government and a central bank that is willing and able to intervene explain why it has not happened yet.

What It Might Take for It to Happen

The United States had a great deal of what we can call "fiscal autonomy" over almost all of the postwar period: there was no need for American policy-makers to be much concerned about adverse foreign reactions to the steps that were taken to contain and reverse episodes of embryonic financial instability and to the deficits that sustained domestic profits.

The situation may well be different now. The United States no longer is as autonomous or as powerful as in the past. Scenarios in which cooperation in maintaining global asset values and profit flows is necessary but not forthcoming can be sketched.

It is only necessary to examine an elaboration of the income accounts à la Kalecki to understand what is at issue. A rather full statement of the profit equation is: profits equal investment plus the government deficit minus the deficit in international trade plus consumption financed by incomes derived from profits minus savings out of wage incomes.

The U.S. deficit on trade account is a drain on domestic profits. Further-more, the accumulated deficits have led to large foreign holdings of U.S. financial assets. The large U.S. government deficit in relatively prosperous times means that the deficit that is needed to sustain profits in the aftermath of even an aborted financial crisis may well be enormous. In the environment that now exists, the interventions needed to sustain the economy the next time may well be beyond the combined efforts of the Federal Reserve and the Treasury.

Countries with large positions in offshore assets possess fiscal autonomy. If global profits are to be sustained such countries need to maintain domestic profits even as they run an international trade deficit. This typically requires these countries to be high consumption economies.

Furthermore, these countries need to take a leading position in whatever lender-of-last-resort interventions are needed. It may well be that the next time national responses will not do, and the apt international response may require a profound restructuring of the high-saving export-based economies: containing future economic and financial crises may depend more on what Japan and Europe do than upon the Federal Reserve and the U.S. Treasury.

Addenda

Point 1. The emphasis is upon the behavior of businessmen who manage the firms that "own" the capital assets of the economy and the banking community that arranges for the liability structure of these firms. Households are in the background although savings out of wages and consumption financed by profit incomes are household behaviors. The view can be expressed by paraphrasing Orwell, "All agents are equal but some agents are more equal than others."

Point 2. The economy is envisaged as a nonlinear time-dependent system so that endogenous processes can generate "incoherent" states. Cycles and the crises are not the result of shocks to the system or of policy errors, they are endogenous.

Point 3. As Peter Albin put it, "Agents in the model have a model of the model; a model of the economy." The agents the financial instability hypothesis emphasizes are profit-seeking businessmen and bankers. The model of the economy they have includes the possibility of financial crisis and economic depressions. However, agents recognize that the institutional structure and the structure of possible interventions change, so that the past is an imperfect guide to the present and the future. We can assume that each agent has a contingency plan of how to react to an incipient financial crisis but is not sure as to when the contingency plan should be put in motion.

Point 4. Success in aborting incipient financial crises and in containing economic declines decreases the value of *I* in the subsequent expansion. If an incipient crisis is successfully aborted, then, after a pause, portfolio adjustments that reflect a greater assurance that crises will be contained take place.

Point 5. The *I* of our formulation is a characteristic of both assets and liability structures. Any change in the view of the future that lowers the value placed upon *I* also increases the willingness of units to lever their position, to increase their payment commitments relative to their expected cash flows, and the willingness of bankers to finance such levered positions.

Point 6. The financial instability hypothesis is pessimistic. Capitalism is flawed in that thrusts to financial and economic crises are endogenous phenomena. An institutional structure and a pattern of intervention may attenuate the thrust to malfunctioning, but each success in containment leads to a further elaboration of the financial and economic relations that make the system prone to crisis. Success is a transitory phenomenon, although as the era since 1946 has shown the time in transit can be quite long.

Point 7. Big government is necessary to contain depressions because only the deficits of big government can prevent a collapse of aggregate profits. Policy needs to be directed to constructing apt government: government that is resource creating and that provides real income outside of the fee-for-service markets. We all hope that we are entering a post-cold-war world. In this world the problem of political economy is to create an effective government tax-and-spending structure that can do the job of stabilizing profits. Unfortunately, successful capitalism requires government to be "big" and this, in turn, implies a need for taxes to be high.

Point 8. The recent refinancing of the FSLIC shows that lender-of-last-resort intervention ultimately depends upon the faith and credit of the government. This faith and credit is worth something in the market only as government tax and spending programs lead to net cash flows in favor of government when the economy is functioning well. The government cannot be in a structural "Ponzi financing" posture: the in-place tax and spending programs need to show a surplus, not necessarily now but when things are going well. Thus, while the deficits that big government can run are necessary to sustain aggregate profits, and therefore to contain thrusts to depressions, the viability of lender-of-last-resort interventions depends upon government debt being acceptable in national and international portfolios. Such acceptability ultimately depends upon the government's ability to force a net cash flow in its favor, that is, to run a surplus. Deficits therefore must be transitory and a response to well-defined conditions.

Point 9. There is nothing in principle nor in the facts of an economy with debts that says that the United States cannot become an Argentina—a country whose debts, whether denominated in its own or in foreign currency, are not marketable.

References

Caskey, John, and Steve Fazzari. 1987. Aggregate demand contractions with nominal debt commitments: Is wage flexibility stabilizing? *Economic Inquiry* 25:583–97.
Fisher, Irving. 1933. The debt-deflation theory of great depressions. *Econometrica* 1:337–57.
Giordano, R. M. 1987. *The Federal Reserve's response to the stock market crash.* New York: Goldman Sachs Economic Research Group.
Keynes, John Maynard. 1937a. The general theory of employment. *Quarterly Journal of Economics* 51:209–23.
———. 1937b. The theory of the rate of interest. In *The lessons of monetary experience: Essays in honor of Irving Fisher,* ed. A. D. Gayer. New York: Farrar & Rinehart.
Kregel, J. 1987. The changing place of money in Keynes's theory from the "treatise" to the "general theory." In *Keynesian theory of planning models and quantitative economics,* ed. G. Gandolfo and F. Marzano. Padova: Guiffre.
Minsky, Hyman P. 1975. *John Maynard Keynes.* New York: Columbia University Press.
———. 1982. *Can "it" happen again?* New York: Sharpe.
———. 1986. *Stabilizing an unstable economy.* New Haven, Conn.: Yale University Press.
Sraffa, P. 1932a. Dr. Hayek on money and capital. *Economic Journal* 42:42–53.
———. 1932b. A rejoinder. *Economic Journal* 42:249–51.
Viner, Jacob. 1936. Mr. Keynes on the causes of unemployment. *Quarterly Journal of Economics* 51:147–67.

3. Paul A. Samuelson

A Personal View on Crises and Economic Cycles

Economic science is prone to cycles of theoretical fads. Before 1929, pundits believed that prosperity in agriculture was necessary if the economy was to be prosperous. "Food will win the War and write the Peace." That was First World War boilerplate, still being muttered by Jeremiahs of the mid-1920s who warned that hard times on the farms would bring on a world debacle.

After 1929 the saying that Wall Street crashes cause Main Street slumps became dogma. As recently as 1962, when President Kennedy lost his patience with Roger Blough of U.S. Steel, the resulting crack in the Dow Jones indexes was feared to entail a National Bureau recession for the American economy. At least that is what you would have learned if, trapped in any Sheraton Hotel and having exhausted the Moody Bible, you read the autobiography planted there by Ernest Henderson, the founder of the Sheraton hostelry chain and a self-taught expert in macroeconomics. Henderson, exaggerating my Rasputin powers over J. F. Kennedy, called me in to say: "Tell your man that in six months time we'll be in a real bad recession unless he backs down from his business bashing." I solemnly recorded in my little black COOP book that a recession would arrive by November 1962. But such are my powers over the head of state that by that date the GNP was in a nice recovery from its mini-growth-recession of earlier 1962. The post-Blough hiccough in the production index, by the way, was about what Franco Modigliani's MIT-Penn-Fed model predicted ought to result from the realized loss in consumer wealth and from the increase in the cost in investment funds implied by the drop in price/earnings ratios of common stocks.

Flushed with this imposing sample of victory, I had to wonder when Stan Fischer and Bob Merton scolded us economists for not taking the stock market more seriously as a macroeconomic phenomenon. Lay people take it too seriously. But economists, Fischer and Merton complained, do not take it seriously enough. Nonetheless, Modigliani and I discounted after 19 October 1987 the dire predictions that a worldwide recession was in the cards. (So did *all* of the 50 consensus forecasters followed by Blue Chip Indicators.) True, the drop in share wealth in October 1987 was fully the equal of the drop in share wealth in October 1929; and, internationally, the crisis and price attrition was in 1987 even more uniform than in 1929. True also, after 1929 came the worldwide depression that was not to be exorcised completely until World War II itself. However, although Franco and Jim Tobin and Bob Solow and I knew that Model-T Keynesianism had to add wealth magnitudes to its flow determinants, we also knew that it was only vulgar journalists who believed that the 25 percent rates of unemployment in 1933 United States and Germany were Granger-caused by the exits of capitalists from the unleaning towers of Wall Street.

As hundreds of banks failed, runs on 15,000 banks caused many thousands more of them to fail. The velocity of high-powered money rationally nose-dived as people chose to hold more currency and less deposits; the result was that, despite the contrived increase in the total of high-powered money throughout the early 1930s, the total nominal GNP shrank by half from 1929 to 1933. Monetarists, wise in their later time, indicted the Fed authorities for not creating whatever high-powered money it would have taken to keep money × velocity ahead of the eroding price level. Although no one could have beaten such a tautological rap, I concur in the view that departing militantly from orthodox finance in 1931 could have reduced greatly the historical decline in high-powered velocity and thereby saved much human suffering and economic waste.

Then, If Not Now?

Was there ever a cogent case for the thesis that panics and crises play a key role in economic slumps of real output and employment?

If you read the early literature on good times and bad times, you will get the impression that panics and crises were more important in the mechanism of business cycles back in the nineteenth century than they are now or have been since, say, 1913. I doubt that this is a safe guide to reality. Much of the alleged change in the role of panics must surely be an artifact of economists' previous lack of statistical knowledge about true economic history.

John Hicks in his last book exemplifies the fallacy. In *A Market Theory of Money* (Oxford University Press, 1989), Hicks writes: "Nineteenth-century cycles (were) not statistical cycles but a succession of crises" (vii). "I want to insist that this [concept of a statistical cycle] is not what Jevons and his contemporaries can have had in mind. . . . They were thinking of the sequence of trade crises which had marked the preceding half-century, occurring in 1825, 1837 (especially in America), 1847, 1857, and 1867" (94).

The weight of the evidence to me points otherwise. If a Christina Romer were able to go back and construct a representative index for the nineteenth century of real production, employment, price levels, investment, and profits, Lombard Street would perhaps be no more important in understanding Mitchell-type business cycles than Wall Street was in the 1920s or in the 1945–89 period.

Schumpeter hailed Clement Juglar as a great business-cycle pioneer—and named the intermediate business cycle after him—because he was allegedly the first to move from the crisis paradigm to the Mitchell-Hansen paradigm.

Adam Smith prattled about the division of labor in *The Wealth of Nations* without showing in his text any appreciation that the Industrial Revolution was bursting out around him. Nor could he have learned better from his excellent library.

So it was with Henry Thornton and John Stuart Mill. Their chronicles lack power as evidence for my present query: If Wall Street crashes have limited effects on Main Street in the last few decades of the twentieth century, was it truly different in 1929 and 1889 and 1839 and 1789?

I must be careful not to overstate my doubts. It may well have been the case that in earlier times the ratio of the value of stocks and bonds listed on bourses was *less* in relation to national wealth and GNP than in the post–World War II epoch. The Modigliani-Tobin partial derivatives, (consumption)/(wealth), may also have been smaller then rather than larger. And the effects of Lombard Street on the changes in the cost and availability of funds to finance investment may also have been limited the more we go back in history.

Nonetheless, I do not wish to deny—nay I want positively to emphasize—the fact that before 1930 we were in pure capitalism, whereas in 1987 we are a case of the mixed economy. The ability of a crisis/panic in Wall Street or Lombard Street to tip off a cascade of failures of unregulated banks was assuredly greater in history than it is or has been since 1933. The money supply itself in the old days tended to be a casualty of the crisis in a way that is no longer true. This is major.

Another way of putting things is this. In Gladstone's time, as in the time of Herbert Hoover, there was an effective political presumption toward long-run stability of the price level. Although Britain since 1688 never lived up to its presumption of balanced fiscal budgets, never was there acceptance by the official elite that the gold standard could be ignored as a constraint and that deliberate deficit spending was an admissible and admirable tool of policy.

Why was the prophet Hyman Minsky for so many decades a voice crying out in the wilderness? "A qualitative credit crisis is in the intermediate-term cards. Wolf! Wolf!"

The answer for his long wait has to be found in the laws of behavior of populist democracy in the "Age after Keynes." Every three years when I came to revise my textbook, two main charts would jump off the page to command my attention. One was the trendless behavior of real wages from about 1250 to 1750, followed by a sea change to a rising trend of the real wage rate in the "Age after Newton." The other was the trendless behavior of staple prices in Europe and North America, as postwar deflations undid the peaks of wartime inflation—followed, since 1932 and the "new deals" in America and Europe, by a remorseless upward trend in the cost-of-living index.

On every proper Richter scale, the 1987 crash rivaled that of the 1929 crash. By contrast with journalists, mainstream economists correctly computed that the late-1987 25 percent erosion of worldwide asset values was prone to reduce by about 1 percent per annum the likely 1987–89 growth in global output. Had you told those economists to factor into their IS-LM diagrams the worldwide acceleration of the money supply induced by the October 1987 crash, their regressions would have projected the continuance of the 1982 recovery that history has recorded in 1988–89.

I should not need to say it, but I will say it: Reacting and overreacting to each and every market crisis by macro policy can alter the historic pattern of GNP response to panics. But such Pavlovian responses cannot be guaranteed to give us a pattern of economic history that is aptly described by the Good Fairy who says, "And they lived happily ever afterward, with minimal unemployment, price stability, and growth in output characterized by almost-unit roots." There will return times when markets crash against a background of stagflation. Then engineering more money to prevent drops in real output will add to policy dilemmas connected with increases in prices.

4. William Poole

Macroeconomic Effects of Financial Crises

The problem with the title of this session is that so little is known about the subject. It may be that no government response is required to a market crash other than to maintain money growth and continue with whatever were the optimal policies before the crash. But I know of no one who wants to conduct such an experiment. The issue, then, is what the government's response ought to be to minimize fallout from a crash without causing harmful side effects.

Let me start by noting that studying financial crisis is more important than most people recognize because the government is not nearly as well-prepared as it should be. I can illustrate one reason for this situation by adding a few sentences to the scenario spun out by Larry Summers.

> Heavy selling pressure hit the market at the opening bell. Investors were jolted by an article in the *Washington Post* reporting that the Council of Economic Advisers (CEA) was well along in a secret study of what the government should do if a certain large money-center bank were to fail. The *Post* article was based on a background interview with a high Treasury official. Most Washington experts believed that the interview was with the Treasury secretary himself, who was known to be feuding with the CEA chairman. The president was reported to be furious given his press conference last week where he said that everyone in the administration had complete confidence in the banking system.

> The situation may be better abroad, but in the United States, government-by-leak makes it extremely difficult for senior officials to engage in contingency planning. We should not be surprised when the U.S. government reacts to financial crises in a confused manner or in ways that set damaging precedents. We can agree that a good part of the problem is that the economists do not understand crashes, but having said that, it is important to emphasize what we do know. There are policies that can reduce the damage to the real economy from market crashes.

The most significant single fact is that companies and individuals with no debt rarely go bankrupt. There was no debt-deflation process in the severe recession of 1920–21 because there was so little debt after World War I. At an absolute minimum the government should not provide positive tax incentives as at present for firms and individuals to accumulate debt. For individuals, we should end the tax deductibility of all interest, and for firms we should put interest and dividends on an identical basis. These are old proposals, but we should not leave them out of this discussion simply because they are old and obvious.

Besides the tax law, the other fundamental condition that needs reform is deposit insurance. Deposit insurance worked in the 1980s; the economy has been little troubled by runs on insured banks and thrifts. The taxpayer cost, though, has been high. If deposit insurance is not reformed to provide better private incentives we will inevitably see extension of regulation in an effort to keep taxpayer costs down. Regulation will also be costly, but the costs will be hidden in the form of market inefficiencies. More important, however, I do not see how regulatory approaches can be easily effective in a highly competitive world financial market. There is also a danger that the budgetary damage inflicted by deposit insurance will lead to efforts that will compromise the contribution to stability of deposit insurance. It is for this reason that I do not favor proposals to scale back deposit insurance but instead favor extending coverage with reforms to assure that institutions with insured deposits face the correct incentives to control risk.

Even if Congress were to act today to reform the tax law and deposit insurance, there will necessarily be a long transitional period before reforms become fully effective. In the meantime, and probably permanently anyway, there will be times when the government must be prepared to act, to deal with or head off, financial crises. What should the principles of crisis management be? An important concern should be that crisis responses not set bad precedents.

First of all, we need to decide which markets deserve special emphasis. I believe that we should concentrate on the stock markets, investment-grade bond markets, and money markets. Commercial banks, of course, play the key role in the money markets and so stability of the banking system is of central concern. If we can avoid crashes (including banking panics) in these markets, or insulate the real economy from the effects of the crashes that do occur, then we will have solved the problem. I deliberately leave the foreign exchange market out of this list for reasons I will discuss in a moment.

With regard to crashes themselves, I see no reason why we should not make use of the public finance principle that we tax activities we want to discourage and subsidize activities we want to encourage. I am sympathetic with the idea behind the Tobin tax, but skeptical that this particular proposal is satisfactory. Perhaps a better approach would be to design a tax preference for securities purchased on any day on which a specified market average declines by more than some trigger amount.[1] The argument against a tax incentive of this kind is that economic efficiency calls for prices to adjust rapidly to new information, but I find it hard to believe that much can be lost if the adjustment can be spread over several weeks rather than over a day or a few hours. As with more fundamental reforms to strengthen deposit insurance and to discourage debt, there is an important advantage to building more stability into the system rather than relying on skilled official responses to crisis situations. Building in more financial stability would extend the gains from automatic income stabilization, which Larry Summers rightly emphasizes as being of considerable importance.

Even if we do build more stability into the system we need to be prepared to deal with crisis situations. I agree with Larry's emphasis on what he calls "the modern pragmatic approach," but believe there is more structure in this approach than is apparent on the surface. There is, first, a commitment that the government, and especially the central bank, will do something to deal with a market crisis rather than let things progress "naturally." Second, the government's response will be as narrowly targeted as possible. There are several reasons for a targeted approach. One is that calming the markets often requires that the perceived source of the problem be directly addressed. Another reason is that a narrowly targeted approach has minimal effects in establishing precedents. There is not precedent from a special response to a highly unusual situation. Finally, what is often needed is a response to buy time. There are many problems that cannot be worked out over night but can be worked out over months or years. The difficulty when buying time is to use the time constructively to address the underlying problem, not to run from it. Unfortunately, given the way our political process works it is sometimes necessary to let things boil a bit before obtaining constructive action. I will discuss this point further in a moment.

I can illustrate these ideas with relatively minor market crises, or market "upsets" for those who prefer to use "crisis" for something really big. In June 1970 the commercial paper market had real problems when Penn Central de-

---

1. For the stock market a tax incentive might consist of a capital gains tax break on stock purchased on a day when Standard and Poor's 500 Index declines by a large amount. For example, when the index declines 3 percent the fraction of capital gains excluded might be zero and the fraction excluded might be 100 percent when the index declines 7 percent or more. The exclusion could rise linearly for index decline between 3 and 7 percent to prevent a situation in which investors would hold back from buying in the expectation that the index would fall by a trigger amount. A similar incentive could apply to the 30-year government bond. It is important that an incentive be continuous rather than discrete; current "circuit breakers" that involve trading halts when prices are down by trigger amounts may accelerate declines as investors accelerate sales and/or delay purchases in the expectation that the market will decline by the trigger amount. Much current discussion seems to assume that tax incentives, if any, should apply to long holding periods. Clearly, though, it is socially productive for speculators to engage in short-run trading that stabilizes markets, and the tax law should recognize that short-run trading as well as long-run investing can be socially productive.

faulted on its commercial paper. The Fed responded by suspending interest rate ceilings on large negotiable CDs and by assuring commercial banks that they would have access to the discount window to obtain funds to lend to creditworthy borrowers who were cut off from the commercial paper market. The Fed made it clear that the banks would bear the credit risk. The Fed's response to this situation was narrowly targeted; no precedents were set, no one was bailed out except in the sense that some borrowers in the commercial paper market were saved from financial embarrassment, and there was no change in the Fed's overall monetary policy stance. Nor was there a market perception that the Fed would change its monetary policy. This latter point was very important at the time. The Fed was trying to reduce inflation, and the situation was touchy with capital flowing from the United States and the Bretton Woods system crumbling.

An earlier Fed crisis response worked much less well. In the credit crunch of 1966 the Fed supported emergency one-year legislation extending Regulation Q interest rate ceilings to thrift institutions. That step bought time, but the time was not well used. Extension of Regulation Q also set a bad precedent. It is always hard to know how things would have gone if a different action had been taken, but it seems to me that it would have been better if the Fed had stalled on extension of Regulation Q and let a few thrifts fail in 1966 before the government moved in to protect the industry. I realize that it is a lot easier to talk here of playing chicken than to actually play, but that is why we pay central bankers such high salaries.

The Fed's response to the October 1987 crash was successful precisely because it was well-tuned to the circumstances. The Fed reaffirmed its earlier sound precedents that it would provide liquidity to the markets as necessary. At the same time the Fed was successful in making clear that extra liquidity would remain only so long as necessary and would not lead to a change in the longer-run path of monetary policy. No one was bailed out; many lost a lot and some securities firms went out of business but the financial system itself was protected.

These comments bring me to an important issue neglected by all the authors of our background papers. At least some of the financial upsets we observe arise because the government is at war with itself. No one knows the importance for last Friday's [13 October 1989] market break of the position taken by the Department of Transportation restricting the amount of foreign investment in U.S. airlines, or of the wrangling in Congress over the capital gains tax, or of the dispute between the Treasury and the Fed over current monetary policy. Policy disputes occur all the time. The point I want to emphasize is that any policymaker who is unwilling to play chicken with the markets on the issues will be conceding a lot in Washington infighting over policy. This is another reason why it is so important to change the incentive structure in private markets to promote stability. Government policy involves conflict, and conflict inevitably brings surprises and disappointments to the markets. We need to create an economic and financial environment that is robust to the normal course of governmental conflict.

I will finish with a few comments on the foreign exchange market. The managed float fails to provide the stability of either a credible fixed exchange rate system or of a freely floating system. Many exchange market uncertainties and instabilities are caused by unresolved policy conflicts over exchange market intervention and over monetary, fiscal, and trade policies. The major problem at present is the effort to use sterilized intervention to influence the exchange rate. This situation will be unstable until the authorities face up to the fact that sterilized intervention makes little difference and that the exchange rate can be influenced only through monetary and fiscal policy changes.

The issue, then, is how far we should go in changing domestic policy to influence the exchange rate. In my view, it is terribly important, for the United States anyway, that there be no compromise of domestic stability for the purpose of attempting to achieve an exchange rate target. There is no conflict whatsoever between international objectives and domestic objectives; achieving stability at home is the most important thing the United States can do to further the objective of international economic stability. The argument that we will have to pay increasing attention to the exchange market as the amount of foreign-owned capital in the United States rises does not make good sense to me. U.S.-owned capital is just as mobile as foreign-owned capital. Capital flows respond to relative risks and returns; policy constraints from international capital flows have changed little over the last decade.

In sum, while economists do not have a lot to offer as yet in explaining market crises, we do have a lot to offer in explaining how to minimize the risk of crises and how to deal with them in constructive ways. In both endeavors we rely on economic fundamentals that the profession understands pretty well.

5. *Paul A. Volcker*

Financial Crises and the Macroeconomy

Martin Feldstein asked me to explain today why I was so worried about financial crises, and I confess to some historical worries about them. I indeed think that the economy is becoming more crisis-prone, more overextended, as Ben Friedman suggested. However, we also have more and more devices for dealing with incipient crises—the FDIC, the FSLIC and its successors, the Federal Reserve—and we seem to be on something of a hair trigger in using these tools. This leaves me with the disturbing question of whether by using these tools repeatedly and aggressively we end up reinforcing the behavior patterns that aggravate the risk in the first place. That is the dilemma that we face. I did not expect to find much sympathy for that point of view, but the background papers at the conference seem to support it. Some people think that if the money supply is more or less stable, then the lending officers will keep pouring it out. However, I will defend the social utility of worrying about financial crises even in a friendly audience.

Ben Friedman, Larry Summers, and Paul Krugman set out my case more eloquently than I can, and more impressively, and I do not want to repeat all of that. I think that they set out a vision of what may be called the "stabilization" crisis, where there are no "right" answers, because the general tools that one uses to deal with the crisis, particularly easing the money supply, may undermine confidence. Further, the international financial repercussions can lead to a depreciation of the dollar which feeds back to internal inflation. So all of these crises inevitably push the Federal Reserve toward an inflationary posture. I think that is the most likely scenario that one has to guard against in terms of the translation of actual and potential financial crises into the real economy.

I woke up this morning and had the *Boston Globe* delivered to my hotel room, as the rest of you did, and I was interested in the editorial page. After the 200 point drop in the stock market on Friday [13 October 1989], there were press reports about an anonymous Federal Reserve spokesman saying that there would be an increase in the money supply as and when necessary over the weekend. Today there was a cartoon titled "Federal Reserve Issues Money to Calm Nervous Markets." It had a caricature of a dollar bill with President Bush on it, the name "United States of Amnesia," and the slogan, "A penny leveraged is a penny earned." Not only Federal Reserve chairmen, but other people as well, worry about this confidence effect translated into external depreciation and then giving rise to an inflationary recession that is very difficult to deal with. We are not quite Argentina, but I think the Latin American model is not irrelevant to concerns about how financial crises affect the real economy.

During these remarks, however, let me mostly ignore the external dimension in discussing my concerns about financial crises. How realistic are these concerns? Let us assume that we stabilize the money supply, which is what everybody says we ought to do in response to financial pressures. The first question I have to ask is, "*What* money supply is being stabilized?" That question sounds very easy *after* a crisis but is hard to answer during one. Say that the rule is high-powered money, which is very fashionable with the Shadow Open Market Committee and many other monitors these days. By this rule, the Federal Reserve did a superb job in the Great Depression, and it is only in retrospect that one can say, "Well those dumb bunnies, why didn't they recognize that velocity was going way off course; why didn't they react more intelligently?" Milton Friedman says that normally velocity is very stable, that it changes once every 40 years. The question is, how can policymakers recognize that change until the 40 years have gone by? I think it is very likely that with a severe financial crisis affecting confidence in the banking system, there would be quite different behavior between high-powered money, narrow measures of the money stock, and broad measures of the money stock.

My second question is, "Even if we could figure out exactly what money supply was right, does that solve the problem?" I think what Larry Summers's paper said was that the amount of money needed to provide reassurance and to properly reduce real interest rates may be too much not only to stabilize the currency externally but to stabilize prices internally. That is a little bit what the cartoonist in the *Boston Globe* is worried about. There may be no correct answer as to what the money supply should be, or, at best, policymakers may be on a knife edge—if they go a little too far they are inflating, and if they do too little they have a financial crisis translating into problems in the real economy. If we are on the edge of a knife for too long—if correct policy requires such fine and precise judgments over a period of time—then it is not surprising that mistakes will be made in one direction or another. Perfection is not in this world, and we will have a translation, therefore, of the financial pressures into problems in the real economy.

Let me try to arrive at a little more constructive position as to how we can approach this problem by looking at a little bit of experience. In one case, I will overlap what Bill Poole said, and with a slightly different conclusion, which shows that different observers can arrive at different answers. From 1945 to roughly 1970, there was literally no worry about financial crises, that I am aware of, in this country or in most other countries. The system was very liquid, there was a lot of equity relative to debt, interest rates were low, and there were few real pressures. In my judgment, it did not make any difference whether we had deposit insurance or not in terms of maintaining confidence in the banking system.

That was first questioned in 1970 with the Penn Central crisis, which had two aspects. First, the judgment was made in the end by Hasbrett not to rescue Penn Central directly but to take the risk and let it go bankrupt. There was a lot of fear of letting this happen, though. It is strange to think of a railroad being big, but in 1970 Penn Central was still a fairly important and diversified company, and it had a lot of commercial paper outstanding for those days. Whether it should be rescued was debated for two weeks, and the owners almost saved it with an extraordinary interpretation of Defense Department loan authorities. The second aspect was that the Federal Reserve issued a lot of reassuring statements and, I thought, eased policy a little bit. I differ from Bill a little bit in thinking that psychologically they overdid it. They did a little more than was necessary to provide reassurance, and I think they did create something of a precedent out of what was, in retrospect, a pretty limited experience.

I say that with a certain humility, because as the financial system became more clearly overextended by the late 1970s, and I found myself as president of the Federal Reserve Bank of New York, I often said to myself, "What this country needs to shake us up and give us a little discipline is a good bank failure. But please, God, not in my district." I think that is the typical attitude of a regulator. My district became somewhat larger shortly thereafter.

This brings me to the silver crisis in 1980 that people sometimes forget about. This crisis broke very suddenly in its financial ramifications one Wednesday afternoon. The price of silver had fallen $38, and it seemed clear that if the price fell $2 more (as I recall), one of the leading brokerage houses in the United States, which held a lot of uncovered silver positions, would have to close its doors and go bankrupt. That firm would have failed to meet its capital requirements with the SEC and probably would have failed to meet its obligations more generally. We had great emergency meetings and all of the confusion normal in government, and whether by good judgment or by failure to make a decision, we decided not to have a "circuit breaker" in the form of closing the markets, which was of doubtful legality in any event. So the markets stayed open, the price stayed $1 above the critical point, the brokerage house liquidated its position, and shortly thereafter it reported record earnings for the quarter, which galled me. There was really no official action taken except a blessing afterward by the Federal Reserve of a consolidation loan in the banking system.

What was at stake in this situation? There was the big brokerage house immediately and another, even larger, brokerage house that would have been in trouble with a drop in price of a few more dollars, all after a $38 decline. There was at least one large money market bank that was heavily exposed in silver directly, and others who, because of the silver speculation, were considered (not today, but in the context of those days) to have impaired capital. The rest of the scenario was never played out and not much was done in fact by the government, except blessing this consolidation loan, which seemed fairly straightforward. We went on to the next crisis more or less happily.

The next crisis, I think, was Penn Square, and then the rescue of the depositors and creditors of Continental Illinois in 1984 that was discussed earlier. What was the rationale for that reaction? Well, at that point there was concern about a systemic crisis, because the banking system in general was commonly understood to have some weak assets in various directions, including most explicitly Latin American loans. Having a big bank's depositors lose money was judged to present too large a risk to the rest of the banking system and too large a risk to the real economy, to which I will return in a moment. Further, this crisis occurred during the ongoing international debt crisis (which began in 1982), a crisis that could have impaired the capital of all of the 10 or so leading banks in the United States and most of the leading banks in the rest of the world. Was that a situation that really justified what would have indeed been extraordinary official efforts to maintain stability? Would it have been enough to simply maintain the money supply of the United States and other countries, let the banks take their losses, and go on about our business? What would have happened?

Well, it is very hard to describe what would happen in these counterfactual situations. There would have been very low interest rates for very high grade pieces of paper, but the real question is what would have happened to the kind of lending activity, and indeed in the stock market itself, that really drives the economy over a period of time. I think that the risk premiums would have been enormous on private paper of all kinds and particularly of greater maturity. Consider the complaints that I hear from Texans about the banking system in Texas following the rescue (or in another sense, the debacle) of the Texas savings and loan system. The complaints are that the banks and savings and loans had lubricated the growth of Texas, and today people cannot get credit. Credit is unavailable because everybody is scared to death after going through a crisis or potential crisis that was resolved favorably from the standpoint of the depositor, most lending officers, and almost everybody *except* the stockholders of the institution. If that kind of crisis had occurred on a wider scale, would the resulting climate have supported continuing economic activity in the fairly regular way that we have seen in recent years? I doubt it, but I think the mechanism would have been very high risk premiums, not all of which can be captured in interest rates with some refusal to lend for private credit.

Finally, let me discuss the stock market crash in 1987. There was great concern about the wealth effects of the crash, and the Federal Reserve reaction was to provide some assurance of liquidity in the economy. I would say, not so unexpectedly, that this potential crisis was reasonably well absorbed and did not really affect the continuing growth in the economy. The wealth effects were offset by monetary and other changes. I think that the central reason this potential crisis did not develop more fully is that there was no institutional discontinuity in the crash. In this way, the crash was similar to the silver crisis in 1980 but different from other potential financial problems.

After the crash a leading banker asked, "Where was the blood on the street?" which I think was apropos. A lot of stockholders lost money—endowment funds, universities, and individuals. However, they are not the kind of people who create a systemic problem in the financial system. In contrast, there is quite a different potential for crisis when one thinks about banks and the interconnections between banks, because then not only is the money supply at stake, but also the payments system, transfers of credit, and the whole lending apparatus.

What are the implications of this distinction for policy? I think that what we have said in the past is that we must protect the core of the depository system, using the FDIC, the FSLIC, and the Federal Reserve as the lender of last resort. It is important that the protected part of the system be big enough, be a critical mass, to maintain stability in the system, but it is not good to protect everybody in the whole system. We make a choice as to what to protect and what not to, and the strategic element to protect is essentially the banking system. Some of the discussion this morning was about how to accomplish that. I believe that we need to restore a greater sense of risk then we have had recently, but obviously we need that greater sense of risk within a structure of stability and resiliency—and it is awfully easy to say that and awfully hard to do.

On a practical level, it is appropriate to emphasize capital, as was mentioned this morning. There could be a much larger role for subordinated debt, which was also discussed earlier. I would like to see some experimentation with marginal coinsurance for bigger deposits. I do not think that this coinsurance can be very substantial, but it ought to be possible to at least put the interest earned at risk. Then maybe, if we became progressively bolder and the system seemed to improve in stability, we could consider insuring only 99% or 95% of the deposit. I think that if we moved much below that, we might as well not insure it at all, because the depositor will act as if it is uninsured. We could insist upon deposit of preference so that we get some discipline from other creditors, and there are a variety of devices of this sort.

I think also that we need some reinvigoration of regulation and supervision to the extent that it affects safety and soundness. I wonder, however, whether that is really a lesson for the 1950s and the 1960s rather than for the future. Can we exercise very careful supervision when people can be something very close to a bank without calling themselves a bank and being regulated like a bank? Or when international movement of bonds and international competition among financial institutions is as pervasive as it is now? Being successful in regulation and supervision requires pretty good agreement among a number of key countries, and the evidence is mixed on that possibility. We have taken a step to provide uniform capital requirements, which, looked at from one direction, is quite an achievement for the first time. Looked at from another direction, though, these capital requirements are the easiest, simplest, and most straightforward thing on which to get international agreement. What are the prospects for achieving the more diffuse and sophisticated kind of supervision that is probably required if we adopt this philosophy of focusing protection on the banking and depository system rather than on the rest of the markets? We need to move to a stable financial system partly so that monetary policy itself can be free to act more in response to concerns about inflation and the stability of the currency instead of in defense of the financial system itself.

Summary of Discussion

Summers began by discussing the current views of some financial market participants affected by the crash of 1987. First, they report little change in their investment behavior. Second, they report that they paid out money during the crash before being paid themselves and were lucky not to lose their shirts as a result. It is a bad sign for the future of the payments system that they say they will not act that way again. Summers continued by contrasting two views about the role of monetary policy and the value of the dollar in spurring the 1987 crash. Many economists believe that high U.S. interest rates designed to maintain an arbitrary level of the exchange rate reduced liquidity in the financial markets and led to the crash. The opposing interpretation of events in 1987 is that a fear of the dollar going into a free fall led to the crash.

Bennett T. McCallum raised two questions concerning the scenario analysis used in Summers's paper. First, does the lender of last resort need to use the discount window to direct loans to particular banks, or is it enough to control the magnitude of some monetary aggregate or interest rate? Second, is it appropriate to analyze events and policies during a crisis, in the design of policy, or must one study ongoing processes?

Robert E. Hall remarked that, as a general matter, governments turn socialist in crises, including for example the U.S. government's planned economic strategy after a nuclear attack. He believes that monetary policy is central to a free-market response to a financial crisis, but the Federal Reserve should not attempt to stabilize any particular monetary aggregate. Instead they should adjust monetary policy to maintain the same consensus forecast of nominal GNP (for one to two years in the future) as before the crash. In the 1987 crash, for example, the consensus forecast fell slightly but not by much, due to a vigorous monetary response. This policy has several advantages. First, the consensus forecast adjusts quickly to current events, as opposed to actual nominal GNP, which adjusts to both crises and monetary policy with a substantial lag. Second, the proposed policy would generate a big surge in liquidity during a crisis, but it does to require intervention on behalf of any particular institutions. Finally, a nominal GNP target is inherently noninflationary.

Poole wondered what would happen to the economy if forecasts were based on the assumption that the Federal Reserve would take some action that it does not in fact take. *Hall* replied that this uncertainty would be quickly resolved due to the short feedback loop.

Friedman responded to Hall that there is no more reason to think there will be an informative consensus forecast than to think that there is one useful measure of the money supply.

Alan A. Walters described the background of a possible currency crisis in Britain. From 1981 to 1986, British monetary policy maintained a growth rate of the monetary base between 2.5 and 5 percent. In 1987, policy switched to targeting the exchange rate, particularly in the Deutschmark-pound rate. Sterilized intervention was used in an attempt to offset the pressure for a pound appreciation but it failed. The exchange rate was contained only by lowering interest rates from 11 or 12 percent in early 1987 to about 7.5 percent in 1988. Inflationary pressures and resulting monetary tightening have since raised interest rates to roughly 15 percent today.

Now, as the next Parliamentary election approaches in 1991 or 1992, there is a significant moral hazard problem for monetary policymakers. An increased probability of the Labor party winning the election will lead to more capital flight and downward pressure on the pound. The government will have to raise interest rates to prop up the pound, thereby increasing the probability of a recession and thus the probability of the Labor party winning the election. But this worsens the capital flight and so on. An attempt to peg the currency, in this political environment, risks generating a fierce monetary squeeze and a severe recession.

Samuelson warned the group not to be misled by the monetary policy successes of Paul Volcker in 1982 and Alan Greenspan in 1987, which he attributed to the "genius" of the Federal Reserve Chairmen.

Robert J. Gordon argued that the United States has recently conducted a controlled experiment of wild dollar gyrations and found, contrary to Summers's scenario, that the effect on domestic inflation was minimal. He cautioned that this experience may not be generalizable to other economies, because U.S. imports have distribution systems that buffer the effect on prices of exchange rate changes. He concluded that monetary policy in crises should focus on domestic targets and not worry about international effects. Gordon contended that the virtues of nominal GNP targeting are irrelevant to the microeconomic allocation and intervention issues of the conference.

Kindleberger noted that not all crises are alike, and different policy responses are needed at different times. He agreed with Volcker and Krugman that contagion crises are the critical problem; nominal GNP targeting does not address this issue.

Mussa discussed the "non-crisis" of the financial system in late 1981 and early 1982, during which high interest rates left the banking system liquid but insolvent on a market-value basis. Because a major failure at that time could have produced a run on the system, policymakers would have had to put out any "brush fires" that occurred. Luckily, no serious fires broke out until the Federal Reserve's anti-inflation credibility was established in 1982.

Krugman commented to Hall that society intervenes in free markets during crises to prevent massive income distribution effects, even though efficiency suffers as a result. *Hall* responded that the beneficiaries of the Continental Illinois bailout were at the top of the income distribution.

Robert D. Reischauer emphasized the important role of political dynamics in dealing with failing financial and nonfinancial institutions. The interests of these institutions will be defended by the political representatives for their geographic locations.

Hall reminded the group that a nominal GNP targeting procedure would have produced a *more* expansionary monetary policy in October 1987 than was actually pursued. This is a consistent framework of monetary policy that responds to crises effectively and thereby reduces the risk of "brush fires." Further, it is "uncanny" how government bailouts go to the rich.

Syron pointed out that the income distribution effects of institutional bailouts depend critically on the importance of contagion in the economy. If the real economy falters, then people at the bottom of the income distribution are the most likely to lose jobs.

Summers concluded the session by stating that the cost of not fighting "brush fires" probably exceeds the cost of fighting them excessively. In particular, the allocative inefficiency resulting from intervention is much smaller than the output loss from a slowdown in the real economy. Further, the argument against bailouts depends on being entirely credible that one will not engage in such bailouts, which is a difficult point to make convincingly. Finally, reputational externalities clearly exist in precarious financial situations, so contagion can be an important problem that is not internalized by individual firms.

Biographies

Robert J. Barro is professor of economics at Harvard University and a research associate of the NBER. He has served as editor of the *Journal of Political Economy* and director of the Rochester Center for Economic Research, and is presently on the Domestic Studies Advisory Committee of the Hoover Institution.

C. Fred Bergsten is director of the Institute for International Economics. He was assistant secretary of the Treasury for international affairs, 1977–81, and assistant for international economic affairs on the Senior Staff of the National Security Council, 1969–71. He is a member of the Trilateral Commission, the Council on Foreign Relations, and the International Advisory Board of Chemical Bank.

Ben Bernanke is professor of economics and public affairs at Princeton University and a research associate of the NBER.

Ralph C. Bryant is a senior fellow in economic studies at the Brookings Institution. Before joining Brookings, he was director of the Division of International Finance and associate economist to the Federal Open Market Committee at the Board of Governors of the Federal Reserve System.

Geoffrey Carliner is executive director of the National Bureau of Economic Research. Prior to coming to the NBER, he was a senior staff economist at the Council of Economic Advisers working on labor issues and international trade policy.

Richard N. Cooper is the Maurits C. Boas Professor of International Economics at Harvard University. He previously served as under-secretary of state for economic affairs, deputy assistant secretary of state for international monetary affairs, and senior staff economist at the Council of Economic Advisers. He is currently deputy chairman of the Federal Reserve Bank of Boston, a director of the Institute for International Economics, and a member of the Trilateral Commission and the Council on Foreign Relations.

183

E. Gerald Corrigan is the president of the Federal Reserve Bank of New York. He is a member of the Trilateral Commission and the Council on Foreign Relations.

Rudiger Dornbusch is the Ford International Professor of Economics at the Massachusetts Institute of Technology and a research associate of the NBER.

Barry Eichengreen is professor of economics at the University of California at Berkeley, a research associate of the NBER, and research fellow of the Centre for Economic Policy Research. He also is a member of the National Academy of Sciences Committee on the Contributions of the Behavioral and Social Sciences to the Prevention of Nuclear War.

Douglas W. Elmendorf is an assistant professor of economics at Harvard University.

Richard D. Erb is deputy managing director of the International Monetary Fund. He has held positions at the U.S. Treasury Department, the White House staff, and the Federal Reserve Board. He is a member of the Council on Foreign Relations and a trustee of the Washington International School.

Martin Feldstein is the George F. Baker Professor of Economics at Harvard University and president and chief executive officer of the NBER. He served as chairman of the Council of Economic Advisers, 1982–84.

Jeffrey Frankel is professor of economics at the University of California, Berkeley, and a research associate of the NBER. He has served as an economist and consultant for the Council of Economic Advisers, the International Monetary Fund, the Federal Reserve Board, the Institute for International Economics, and the World Bank.

Jacob A. Frenkel is economic counsellor and director of research at the International Monetary Fund. Prior to assuming his current position in 1987, he was the David Rockefeller Professor of International Economics at the University of Chicago. He is a fellow of the Econometric Society, a research associate of the NBER, a member of the Group of Thirty, and a member of the Advisory Committee for the Institute for International Economics.

Benjamin M. Friedman is the William Joseph Maier Professor of Political Economy at Harvard University, and director of the Financial Markets and Monetary Economics Program at the NBER. He is also a director of the Private Export Funding Corporation, a trustee of the Standish Investment Trusts, and a member of the Council on Foreign Relations.

Robert J. Gordon is the Stanley G. Harris Professor in the Social Sciences at Northwestern University and a research associate of the NBER. He serves as a member of the Boston Company Economic Advisers Economic Advisory Council, as treasurer of the Econometric Society, and as coorganizer of the NBER's annual International Seminar on Microeconomics.

Joseph A. Grundfest, formerly a commissioner of the U.S. Securities and Exchange Commission (1985–90), is currently a member of the faculty of Stanford Law School. An attorney and economist, he has served on the staff of the President's Council of Economic Advisers, practiced law with Wilmer, Cutler and Pickering, and worked as an economist at the Rand Corporation.

David Hale is chief economist of Kemper Financial Services in Chicago. He holds a degree in international economic affairs from the Georgetown University School of Foreign Service and an M.Sc. (economics) from the London School of Economics. His articles have appeared in the *Financial Analysis Journal,* the *Financial Times* of London, the *Wall Street Journal,* the *Far Eastern Economic Review, Foreign Policy,* and other publications. He is a member of the financial instruments steering committee of the Chicago Mercantile Exchange and the U.S.-Japan Consultative Committee on International Monetary Policy.

Robert E. Hall is professor of economics at Stanford University and a senior fellow at the Hoover Institution at Stanford. He is director of the Economic Fluctuations Program at the NBER and a director of the Center for Policy Research of the American Council for Capital Formaation.

William S. Haraf is director of Policy Analysis for Citicorp. Previously he was a scholar with the American Enterprise Institute, and he served on the staff of the President's Council of Economic Advisers, 1983–85.

R. Glenn Hubbard is professor of economics and finance at the Graduate School of Business at Columbia University and a research associate of the NBER. Previously he taught at Northwestern University and Harvard University. He has been a consultant to numerous government agencies.

Michael Jensen is the Edsel Bryant Ford Professor of Business Administration at the Harvard Business School. He is the founding editor of the *Journal of Financial Economics* and founder and director of the Managerial Economics Research Center at the University of Rochester Simon School of Business.

Sidney Jones is assistant secretary of the Treasury for economic policy. He has served in various government economic policy positions since 1969, and has been a professor at the University of Michigan and associate faculty of the Brookings Institution.

Edward J. Kane is the Everett D. Reese Professor of Banking and Monetary Economics at Ohio State University and a research associate of the NBER. He has consulted for the Federal Deposit Insurance Corporation, the Federal Home Loan Bank Board, the American Bankers Association, the Department of Housing and Urban Development, the Federal Reserve System, and the Congressional Budget Office. He is a past president of the American Finance Association, a former Guggenheim Fellow, and a member of the Shadow Financial Regulatory Committee.

Charles P. Kindleberger is professor of economics emeritus, Massachusetts Institute of Technology. His recent books bearing on the subject of the conference are *The World in Depression, 1929–1939,* (rev. ed., 1986), and *Manias, Panics and Crashes: A History of Financial Crises* (2nd ed., 1989).

Mervyn King is professor of economics at the London School of Economics, where he is also codirector of the LSE Financial Markets Group. He is a research associate of the NBER. Until this year he was an independent board member of the Securities Association and is the first academic to be invited to be a member of the City Capital Markets Committee.

Paul Krugman is professor of economics at the Massachusetts Institute of Technology and a research associate of the NBER. He was the international policy economist at the

Council of Economic Advisers in 1982 and 1983 and is a member of the Group of Thirty. He has served as an economic consultant to the International Monetary Fund, the World Bank, and the United Nations.

Lawrence B. Lindsey is special assistant to the president for policy development and the executive director of the President's Council on Competitiveness. He is an associate professor of economics on leave from Harvard University and has served as a senior staff economist at the Council of Economic Advisers.

Robert E. Lucas, Jr., is the John Dewey Distinguished Service Professor of Economics at the University of Chicago. He is an associate editor of the *Journal of Monetary Economics.*

Bennett T. McCallum is the H. J. Heinz Professor of Economics in the Graduate School of Industrial Administration at Carnegie-Mellon University and a research associate of the NBER. He has been a visiting scholar at the Board of Governors of the Federal Reserve System and the International Monetary Fund, and a consultant at the Federal Reserve Bank of Richmond, Virginia. He currently serves as coeditor of the *American Economic Review.*

Brian Maddigan is a senior staff economist at the Council of Economic Advisers. He is on leave from the Board of Governors of the Federal Reserve System.

N. Gregory Mankiw is professor of economics at Harvard University and a research associate of the NBER. He has previously served as a staff economist at the Council of Economic Advisers.

Hyman P. Minsky is professor of economics at Washington University in St. Louis, and a member of the International Advisory Board and professor at the International Center for the Study of Political Economy, Trieste, Italy.

Michael Mussa is the William H. Abbott Professor of International Business at the University of Chicago and a research associate of the NBER. From 1986 to 1988, he was a member of the Council of Economic Advisers. He has been a consultant to the World Bank and the International Monetary Fund.

William Poole is the Herbert H. Goldberger Professor of Economics at Brown University and director of the Center for the Study of Financial Markets and Institutions. He was a member of the Council of Economic Advisers from 1982 through 1985. He is a research associate of the NBER and is an adjunct scholar at both the American Enterprise Institute and the Cato Institute.

Douglas D. Purvis is professor and head of the department of Economics at Queen's University in Kingston, Canada. He is the author of numerous academic articles in professional journals, is coauthor of a widely used principles of economics textbook, and has written extensively in the public press on economic policy. Previous positions he has held include director of the John Deutsch Institute for the Study of Economic Policy and Clifford Clark Visiting Economist at the Department of Finance, Ottawa.

Robert D. Reischauer is the director of the Congressional Budget Office. He has been a member of the Economic Studies Program staff of the Brookings Institution and the senior vice president of the Urban Institute.

Paul A. Samuelson is Institute Professor Emeritus at the Massachusetts Institute of Technology. He was awarded the Nobel Memorial Prize in Economic Science in 1970.

Robert J. Shiller is the Stanley B. Resor Professor of Economics at the Cowles Foundation, Yale University, and a research associate of the NBER.

Irvine H. Sprague, in a long government career, served as special assistant to President Lyndon Johnson in the White House, as deputy director of finance for California Governor Pat Brown, as executive director of the House Policy Committee for Speaker Tip O'Neill, and for eleven and a half years as either chairman or director of the Federal Reserve Insurance Corporation.

Norman Strunk was the chief executive officer of the U.S. League of Savings Institutions from 1952 to 1979. He later served as secretary-general and Congress secretary of the International Union of Building Societies and Savings Associations. He has served also as a director of the Federal Home Loan Bank of Chicago.

Lawrence H. Summers is vice president of development economics and chief economist of the World Bank. He is currently on leave from his position as the Nathaniel Ropes Professor of Political Economy at Harvard University. He served as domestic policy economist at the Council of Economic Advisors from 1982 to 1983, and as editor of the *Quarterly Journal of Economics* and a number of other journals.

Richard F. Syron is president of the Federal Reserve Bank of Boston and a voting member of the Federal Open Market Committee. He has served as president of the Federal Home Loan Bank of Boston, assistant to the chairman of the Federal Reserve Board of Governors, and deputy assistant and acting assistant secretary for economic policy, U.S. Treasury.

Paul A. Volcker is chairman of James D. Wolfensohn, Inc., and the former chairman of the Board of Governors of the Federal Reserve System. He has served as the president of the Federal Reserve Bank of New York and as the Undersecretary of the Treasury.

Alan A. Walters is a senior fellow at the American Enterprise Institute and a professor of economics at Johns Hopkins University. He has been a consultant to the World Bank and a number of central banks and served as the personal economic adviser to the prime minister of the United Kingdom.

Contributors

Robert J. Barro
Department of Economics
Littauer Center
Harvard University
Cambridge, MA 02138

C. Fred Bergsten
Director
Institute for International Economics
11 DuPont Circle, NW, Suite 805
Washington, DC 20036

Ben Bernanke
Woodrow Wilson School of Public and
   International Affairs
Princeton University
Princeton, NJ 08544

Ralph C. Bryant
The Brookings Institution
1775 Massachusetts Avenue
Washington, DC 20036

Geoffrey Carliner
Executive Director
National Bureau of Economic Research
1050 Massachusetts Avenue
Cambridge, MA 02138

Richard N. Cooper
Center for International Affairs
Harvard University
1737 Cambridge Street
Cambridge, MA 02138

E. Gerald Corrigan
President
Federal Reserve Bank of New York
33 Liberty Street
New York, NY 10045

Rudiger Dornbusch
Department of Economics
Massachusetts Institute of Technology
Room E52–357
Cambridge, MA 02139

Barry Eichengreen
Department of Economics
University of California
250 Barrows Hall
Berkeley, California 94720

Douglas W. Elmendorf
Department of Economics
Littauer Center
Harvard University
Cambridge, MA 02138

Richard D. Erb
Deputy Managing Director
International Monetary Fund
700 19th Street, NW
Washington, DC 20431

Martin Feldstein
President and Chief Executive Officer
National Bureau of Economic Research
1050 Massachusetts Avenue
Cambridge, MA 02138

Jeffrey Frankel
Department of Economics
Evans Hall
University of California
Berkeley, CA 94720

Jacob A. Frenkel
Economic Counsellor and Director
Research Department
International Monetary Fund
700 19th Street, NW
Washington, DC 20438

Benjamin M. Friedman
Department of Economics
Harvard University
Littauer Center 127
Cambridge, MA 02138

Robert J. Gordon
Department of Economics
Northwestern University
2003 Sheridan Road, Room G-174
Evanston, IL 60208

Joseph A. Grundfest
Stanford University Law School
Stanford, CA 94305

David Hale
First Vice President and Chief
   Economist
Kemper Financial Services, Inc.
120 South LaSalle Street
Chicago, IL 60603

Robert E. Hall
Hoover Institution
Stanford University
Stanford, CA 94305

William S. Haraf
Director of Policy Analysis
Citicorp
1275 Pennsylvania Avenue, NW
Suite 503
Washington, DC 20004

R. Glenn Hubbard
Graduate School of Business
Columbia University
Uris Hall 609
New York, NY 10027

Michael Jensen
Harvard Business School
Cotting House, Room 202
Boston, MA 02163

Sidney Jones
Assistant Secretary
U.S. Department of the Treasury
1500 Pennsylvania Avenue, NW
Washington, DC 20220

Edward J. Kane
Department of Economics
Ohio State University
410 Arps Hall
1945 North High Street
Columbus, OH 43210

Charles P. Kindleberger
Brookhaven at Lexington
Amherst 406
Lexington, MA 02173

Mervyn King
London School of Economics
510 Lionel Robbins Building
Houghton Street
London WC2A 2AE, England

Paul Krugman
Department of Economics
Massachusetts Institute of Technology
50 Memorial Drive
Cambridge, MA 02139

Lawrence B. Lindsey
Office of Policy Development
Executive Office of the President
Old Executive Office Building
Washington, DC 20500

Robert E. Lucas, Jr.
Department of Economics
University of Chicago
1126 East 59th Street
Chicago, IL 60637

Bennett T. McCallum
Graduate School of Industrial
   Administration
Carnegie-Mellon University
Pittsburgh, PA 15213

Brian Maddigan
Council of Economic Advisers
Old Executive Office Building
Washington, DC 20500

N. Gregory Mankiw
National Bureau of Economic Research
1050 Massachusetts Avenue
Cambridge, MA 02138

Hyman P. Minsky
Department of Economics
Washington University
St. Louis, MO 63130

Michael Mussa
Graduate School of Business
University of Chicago
1101 East 58th Street
Chicago, IL 60637

William Poole
Department of Economics
Brown University
Providence, RI 02912

Douglas D. Purvis
Department of Economics
Queen's University
Kingston, Ontario K7L 3N6
Canada

Robert D. Reischauer
Director, Congressional Budget Office
House Annex 2, Room H2–402
2nd and D Streets, NW
Washington, DC 20515

Paul A. Samuelson
Emeritus
Department of Economics
Massachusetts Institute of Technology
Room E52–383C
Cambridge, MA 02139

Robert J. Shiller
Cowles Foundation for Research in
  Economics
Yale University
Box 2125 Yale Station
New Haven, CT 06520

Irvine H. Sprague
962 Millwood Lane
Great Falls, VA 22066

Norman Strunk
1468 Parkside Drive
Park Ridge, IL 60068

Lawrence H. Summers
The World Bank
Room S-9035
1818 H Street, NW
Washington, DC 20433

Richard F. Syron
President
Federal Reserve Bank of Boston
600 Atlantic Avenue
Boston, MA 02106

Paul A. Volcker
Chairman
James D. Wolfensohn, Inc.
599 Lexington Avenue, 40th Floor
New York, NY 10022

Alan A. Walters
American Enterprise Institute
1150 17th Street, NW
Washington, DC 20036

Name Index

Aftalion, A., 95
Altman, Edward I., 36n13
Amihud, Y., 68n7
Asquith, Paul, 36

Bagehot, Walter, 117, 119, 130–31, 136, 146–47, 150–51
Barsky, R., 141
Becker, Gary S., 77n17
Bergsten, C. Fred, 115n10, 116n11, 133
Bernanke, Ben, 23, 29–30, 103
Brady, Nicholas, 5
Brumbaugh, R. Dan, Jr., 38, 39n15, 40
Bryant, Ralph C., 134
Burton, T., 117

Campbell, John, 29
Case, Fred, 57–58
Caskey, John, 163
Cline, William R., 113n5
Cutler, D., 141

De Long, J. Bradford, 141
Diamond, Douglas, 147
Dornbusch, Rudiger, 103, 122n1
Dybvig, Philip, 147
Erb, Richard D., 82

Fazzari, Steven, 163
Feldstein, Martin, 80, 81, 83, 134
Feltus, William J., 65n1
Fisher, Franklin M., 65–66
Fisher, Irving, 23, 158
Flood, Robert, Jr., 93, 94

Fox, Christopher J., 34n9
Frankel, Jeffrey, 103, 133–34
French, Kenneth, 34n10
Friedman, Benjamin, 24, 28n7, 79, 83, 180
Friedman, Milton, 22, 23, 102
Froot, Kenneth, 94

Galbraith, John K., 22n1
Garber, Peter, 93, 94
Garcia, G., 143, 151
General Accounting Office (GAO), 40
Gennotte, Gerard, 68n9, 74n16
Gibbon, Edward, 22n2
Gilson, R., 67n3
Goldsmith, R., 137
Goodfriend, Marvin, 148
Goodhart, C., 146
Gordon, Robert J., 133, 181
Grossman, Sanford, ix, 68n9
Grundfest, Joseph, 82
Gurel, Eitan, 72n13

Hale, D., 155
Hall, Robert E., 82–83, 180, 181
Hamilton, Mary, 68n8
Haraf, William S., 79, 134
Harris, Lawrence E., 72n13
Henderson, D., 93
Hertzberg, D., 155
Hicks, John, 168
Hoyt, Homer, 130
Hubbard, R. Glenn, ix
Humphrey, David, 152

Subject Index